D-Day to Victory

The Diaries of a British Tank Commander

Sgt Trevor Greenwood

Edited by S. V. Partington

**SIMON &
SCHUSTER**

London · New York · Sydney · Toronto · New Delhi

A CBS COMPANY

First published in Great Britain by Simon & Schuster UK Ltd, 2012
A CBS COMPANY
In association with Imperial War Museums

Text copyright © The Trevor Greenwood Archive
and Imperial War Museums 2012

1 3 5 7 9 10 8 6 4 2

Simon & Schuster UK Ltd
1st Floor
222 Gray's Inn Road
London WC1X 8HB

www.simonandschuster.co.uk

Simon & Schuster Australia, Sydney
Simon & Schuster India, New Delhi

Maps © Peter Beale

Cover image is a composite of more than one photograph.

A CIP catalogue record for this book is available from the British Library

ISBN: 978-1-47111-068-9

Typeset by Hewer Text UK Ltd, Edinburgh

Printed and bound by CPI Group (UK) Ltd, Croydon, CR0 4YY

Editor's Note

As is often the case with diaries, Trevor Greenwood's original notebooks contain a great many abbreviations and contractions in the writing. These have been spelt out in full wherever necessary, either for clarification – for example, where Trevor wrote 'going to S.' for 'going to the Solent' and 'W–K–M' for Wickham – or for ease of reading.

Many of the abbreviations and acronyms were common army usage – and, indeed, still are so – and these have been left as Trevor wrote them. Readers from a non-military background will find the List of Abbreviations that precedes the diary useful in deciphering their meaning.

The weapons, vehicles and aircraft mentioned in the diary are identified and, where helpful, explained, in the Glossary of Military Terms and Equipment. The brief note on The Organisation of 9 RTR explains the higher formations to which the battalion belonged, as well as the role of the echelons into which it was divided, since these can otherwise be confusing to the general reader.

The diary itself is followed by a superbly informative essay on 9 RTR in Normandy by John Delaney of the Imperial War Museum, which sets the events recorded by Trevor in their historical context, expanding on the battles in which he took part and explaining the role of the tank as infantry support.

Trevor used underlining for emphasis and quotation marks for names of ships, films, foreign words and so on, and these have been replaced throughout by italics. I have, however, kept the quote marks he used when writing about the echelons into which 9 RTR was divided, 'A', 'B' and 'F'. This is to distinguish them from the squadrons A, B, and C, since the diary sometimes refers to both echelons and squadrons by letter alone.

The occasional spelling has been modernised: 'loudspeaker', for instance, has long since lost the hyphen it possessed in the 1940s: to retain it would read rather quaintly to us today.

The diary refers in places to Trevor's family and friends, and in order to avoid the need to footnote them, these purely personal connections are identified below.

Dorothy, Kath and Marjorie were Trevor's sisters. Tod, or Toddy, was his brother, married to Olive. Bob and Fred were married to Kath and Marjorie respectively. Garsden was a work colleague in England, as was Mr Morgan. Trevor's son, Barry, (aka 'Poppet') was eleven weeks old when the diary opens, and Trevor had seen him briefly just once before leaving England. Haydn Dewey was Trevor's cousin; Aunt G or Aunt Gertie was Haydn's mother, and Trevor's father's sister. Johnny was the younger brother of Jess, Trevor's wife. Phyl was Phyllis Lambert, Jess's cousin, who later married Lance Corporal Ernest Bland. Wilf Colclough was a close friend of Trevor's, who wrote to him often, and with whom he shared an active interest in politics. Stan Smith was a lifelong friend who shared Trevor's deep love of music: several of his letters to Trevor survive.

Military personnel who were also known to Trevor and Jess outside of Trevor's army life include Noel Wright, Dave Lubick and Jimmy Aldcroft. The Wrights were near neighbours, and Jess was in close touch with Mrs Wright and with Mrs Aldcroft throughout the war. Bob Plowman also appears to have been both a friend and a one-time army colleague, although his precise connection is less certain.

Space precludes the individual identification of all the army colleagues who are mentioned in the diary. Readers who wish to know more about 9 RTR and the men who served with it can find a wealth of information on the official website of the Royal Tank Regiment Association at www.royaltankregiment.com, which contains within it a site dedicated to 9 RTR under the link to Disbanded Regiments. Amongst the admirable resources to be found here are the complete 9 RTR War Diary, a privately published *History of the 34th Armoured Brigade* and the full text of *Tank Tracks*, a history of 9 RTR in action, written by Peter Beale, a veteran of B Squadron.

The assistance provided by Peter Beale has been especially valuable in helping to bring the diary to publication; both in explaining and identifying many of the more puzzling or obscure references, and in allowing us to use his wonderfully clear and comprehensive maps.

Contents

Sergeant Trevor Greenwood.
Photograph © The Trevor Greenwood Archive.

Foreword

Our parents, Richard Trevor Greenwood (1908–82, known as Trevor) and Jessie Whitaker (1910–99, known as Jess) lived in Reddish, near Manchester, and moved to a house in Hazel Grove, near Stockport, after their marriage. Trevor worked for the Ediswan Electrical Company as an electrical sales engineer and Jess was a clerk at the Public Trustee Office until their son Barry was born in March 1944.

Trevor was amongst the first batch of conscript recruits to arrive in Gateshead on 27 November 1940, when the 9th Battalion Royal Tank Regiment was reborn. From then until his demobilisation in December 1945 he kept up an almost daily correspondence with our mother which records in great detail his progress through the war, from the long period of training in Britain, through to active service in Europe and post-war policing duties in Germany. He also kept a diary which provides a detailed, uncensored eye-witness account of events from D-Day (6 June 1944), to 17 April 1945.

The letters reveal that Trevor was selected for a fast-track course in 'D&M' (Driving and Maintenance). Thus began his army career in Churchill tanks, and his training took him all over the country. From 13 April 1944 until the end of the war, the whereabouts of 9 RTR could not be revealed. In fact, the regiment's final preparations took place in Lee-on-Solent near Gosport, where they awaited embarkation for Normandy. In Trevor's case, active service in Normandy began on D-Day +16.

The diary consists of seven notebooks, some left with blank pages. Trevor knew that he was contravening regulations by keeping a diary, and took any opportunity to send these volumes back with trusted colleagues returning to England on leave or through injury. The sixth volume ends on 14 February 1945, with many unused pages. This was the day Trevor went on leave, his only home visit during the period covered by the diary. Why he risked keeping a diary is a mystery, but he was certainly conscious of the momentous importance of the events he was witnessing, and wanted to deliver an accurate account for posterity. His incessant writing, particularly in the more intimate context of his letters to Jess, also fulfilled a cathartic need to keep closely in touch with the preferred reality of his home life. In recent years his former friend and squadron colleague Dicky Hall told us of the many hours spent by Trevor sitting in his tank turret with pen and notepaper. It is interesting to note that long descriptions in the diary, particularly of battles, are sometimes reproduced verbatim in a letter a few weeks later. This delay was to comply with the strict rules of censorship; for example, the battle for Le Havre: diary entry 12.9.44, letter 9.10.44. Presumably Trevor had in mind that this approach would fulfil two purposes: it provided interesting material for long letters to Jess, and preserved accurate accounts of significant events in case his diary did not survive.

But why did he write no more entries after 17 April 1945? There is a clue in the entry for 14 April. Patrol work and guard duties in Germany during and after the final phase of hostilities kept the squadron far more continuously busy than previously. There is also an unusual gap of four days (13 to 16 April) in his letters to Jess, coinciding with the upheaval of 9 RTR's move to Schüttorf. It seems likely that from 17 April onwards, with the end of hostilities clearly in sight, he felt that his duty to 'posterity' was over and his daily correspondence with Jess became his main leisure-time priority.

After the war Trevor resumed his former career and stayed with the same firm until his retirement. His daughter Julie was born in 1948 and the family moved to Watford, Hertfordshire in 1956 after his promotion to a new post in the firm's London office. During our childhood we were aware of some boxes in the loft containing wartime material, but it was not until a few years after Trevor's death that we came to appreciate the full extent and significance of this archive. Barry set to work transcribing the diary, and a few photocopies were made in 1988 with a revised edition in 1994. The seven notebooks were then given to the Imperial War Museum. We are still in the process of transcribing the letters, after which they will also be given to the IWM.

From the early days as a raw recruit, to his final rank of Sergeant and Churchill tank commander, Trevor was always a reluctant soldier, resigned to doing his duty and gaining solace mainly from his copious correspondence with Jess. Through the legacy of his writing we can follow in great detail the journey of one man from civilian to battle-hardened soldier. There are harrowing accounts of battles, and vivid descriptions of the activities of his fellow soldiers. His comments give a fascinating insight into the lives of ordinary people in war-torn Europe, particularly in his descriptions from the various homes where he was billeted in Holland and Belgium. The gratitude of these newly liberated people provided a heart-warming respite and the opportunity to foster real friendships; in Trevor's case, notably with the Cornelese family of Eindhoven, from whom several letters and cards to Trevor and Jess have survived. Some of these, along with other documents, photos and background material can be seen at the website for Trevor's war archive: http://trevorgreenwood.co.uk.

Above all, the one constant theme pervading this archive is Trevor's unflinching devotion to Jess, and his longing to be reunited with her and Barry. Without this driving force the diary and letters would not have been written, and without Jess's reciprocal devotion, they would not have been so lovingly preserved.

We would like to dedicate this book to the memory of all those who served with Trevor in the 9th Battalion, Royal Tank Regiment, from those who tragically lost their lives in service, to those like Trevor who survived, but whose lives were changed forever by the traumatic experience of active service on the front line.

Barry Greenwood and Julie Schroder (née Greenwood)

Introduction

'You are about to embark upon the Great Crusade, toward which we have striven these many months. The eyes of the world are upon you. The hopes and prayers of liberty-loving people everywhere march with you. In company with our brave Allies and brothers-in-arms on other Fronts, you will bring about the destruction of the German war machine, the elimination of Nazi tyranny over the oppressed peoples of Europe, and security for ourselves in a free world.'

Message from General Eisenhower to the Allied
Expeditionary Force, 6 June 1944

In the summer of 1944, more than two million British, US and Canadian soldiers underwent intensive preparation for the invasion of Normandy and the subsequent campaign in north-west Europe; an invasion that had been many months in the planning.

For us today, in an era of professional career soldiers, when war in Western Europe would be unthinkable, it is hard to imagine what it was like for the ordinary men and women of Britain whose lives were transformed and who made such enormous sacrifices during the Second World War. It is harder still to put ourselves in the shoes of the men who were heading for the front line: men of all ages and walks of life who now awaited embarkation on the troop ships and landing ships that crowded the Solent ports, not knowing what lay ahead of them in Normandy, but all too aware that, whatever the outcome, they were about to participate in the most crucial phase of the war.

Trevor Greenwood was one of those men. Leaving behind his much-loved wife, Jess, and their baby son, Barry, who was just twelve weeks old, he sailed for France with the 9th battalion of the Royal Tank Regiment on 22 June as part of the follow-up to the first wave of the invasion.

From D-Day, 6 June, until 17 April 1945, by which time he was in Germany, he kept a diary which gives us a remarkable insight into the experiences of the ordinary soldier.

Other veterans have left accounts of individual actions and engagements, and the proliferation of online regimental histories and collections of wartime memoirs allows us ever-increasing access to them. But what makes Trevor Greenwood's diary such a valuable addition to our understanding of the Second World War is that, except for his nine days' leave in February 1945, he kept an unbroken daily record of his active service, from the beginning of the invasion right up until the point at which the war in Europe was won.

Trevor's war took him through Normandy, into Belgium and Holland and finally over the Rhine and into the heart of Germany. 9 RTR, as the 9th Battalion, Royal Tank Regiment was known, were in action more or less continually for the duration of the campaign in north-west Europe, and took part in several of the most famous and important battles of the war. In Normandy they fought in the Battle for Caen, at Hill 112, and at what came to be called the

Falaise Pocket. They were involved in the capture of Le Havre, a success which did much to boost morale, and in the capture of Antwerp, which was to prove crucial in the longer term. In a series of complicated movements to and fro across the Dutch and Belgian border, they helped to keep the Scheldt estuary free of German blockades, liberating the Dutch towns of Eindhoven and Roosendaal. Through the winter months they were part of the long struggle in the Ardennes, followed by the breaching of the Siegfried line at the Reichswald Forest. Trevor's is thus the most complete, first-hand soldier's-eye view that we have of the whole campaign.

The 9th Battalion, Royal Tank Regiment, which Trevor had joined on his call-up in December 1940, was one of the first units in the British army to receive the newly designed Churchill tanks. It was what was known as a 'hostilities-only' battalion; that is, it was not a regular army battalion, but was raised specifically in times of war. Many of its recruits were drawn from the same regions of the north-east, and many were men well into their thirties, with several years' experience of working life. This meant that there was an element of maturity and a strong sense of unity and identity within the battalion, even before they had completed their three and a half years' training at camps and on gunnery ranges the length and breadth of England. From its rebirth at Gateshead in 1940, at various times in the lead-up to June 1944 9 RTR was based at Otley in Yorkshire, Eastbourne and Lancing in Sussex and Charing in Kent, and finally Farnborough and Aldershot in Hampshire.

Although he had a circle of close friends who shared his passion for music and for politics, Trevor thought of himself perhaps as something of a loner. He was well liked, however,

and clearly made an impression on the younger members of
the battalion, one of whom, recently posted to the 9th from
the 58th Training Regiment, wrote: 'In the 58th we were all
young soldiers. Here, we had a smattering of older men
among us ... Trevor Greenwood, for whom I had a great
respect, and several others from whom I learned much.'

Trevor was a thinker, but also a deeply practical man, able
to turn his hand to all sorts of things. His skills were to
come in useful on many occasions, wiring up electrical
circuits and keeping tanks on the road – no easy task for a
vehicle that weighed 38 tons, was known for the complexity
of its gearbox, and was liable not only to be damaged by
enemy fire, but was all too frequently ditched or otherwise
disabled. Several times in the diary we find him in one place
in charge of patching up a vehicle or waiting for fitters or
parts while the rest of the battalion is somewhere else.

The realities of tank warfare meant that tank crews had to
be adaptable and independent, able to use their initiative
and to think on their feet. These were qualities Trevor had in
abundance. What he was not was a natural soldier. The business of war was morally repugnant to him, and his first taste
of army life had done nothing to change his mind. But he
had no doubts at all about why he was fighting. In common
with many of their generation, both Trevor and his wife Jess
took a keen interest in politics, and Trevor had regarded the
rise of Adolf Hitler and the developing situation in Europe
with growing unease long before war had broken out.
Whatever the personal cost to himself, he believed with
absolute conviction that Nazi Germany had to be defeated.

On 26 June, four days after they landed on Juno beach,
9 RTR faced their first action, at the village of Cheux, just

west of Caen. The next several entries in the diary – many of them long and detailed – are a more or less continuous record of the fighting, punctuated only by fractured sleep, out in the open with only the tank for shelter – a luxury which Trevor was conscious the infantrymen did not have. It is astonishing that he was able to write at all in such circumstances, let alone with such force and immediacy. At one point he says, 'I am writing this in a hole, beneath tank, with mortars falling uncomfortably close . . .'

Impressions come thick and fast, with bewildering intensity: burning tanks, their crews baling out; the whine of lethal mortars overhead; a shot-down plane, its pilot beyond help; 'smoke . . . fire . . . death'. Reading these pages, we are powerfully transported onto the battlefield, and begin to feel that, yes, we *can* understand something of what it was like.

Trevor was lucky enough to go through the war without serious injury. However, he did not remain unscathed. The Second World War was more enlightened than the Great War had been regarding the mental health of men who had spent time under sustained fire, and stations were set up behind the lines to which those considered to be at risk of battle fatigue could be sent. Trevor was ordered back behind the lines on 1 July. In his diary he only notes that, somewhat to his surprise, he has been sent back to 'B' Echelon for a rest, although he does admit on 29 June that 'after only one day, I feel worn out. There is the constant physical effort of diving for safety, plus the awful mental strain of waiting for the explosion.'

From the safety of 'B' Echelon, he merely writes that away from the front line, he is able to sleep for the first time without his trousers on, and comments on how peaceful it is away from the noise of the mortars. Even to Jess, from whom he seldom hid his feelings, he wrote 'I am quite well.'

Jess Greenwood.
Photograph © The Trevor Greenwood Archive.

In fact he was far from well, although it was not until many years later that his daughter, Julie Schroder, discovered the truth from Dicky Hall, who had served with him in C Squadron. Trevor was more than exhausted; he was traumatised by his first few days in action. Dicky Hall and his colleagues thought that he might not be fit to return to front-line service, but were delighted when he did so, in Julie's words, 'presumably, sufficiently hardened to cope with all that the rest of the war threw at him.'

It was just as well that he made a full recovery, for there followed another two months of intensive fighting before 9 RTR gained its first respite as they moved up the coast towards Le Havre. On 3 August he was able to write with equanimity, though not with pleasure, 'have been in every action so far . . .'

In a letter, which allowed him more time to analyse his thoughts than did the diary, he writes instructively about fear on the battlefield:

> '*At any moment the troop officer may appear, face tense, maps beneath his arm, to announce "we are going into action". These are dreadful words to me. Whenever I hear them, I seem to experience a momentary mental paralysis, and my whole inside contracts in a peculiar way. I imagine a criminal must suffer similar physical reaction when he hears his death sentence. I think it must be caused by fear: not just ordinary fear, but a more violent brand which has its kinship in death. I can find no antidote to this experience: it seems to be an inevitable part of my role as a front line soldier.*
>
> *Strangely enough, the initial spasm of fear soon wears off, and I usually find myself taking a grim interest in the plans for action . . .*'

He writes in similar vein about the aftermath of combat: 'I find it terribly difficult to write immediately after we have been in action. I think I must suffer from some sort of reaction under the strain. My brain simply will not function.'

On 20 August, he had his closest brush with death. It was near the village of Crèvecoeur, when, returning on foot from taking two injured crewmen for medical attention, he found himself facing a barrage of high explosive shells. The only cover was a single log: two infantrymen who were crouched behind it were both hit beside him one after the other, but somehow Trevor survived. He writes: 'Meanwhile the shells came down relentlessly. I could feel the hot blast from each one: the air became thick with the acrid fumes of cordite. I knew I should have been blown to smithereens, by all the laws of explosives ... but all the time I remained conscious of being alive.'

Vivid as these sequences are, Trevor's diary is more than a straightforward record of the fighting.

There is a wealth of incidental detail about the minutiae of life lived largely inside (or, during night-time mortar attacks, underneath) a tank, in close quarters with four other crew members.

And outside the confines of his Churchill, Trevor took a lively interest in everything he encountered. He mourns the devastation of the fine French farmland across which the Normandy battles are taking place. He is moved by the plight of the refugees who are fleeing or in some cases returning to shattered towns and villages, many of their houses obliterated, others still standing but filled with the pitiful remnants of abandoned lives: scattered belongings, family photographs and children's toys.

Always aware of the wider picture, he reflects frequently on his concerns for the future, agonising over his attitude to the German people, and worrying for a Europe torn apart by hatreds, even if the war should be won. He keeps up assiduously with the news at every opportunity, and even in the thick of the action, he cannot help but comment, often acerbically, on items he has read or heard.

On 14 December 1944, for example, despairing at the attitude of the Allied Powers to the left-wing resistance movement in Greece, he writes with extraordinary prescience: 'Are we trying to "impose" suitable governments upon liberated territories? It seems like it . . .'

There are moments of comedy, too, such as the occasion when, to his great consternation, what seems to be half the female population of the village of Nampont insist on hitching a ride inside his tank.

There is the motley collection of animals that the tank crews acquired wherever they went: from somewhere a milking goat, from somewhere else an orphaned puppy, and the ever-increasing flock of chickens, useful providers of fresh eggs, which accompanied them everywhere except into battle (some of them living in compo boxes, others travelling in sacks). Not to mention the cow whose byre was attached to the kitchen in one of their Belgian billets, adding her distinctive aroma to the smells of farmhouse cooking.

In Belgium and then in Holland, with the liberation first of Eindhoven and then Roosendaal, conditions were easier than they had been in France, with troops billeted in the houses of the local population at night, rather than having to sleep in the open or beneath their tanks. Later in the winter, at least, there were longer spells of rest and regrouping in between engagements.

But the fighting continued as fiercely as before, as the Allies continued to push the Germans north and east. Of one action on the borders of Belgium and Holland Trevor writes: 'The day's battlefield reminded me of Normandy. So many dead cattle: broken fences, shell holes – dead bodies, mostly Jerries – noise of artillery, of aircraft – burning buildings. A beastly business. At night, we counted 16 fires on the immediate horizon – 16 farms and homes ruined in a few hours . . .'

And again two days later, on 22 October: 'It was like hell let loose. There were twelve vehicles, all going flat out, and firing their guns in all directions except to the rear. Hedgerows, ditches, trees, houses – any mortal thing that could provide cover for Jerries was saturated with MG fire and HE . . . our own vehicles lumbered over ditches, through hedges, across ploughed fields, turnip fields, crashed through plantations, uprooted trees: it was sheer destruction, but rather thrilling – and how terrifying for the enemy!'

There were other difficulties to contend with. The winter of 1944–5 was bitterly cold, with biting winds and sub-zero temperatures for weeks on end. Fuel for warmth was in short supply, and movement for tanks on the icy roads was extremely difficult.

One member of 34 Tank Brigade recorded that 'by "moving" at this time it should be understood that more endurance was often demanded of the tank crews than in many battles. Ten miles in 24 hours of continuous effort was considered quite good going. Deep snow across country was friendly but when, as frequently occurred, tanks were forced onto a road, Churchills without ice-bar tracks travelled in any direction as easily as curling stones on polished ice.'

Trevor contracted a chest infection, possibly pneumonia,

severe enough to keep him from the front line for a month; although with characteristic understatement, he refers to his illness in the diary as 'a bad cold' and 'a mild dose of flu', and is frustrated that he is confined to bed.

In February 1945 9 RTR, under the command of the 53rd Welsh Infantry Division and the overall control of the First Canadian Army, mustered west of Groesbeek in preparation for an assault on the Reichswald Forest.

The Reichswald barred the route from Holland into Germany. The only roads through it ran on a north–south axis, on the German side of the border. The Allies' plan was to advance directly through the forest from west to east.

This meant driving the tanks straight through the plantations of mostly coniferous softwood trees, although there were also stands of hardwoods, chestnut and beech. Such an action had never been attempted before, and indeed it was entirely unexpected on the part of the German defenders, who had considered the Reichswald to be impenetrable to tanks.

In the limited edition of Trevor's diary which was published in 1988 under the title of *One Day at a Time*, Barry Greenwood writes:

When, infrequently, my father used to relate his wartime experiences (usually at my request), it seemed to me that the action through the Reichswald had left the most vivid and abiding impression on his memory. I recall his describing the scene – dozens of tanks proceeding forward in lowest gear on a wide front through this dense forest of tall, mature trees, crashing and smashing everything in their path. He related the noise as beyond anything he had ever experienced both for sheer volume and for terror. Try to

*picture it: dozens of tanks in close proximity, with engines
screaming hard in the confined acoustic of dense forest, and
the continuous ear-splitting cracks of trees being smashed
to the ground by brute power. And the thought that you
are, at long last, heading towards the enemy on his home
ground, with unknown terrors ahead.*

The Reichswald offensive was successful, but before it was
finished Trevor was sent home on nine days' leave. Leave
was allocated on a strict rota basis, and Trevor had known
for some time that his was due. It was something to which
he looked forward with a curious combination of longing
and dread, writing to Jess when the leave scheme was first
announced: 'Naturally I will not refuse leave. If it meant
being with you for only an hour, I would accept gladly. But
my mental state will be a queer one. I will not be able to
forget this hell, this bloody beastliness ... How much
worse will it be to return to it from home ... from all that
matters in life. I mustn't think about these things, Jess. No
soldier has any right to think of the future ... it is the way
to insanity.'

The Reichswald was the final major action of 9 RTR in
the Second World War, although there were a number of
mopping up operations throughout March both in Holland
and in Germany, and several remaining areas of stubborn
German resistance to be overcome.

On 7 April Trevor crossed the Rhine, following the initial
Allied crossing by the US First Army on 7 March, and the
main crossings by the US Third Army on 22 March and the
British 21st Army Group on 23 March. On 14 April 9 RTR
were transferred to the town of Schüttorf, roughly ten kilometres from the Dutch border, there to begin what were in

effect policing duties as part of the Allied Military Government of Occupied Territories; and on 17 April 1945 Trevor wrote the final entry in his diary. Although the war was not yet over – another three weeks would pass before the Allies formally accepted Germany's unconditional surrender on 8 May – it was clear that it was as good as won, and it is more than likely that Trevor stopped keeping the diary because he felt that he was no longer on 'active' service. Part of his reason for writing it in the first place was so that something of him should survive in the event of his death, and in Schüttorf he no longer had cause to feel that death was imminent.

Trevor was not entirely comfortable with his new role of policing a defeated people, writing to Jess that as an occupying force, he felt as though the Allies were no longer liberators, but conquerors.

His post-war duties took him from Schüttorf via Bentheim and Lengerich to a two-month spell at the British Army Exhibition in Paris. Returning to Germany, he rejoined his unit at Gummer, moving with them near to Ringelheim, Hannover, until his demobilisation on 1 December.

Was Trevor hardened by his ten months of fighting on the battlefields of north-west Europe? As a soldier, certainly. In the diary, we can trace his transformation from the shaken man of June 1944 into the highly competent tank commander of the later months. But even in the worst times, he never once lost his humanity or his sensitivity.

On 11 November 1944, he writes home: 'There was a beautiful moon last evening: I gazed at it for an hour through my binoculars: I could see the craters quite easily. How trivial seemed my present life. How worthless we poor ignorant fools who have nothing better to do than slaughter each other. There is such beauty in the universe, Jess. And so much happiness for everyone . . . enough for everybody. Why are we so mad?'

It would be impossible to endure what he and the men who fought alongside him went through and remain unchanged by the experience. Nevertheless, the Trevor Greenwood who finally came home to Jess and Barry at the end of 1945 was the same loving husband and father who had left for the beaches of Normandy eighteen months before, and was able to resume a happy and fulfilling civilian life. His second child, Julie, was born in May 1948.

Trevor did not write his diary for the public eye. Writing for him was a necessary act, as if by committing what was happening to him and around him to paper, he was able to retain his sense of self, his strength and equilibrium, in the face of what he saw as a deadly chaos. He would never have dreamt that almost seventy years on, a generation who were not yet born at the time at which he was writing would be reading his words.

Posterity, though, is infinitely richer for the account he left us. We owe a debt of gratitude to Trevor's family, who first of all kept the diary safe, and then lovingly and carefully transcribed it, making it available to us all to read, so that it can take the place it so fully deserves in the literature of the Second World War.

List of Abbreviations

AA	Anti-Aircraft (guns or shells)
AFV	Armoured Fighting Vehicle
AP	Armour Piercing (shell). Also Anti-Personnel (mine)
ARV	Armoured Recovery Vehicle
AT	Anti-Tank gun
AVRE	Armoured Vehicle Royal Engineers (a modified Churchill tank)
AWD	Allied War Department
BD	Battle Dress
BLA	British Liberation Army
Br	Brigade
Brig	Brigadier, Brigade
BTO	Battalion Technical Officer
BWEF	British Western Expeditionary Force
CB	Confined to Barracks
CI	Current Invalidity (unfit for active service). Also Chief Instructor
CMP	Corps of Military Police
CO	Commanding Officer
D&M	Driving and Maintenance
Dem	Demonstration (e.g. of equipment, new weapons or vehicles)
DM	Driver Mechanic. Also abbreviated to Dr. Mech.

DO	Driver Operator
DP	Destination Point
DR	Dispatch Rider
DSO	Distinguished Service Order
EME	Electrical and Mechanical Engineers
FDS	Forward Delivery Squadron (vehicle and crew replacement). Also Field (or Forward) Dressing Station
FFI	Free From Infection. Also French Forces of Interior (resistance groups)
FUP	Forming Up Point
Fw	Focke-Wulf Fw 190 (see Glossary)
GHQ	General Headquarters
GM	Gunner Mechanic
GO	Gunner Operator
HE	High Explosive shell
HQ	Headquarters
I/c	In command (e.g. 2 i/c, second in command)
IC	Intercom
IO	Intelligence Officer
LAD	Light Aid Detatchment (under REME control)
L of C	Lines of Communication
L/Cpl	Lance Corporal
LCT	Landing Craft, Tanks (smaller vessel to carry 4 to 6 tanks)
LOB	Left Out of Battle (official rest period)
LST	Landing Ship, Tanks (large vessel to carry up to 20 tanks)
M&V	Meat and Veg (tinned staple in compo packs)
MC	Military Cross. Also Military Convoy
ME	Messerschmidt ME 109 (see Glossary)
MG	Machine Gun. Also machine-gun fire

Mk IV	German Mark IV tank (see Glossary)
MM	Military Medal
MO	Medical Officer
MP	Military Police
MT	Motor Transport
NCO	Non-Commissioned Officer
OC	Officer Commanding
OD	Other Denomination
OP	Observation Post
OR	Other Rank
PC	Postcard
PIAT	Projector Infantry Anti-Tank (hand-held bomb launcher)
POW	Prisoner of War
PT	Physical Training
Q	Quartermaster, short for SQMS
RAC	Royal Armoured Corps
RAF	Royal Air Force
RASC	Royal Army Service Corps
REME	Royal Electrical and Mechanical Engineers (same as EME)
RO	Reconnaissance Officer
RSM	Regimental Sergeant Major
RTR	Royal Tank Regiment
SP	Self-Propelled gun (for anti-tank work)
SQMS	Squadron Quarter Master Sergeant (Q for short)
SSM	Squadron Sergeant Major
TDU	Tank Delivery Unit
TP	Tank Park
Tpr	Trooper
Trp	Troop
WO	Warrant Officer

Glossary of Military Terms and Equipment

5.5

British field gun first used in 1941. In 1944 a lighter shell was introduced which increased its maximum range from 16,000 to 18,000 yards. The BL 5.5 remained in service until the 1980s.

50mm

German anti-tank gun. The 5 cm PaK (Panzerabwehrkanone) 38 was gradually replaced by the heavier, more powerful **7.5cm** PaK 40, but still remained in use until the end of the war.

7.9

German hand-held anti-tank gun developed from the 7.9mm rifle.

88

88mm (8.8cm) German anti-tank and anti-aircraft gun, used both freestanding and, later, tank-mounted, and highly effective against Allied tanks, most of which were equipped with 75mm guns.

Aerial tugs: *see* gliders

Air-burst
Artillery shell designed to detonate in mid-air, causing damage over a wider area than ground-bursting shells, and more effective against cover.

Amgot
Allied Military Government of Occupied Territory, as implemented in Germany, Italy, Austria and Japan.

Auster AOP
The Taylorcraft Auster Mark III, IV and V was a light monoplane used chiefly by both the RAF and the Royal Canadian Air Force as an Air Observation Post to aid in the direction of artillery fire.

Bailey bridge
A portable bridge system of steel and timber sections, used for the first time in 1942. Easy to transport and assemble, the Bailey bridge was able to carry tanks.

Barrage balloons
Large balloons tethered by cables to vulnerable targets to deter low-flying enemy fighter aircraft.

Bazooka
Now a generic term for any shoulder-fired rocket launcher, the name initially referred to the M1 portable rocket-propelled anti-tank weapon first used by the US Army in 1942.

Besa

A 7.92mm machine gun mounted co-axially with the main turret gun. Also used to mean machine-gun fire. The name comes from the Birmingham Small Arms Company (BSA), who manufactured the weapon from 1939.

Bivvy

Short for bivouac, a temporary outdoor sleeping arrangement, without the benefit of tents.

Blockhouse

A fortified building designed to withstand artillery. Similar in purpose and construction to a bunker, but built above ground rather than below.

Bren

A light machine gun used by British and Commonwealth infantry throughout the Second World War, still in use up to the first Gulf War in 1991.

Brigade

Used as in 'at Brigade' to mean Brigade Headquarters.

Churchill

British heavy infantry tank, of which more than 7,000 were built between 1940 and 1945. The Churchill weighed just over 38 tons and was one of the heaviest Allied tanks of the Second World War.

Compo pack

Short for 'composite rations', the compo pack was designed to provide sufficient daily nutrition for highly mobile units.

The 9 RTR 15-man compo pack typically contained canned meat and vegetables, biscuits, margarine, tea, sugar, salt, chocolate, matches and cigarettes. Vehicle crews were issued with a small portable stove on which the canned food could be heated.

CROCODILE
A modified Churchill Mk VII tank converted into a flamethrower. Crocodiles used specially thickened petroleum supplied by means of an armoured fuel trailer.

Dakota
The Douglas C-47 Skytrain, a military transport aircraft developed from the Douglas DC-3 civilian airliner. The plane acquired its name as an acronym of *Douglas Aircraft Company Transport Aircraft* (DACoTA).

Demob scheme
An organised programme of courses designed to help demobilised servicemen return to civilian life.

Dummy tanks
Dummy tanks were used to draw enemy fire, or to mislead the enemy as to the number of tanks in the field and where the real tanks were deployed. Some were made of inflatable rubber, and some from wheeled vehicles covered with a wire and canvas skin.

Ensa
The Entertainment National Service Association was set up in 1939 to provide entertainment for British services personnel. Many stars of stage and screen appeared in Ensa productions.

Field service card
Pre-printed postcard issued to British forces to send home containing minimal information such as 'I am quite well/I have been wounded', and so on.

Flame-thrower: *see* Crocodile

Flying bomb
The V-1 flying bomb, also known as the doodlebug. More than 9,500 were fired on London and south-east England from mid-June 1944 until October, when all the launch sites within range of Britain were destroyed. A further 2,500 were fired on Antwerp between October 1944 and March 1945.

Fortress
The Boeing B-17 Flying Fortress was an iconic long-range American heavy bomber which played a decisive role in the strategic bombing of key German industrial and military targets.

Fw 190
The Focke-Wulf Fw 190, a single-seater single-engine German fighter aircraft, amongst the most formidable and versatile fighter planes of the war.

Fwd. rally
A place away from immediate enemy contact behind the front line.

Gliders
Military gliders towed by transport planes or by bombers on secondary duties were used to transport both troops and equipment.

Green envelope

British forces were given 'green envelopes' in which to send private uncensored letters to their nearest and dearest. All other letters were subject to the standard military censorship. The green envelope was intended solely for personal family correspondence, and to use it for any other purpose was a serious infringement.

Half-tracks

Armoured vehicles with wheels on the front axle and caterpillar tracks on the rear, combining the manoeuvrability of a wheeled vehicle with the all-terrain capacity of a tank.

Halifax

The British Handley Page Halifax four-engined long-range heavy bomber, also used by the Special Operations Executive (SOE) to parachute agents and supplies into occupied Europe.

Harbour

All-purpose military term – despite its apparent naval or maritime connotations – for a safe place in which to park vehicles overnight.

Honey

British forces nickname for the Stuart M3 and M5 light reconnaissance tank.

Hull down

Position in which the tank is screened by rising ground or similar, so that only the turret is visible to the enemy.

Jack Panther
The Jagdpanther self-propelled heavy tank destroyer. Generally the tank destroyer was lightly armoured, if more heavily armed than a conventional tank, but the Jagdpanther combined the armour of the Panther with a long-barrelled 88mm anti-tank gun which made it effective against any Allied tank.

Laager
Tank harbour, all-round defensive position. From the Afrikaans word for the protective wagon circles of the nineteenth-century Dutch *voortrekker* settlers in South Africa.

Lancaster
British bomber designed and built by Avro: first used in 1942, it went on to become the best-known heavy bomber of the war, flying over 150,000 sorties.

Liberator
The Consolidated B-24 Liberator American heavy bomber, the mainstay of the US Eighth Air Force in the Combined Bombing Offensive against Germany.

Liberty truck: *see* Passion truck

Lightning
The Lockheed P-38 Lightning, an American fighter-bomber known as '*der gabelschwanzteufel*' – the forktailed devil – to the Germans.

Mk IV
The German medium Panzerkampfwagen IV or Panzer IV was in production throughout the war and was widely used on the Western Front alongside the newer Panther. Not to be confused with the British Mk IV tank of the First World War.

Mauser
The Mauser K98 bolt-action rifle was the standard infantry weapon of the German Wehrmacht from 1935 to 1945.

ME 109
The Messerschmidt Bf 109, a supremely adaptable and effective fighter aircraft of which more than 33,000 were built from 1936 to 1945.

Minesweeper
A warship specifically designed to detect and clear mines at sea.

Mitchell
The North American Mitchell B-25 was a medium bomber introduced in 1941 and widely used by the USAAF, the Royal Canadian Air Force, and by the RAF both for strategic bombing prior to D-Day and as a support aircraft after the invasion.

Moaning Minnie
Common name among Allied troops for the German Nebelwerfer field mortar, so called because of the high-pitched howling sound made by the incoming mortar rounds. US troops christened it 'Screaming Mimi' and Trevor also refers to it as a 'Singing Sister'.

Naafi

The combined Navy, Army and Air Force Institutes, which since 1921 has provided recreational facilities, clubs, bars, shops and supplies to British servicemen and women. The Naafi was traditionally the preserve of the ordinary soldier, commissioned officers having their needs met by the officers' mess.

Nebelwerfer

German multi-barrelled rocket-launcher, usually translated as 'smoke thrower', although the literal meaning of *nebel* is 'fog'. *See* Moaning Minnie.

Panther

German medium tank first used in 1943: its combination of firepower and mobility made it one of the most successful tanks of the war. Later models with added armour were heavier. Note that Panther and Panzer are not synonymous: the similarity is coincidental, and the German word *panzer* means 'armour'.

Panzerfaust

German portable single-shot light anti-tank projectile launcher.

Panzergrenadiers

German mechanised infantry. From 1942 the name was used both for the infantry units of existing Panzer divisions and for newly established Panzergrenadier divisions.

Passion truck

Trucks which transported troops from their camp or billets into towns for recreation and/or entertainment.

Pay parade
Weekly parade – usually on a Friday, although the day could vary on active service – at which soldiers were assembled to be paid. Pay was given in cash in a sealed envelope to each man in alphabetical order.

Petard
A 29cm mortar mounted on a Churchill AVRE (Amoured Vehicle Royal Engineers) which fired a 40 lb bomb affectionately known as the 'Flying Dustbin'.

Piat
Projector, Infantry, Anti-tank: a British hand-held projectile launcher first used in 1943.

Pillbox
A small concrete defensive post, usually round or hexagonal, so named from their resemblance to the containers in which pills were sold.

Pocket
Part of a salient where the neck is narrow enough for the 'pocket' to be completely surrounded and effectively cut off.

Reveille
Military waking signal, normally sounded on a bugle.

S-mine
German anti-personnel landmine nicknamed the 'Bouncing Betty'. When triggered, the mine sprang upwards into the air and detonated just below waist height, making it a highly effective deterrent against infantry.

Salient
Territory surrounded on three sides by the enemy.

Scammell
The British 30-ton Pioneer semi-trailer tank transporter, manufactured by the Scammell truck company.

Second front
The opening of a new battlefront, so that the enemy has to divide his forces. In the Second World War, specifically the 1944 invasion and subsequent Allied campaign in Western Europe, which diverted German resources from the Eastern Front against Russia.

Sherman
The M4 Sherman, a US medium tank also used by other Allied forces. Although outgunned by heavier tanks, its mobility and durability meant that large numbers were produced throughout the war.

Siegfried defences
A line of bunkers, tank traps and concrete fortifications stretching 400 miles along Germany's western borders. First built in 1938, the defences were reinforced in 1944 as the Allied armies approached.

Singing Sister: *see* Moaning Minnie

Smoke
Tanks fired smoke shells to create a screen and provide concealing cover, either to confuse the target of an attack or to mask a change of direction.

Spandau

Generic name given to the German MG34 and MG42 machine guns. The government arsenal at Spandau was one of two major manufacturers.

Spitfire

Iconic British single-seater fighter aircraft, noted for its speed, produced throughout the war by the Supermarine Aviation Works (Vickers) Ltd.

Stirling

A British heavy bomber which first saw service in 1941, the Short Stirling was largely superseded by the Halifax and the Lancaster, both of which could carry bigger bombs.

Stonk

A heavy barrage of mortar fire.

Thunderbolt

The heaviest of the single-engine fighters, the American P-47 Thunderbolt could carry a bomb load of 2,500 lb and was equally effective both in ground attacks and in the air.

Tiger

The heaviest of the German tanks, the Panzerkampfwagen Tiger Ausführing E was massively armoured and outgunned every Allied tank, but was costly to produce, and fewer than 1,500 were made between 1942 and 1944. The later Tiger II or Konigstiger (King Tiger) was more powerful still.

Tracer fire

Tracer fire carries a pyrotechnic charge which ignites so that the trajectory of the round can be clearly followed, and is largely used to improve accuracy of aiming.

Typhoon

British single-seater fighter-bomber, made by Hawker, which was able to combat the Fw 190 and also enjoyed considerable success as a ground-attack aircraft.

Wolfpacks

Name given to groups of German U-boat submarines, which hunted in 'pack' formations to destroy Allied shipping convoys.

9 RTR C Squadron officers and NCOs, taken at Charing in autumn 1943. Trevor is in the centre of the back row. Among those mentioned in the diary are Seargeant Vic Hewitt, back row far left, SSM Edwards, third row far left, second-in-command Captain Link, second row fifth from left, and Lance Corporal Bert Cousins, who drew the cartoon of Trevor on page 366, front row far right.

Photograph © The Trevor Greenwood Archive

The Organisation of 9 RTR

At the start of its active service in June 1944, 9 RTR was part of 31 Tank Brigade, under the command of Brigadier G. S. Knight. On 31 August 1944, following the decision to convert 31 Tank Brigade to Churchill Crocodile flame-throwers, 9 RTR became part of 34 Tank Brigade, under the command of Brigadier W. S. Clarke.

9 RTR remained with 34 Brigade until the end of the war, except for a brief period between 26 December 1944, when it was detached from the brigade and placed under the command first of 51 (Highland) Division and then 53 (Welsh) Division, and 29 January 1945, when command reverted to 34 Brigade. Also in January 1945, the RTR battalions were renamed regiments, so that 9 RTR became the 9th Royal Tank Regiment rather than the 9th Battalion, Royal Tank Regiment; and 34 Tank Brigade was renamed 34 Armoured Brigade.

Until July 1944, when he was injured in the battle for Hill 112, the CO of 9 RTR was Lt Col Sir Nugent Everard. From then until 9 RTR was disbanded after the war, the CO was Lt Col Peter Norman (Berry) Veale.

9 RTR was divided into four squadrons: HQ Squadron and A, B and C Squadrons. Trevor Greenwood was in

C Squadron, the officer in command of which was Major Ronald Holden.

When in action the battalion was also divided into echelons: 'A', 'B' and 'F'. 'F' echelon comprised the fighting tanks, with the addition of a scout car. 'A' echelon was the supply echelon which kept the tanks functioning, and consisted of half-tracks and 3-tonners with ammunition and petrol, plus a water truck, a fitters' half-track and a recovery vehicle in case of broken-down or otherwise damaged tanks. 'A' echelon operated at some distance behind the front lines and further back still would be 'B' echelon, which carried baggage and blankets, a field kitchen and catering supplies and the officers' mess equipment. When 9 RTR were in action, the echelons remained separate, and 'A' echelon would come up to the tanks as and when required, or when it was possible to reach them.

The supply echelons also contained personnel from the Signals, from the Royal Engineers and from the Army Catering Corps, all of whom worked to maintain both the tanks and their crews in good fighting order.

More detail on the structure of 9 RTR and how it functioned can be found in the concluding chapter by John Delaney: *9 RTR in Normandy, 1944*, beginning on page 367.

Part One

France

303.

D+200. Sat. 23.12.44.

Usual routine & little to report.
Not much news from the 'front', but
everyone seems optimistic. Weather a little
better today: perhaps our aircraft will
have a chance to intervene. It has
certainly been 'funny' weather up to now.
Plenty of mail today. Four letters from
Jess. ... including three 'snaps' of Barry.
Jolly good!
Canuks still at Bilzen — standing by.
Judging by reports, the lads are having
a fairly easy time.
Spent the day reading & writing

D+201. Sun. 24.12.44

Xmas eve! A grand morning: cloudless
sky, no wind, & heavy frost ... very cold.
At last our aircraft will have a chance to

Trevor kept his diary in a series of notebooks, writing in them every day,
often under conditions of considerable difficulty.

D-Day Tuesday 6.6.44

It has happened at last. Heard first rumours at 8 a.m. Much evidence of restrained excitement. We are not affected ... yet! Apart from numerous Lightnings, saw little evidence of 'second front' during day. This evening saw amazing procession of aerial tugs and gliders, all heading south. Several waves of them, many dozens in all. An inspiring sight. Weather fine, but fairly cloudy: breezy. Heard radio 9 p.m. ... King's speech. Sounded like an address by the Archbishop. News later confirmed success of landings: fighting 10 miles inland at Caen. PM addressed Commons twice. Eisenhower* broadcast to France. Wrote to Jess.

D +1 Wednesday 7.6.44

Half day cancelled. More work on vehicle – sealing. Saw film *Tunisian Victory*† this morning: very good. Much aerial activity today: waves of Libs and Forts [Liberators and Fortresses: see Glossary] this evening. Everyone seems quite cheerful ... probably glad to have reached end of deadlock. Learned today that we are scheduled for France, but when? Can't be long now. Letter from Jess; wrote to Jess and Garsden. Weather fine, but fairly cloudy. Stiff breeze.

---

* General Dwight D. Eisenhower, later US President (1953–61), was Supreme Commander of the Allied Forces in Europe from January 1944 until the end of the war.
† A joint production of the British and US governments, this was one of several stirring films specifically designed to boost morale.

D +2 Thursday 8.6.44

Still progressing in France. Spent the day on final sealing. Pay parade – later handed in all cash except 10/– [10 shillings].* Lecture by Captain Link, illustrated with French maps.

Weather fine, but rather dull – strong breeze. Not too good for landing craft. Letter to and from Jess.

D +3 Friday 9.6.44

Still sealing tanks. Yesterday's cash return re-paid in francs plus an extra £1's worth (200 to £1). Weather terrible. Rained most of morning – but after lunch there was a deluge, continuing until evening. Streets and fields flooded afterwards. Heaven help the invasion forces if we have much similar weather. Practically no signs of aircraft all day: must be grounded. Latest invasion news satisfactory. Bayeux taken yesterday, and advances practically everywhere. Caen still held by enemy. Appears to have some armoured stuff there.

Letter from Jess – letter to Jess. Phoned Jess 5 p.m. Heard her voice: lovely thrill.

D +4 Saturday 10.6.44

Sealing completed: we are ready. Weather much better: only a light shower: soon over. Much air activity today – more

* There were twenty shillings to the pound, and twelve pence in a shilling. The old shilling was the equivalent of five new pence in today's currency.

cheerful sign. OC's lecture after lunch – behaviour, discipline, etc. overseas. Billet cleaning preparatory to departure ... when?

All confined to barracks from 8 a.m. Saw Mrs Lubick and Mrs Cove. Lucky husbands! Bought a kettle (Mrs Cove paid and refused my cash!) Expect this will be darned useful.

Evening: CB ban lifted. Tomorrow, Sunday routine. Are we going Monday? Letter from Jess and Dorothy.

Canteen for supper. Heard 9 o'clock news. Still progressing. British and Americans now made contact: 20-mile continuous beachhead. Still fighting for Caen. Enemy reported retreating disorderly in Italy. Good. Wrote to Jess.

D +5 Sunday 11.6.44

This morning we were given a couple of hours to write our last letters ... from this side. Scribbled a hasty note to Jess: but how inadequate were my few words. It is so difficult to say what is in your heart without causing grief. But she will understand. Also wrote a short note to Dorothy. Would have liked to write Kath and Tod and Marjorie, but there was no time.

All tank crews issued with more new clothing during the day, *viz*: suit of one-piece denim per man, 2 shirts, 2 drawers, 2 pair socks – surely we have too much clothing now! Some have already started bartering shirts for socks, etc. Likewise, many fellows have spent all remaining English money and are now selling their francs! If we don't go soon, there will be a few bloated capitalists in the squadron with thousands of francs: the rest will be bankrupt.

Noticed a more hysterical atmosphere this morning: particularly among the younger fellows. I s'pose they are blowing off steam. This delayed departure is getting us worked up. But things are moving now.

This evening, a few A tanks moved out . . . witnessed by many civilians. The watching troops treated this departure hilariously, but the civvies looked very grim – almost strained, particularly the women. No mistaking their anxiety. Our turn tomorrow, maybe. We are now strictly confined after 10.30 this evening. Better to go anywhere than remain here penned up. Went to the YMCA free cinema after tea . . . six 'shorts'. Heard the 9 o'clock news later at YMCA. Still making progress. Record landings in Normandy today. Monty's message sounds optimistic.* Front now 50 miles. Still meeting armour at Caen. Situation in Italy still fine: Germans retreating rapidly. We now hold Pescara.

Weather today mild and fairly cloudy. One or two light showers. Not too good for aircraft over there. Letter from Jess: 'I will not be sad: I have prepared myself for this greatest trial of all.' I will remember her words . . . so brave . . . so sensible . . . so reassuring. And my heart will sing to her closing words – 'I love you so much' – as I shortly approach 'the valley of the shadow . . .' I don't think I can possibly hear from her again until I reach France.

---

* General (later Field Marshal) Bernard Law Montgomery commanded the Allied ground forces from the D-Day landings until the end of the Battle of Normandy, after which he continued in command of the 21st Army in northwest Europe. Throughout the campaign Monty habitually wore a black beret with the badge of the Royal Tank Regiment alongside his rank insignia.

General Montgomery sets foot on the beaches, after coming ashore in a
DUKW, 8 June 1944. Note his trademark black beret displaying the badge
of the Royal Tank Regiment alongside his general's insignia.
Photograph © IWM B5174.

D +6 Monday 12.6.44

More departures during last night. The Tank Park looked
fairly deserted this a.m. But C are still here. First contingent
depart about 2 a.m. tomorrow. Self and others about 4.30 a.m.
Not much sleep tonight. Going to the Solent by rail. Did a
little final stowing this morning, then ceased work for the day.
Weather warm and sunny. Plenty of air activity. Had shower
during afternoon. Cash running short. Most of the men are
now broke – apart from francs, which no one now wants to
buy. But there has been a little more bartering.

Managed to write another short note to Jess. Saw Dave Lubick this morning. He had just said good-bye to his wife. I think it is a good job we are going in a few hours' time. Much more of this inactivity will cause depression. Many of the tank crews proudly wearing new denims today, with various titles and slogans painted on the back. A good sign: the lads are very cheerful and in excellent spirits. Heard the 9 o'clock news. Beachhead now 60 miles. Americans about 15 miles from Cherbourg. Still progressing.

German retreat in Italy continuing. Russians have launched attack on Finland. Have no sympathy for the latter. They had their chance to get out of the war* ... But I think this offensive is only the introduction to Russia's summer campaign.

And now to bed: reveille 2.30 a.m.! Where will I be this time tomorrow? Have missed Jess's letter today: but mustn't moan. Have to get used to it ... YMCA cinema this evening – saw *San Francisco*.

D +7 Tuesday 13.6.44

Left Tank Park about 4 a.m. Train departed 6.30 a.m. Arrived Wickham 10.30. By road to Lee-on-Solent, arriving 1.30 p.m.: thus am now in embarkation area. Road journey here from station about 12 miles through rural villages, etc. Much friendly hand-waving, but no hysterical demonstrations from onlookers: no flags, bands or slogans. Just a calm friendliness: even troops waved to us ... rather

* Finland had initially allied itself with Germany against Russia, from whom it had declared independence in 1917. On 16 March 1944 President Roosevelt called for Finland to disassociate itself from Nazi Germany. The Red Army attack on Finland was launched on 9 June 1944.

unusual, but they knew where we were destined for. Got a secret little thrill from all this; but am glad there were no pretentious farewells. Hot meal served in tent on arrival at Lee-on-Solent . . . and then work: final sealing.

Billeted in camp 4 miles from vehicles: had to walk there for tea. Sleeping in huge vehicle shed: hundreds of us in one long room. Three blankets per man issued, with palliasse and pillow straw, etc. After tea, everyone paid 10/– . . . very welcome. Evening free . . . wrote to Jess: letter not sent . . . too badly censored. Will try again tomorrow. Amazing mass of shipping here, all flying barrage balloons. Rained all morning, but cleared up at lunch time. Afternoon warm and sunny. Strawberry time: much activity in fruit fields around here. Countryside very beautiful. Saw a grand avenue of rhododendrons in flower close by.

D +8 Wednesday 14.6.44

Fine morning: marched to vehicle – about 3 ½ miles along waterfront. Dozens of vessels . . . maybe hundreds, including some very large naval vessels. Completed sealing and stowing by lunch time. One or two heavy showers about noon. Had lunch in town . . . got a lift back to camp later. Afternoon free. Went to camp 'cinema' in evening: accommodated in a queer 'building' of marquees. Saw *The Sullivans*.

Band of East Lancs Regt. played in camp prior to cinema show – quite good. Wrote to Jess. Strawberries very plentiful just now: tasted my first today. Wonder if Jess has yet gathered any at home. Hope they aren't all eaten by visitors! Wonder whether she is worrying much. She won't know definitely that I am still in this country ... but may have an idea. Seems ages since I had a letter. 'A' Echelon may bring some when/if they catch up with us. No signs of any great excitement today, but our departure must be very near. Am amazed that I don't feel terrified about impending events. But I am not looking forward to action.

D +9 Thursday 15.6.44

Lecture this morning by IO ... and then nothing, but plenty of rest. Weather warm and sunny. Pleasant surprise about 5 p.m. – mail arrived. Two letters from Jess, and one from J.W.G. [Garsden] Much news about Barry and Jess ... all happy news. Also about the family ... Kath, Toddy and Olive, Dorothy, etc. A great treat, these letters: seems ages since I last heard from home, but it is only a few days really.

D +10 Friday 16.6.44

Still here ... another day of rest. Only official activity was the issue of 'Mae Wests'* this morning, plus two 24-hour ration packs per man. Also vomit bags: found I had been given three of the latter. Do I look like a good vomiter? Inserted craft Nos. on our embarkation tags.

Wrote to Jess – then read for most of day. Loudspeaker system here is a bit of a nuisance. It operates throughout the camp ... making official announcements, etc. all day. I am

---

* An inflatable life jacket affectionately named after the curvaceous American film actress, who provided a convenient rhyming slang for 'life vest'.

beginning to dread that 'attention all troops' repeated so often throughout the day. Received a further 10/– each.

D +11 Saturday 17.6.44

Still waiting: games this morning ... an effort to prevent boredom, I suppose. Delightful surprise in Naafi at 11 a.m.: heard a really fine pianist playing Chopin, Rubinstein, Mendelssohn, Beethoven. Very rare to hear other than jazz in Naafi ... hope to hear him again. Wrote to Jess: read quite a lot. Went to cinema after tea. Saw *Melody Jim*: not much good.

Air raid warning about 11.30 p.m.: all clear half hour later. Had 10 francs on Derby sweep. Still fair amount of bartering for English money. Francs are being sold pretty cheaply by some fellows. Think they regard the money as partly worthless owing to press controversy regarding note issue. Germans, too, are reported to have paid out francs liberally. But I imagine our currency will be stabilised as we occupy the territory. Fine day, but cool wind.

D +12 Sunday 18.6.44

Aroused early this a.m. by loudspeakers (about 4 a.m., I imagine), calling certain craft numbers to parade. Not ours, thank goodness, – but the numbers are getting very close. Heard later that it was the 7th. So our brigade has started to go at last! Believe they ultimately got away about 7 a.m. The loudspeakers less welcome than ever now: at any time they may call our numbers. Day fine and warm: hot shower before lunch. Read most of morning.

Lecture from OC this morning, reminding us of procedure for crossing, and on arrival. Thinks we may go today. Somehow, I don't think C will go today.

Later. I was wrong. Loudspeakers announced our craft numbers about 4.30 p.m. . . . whole battn. Much excitement: news greeted with roar of cheers . . . don't know why.

Blankets, palliasse, etc. returned to stores. Tea and wash and ready for departure about 5.30. Transport to tanks . . . and then we moved off about 6.15 p.m. Did a circuit along the front, and back via rear of Lee-on-Solent. Seemed to be people waving from every house. Also many people in streets waving to us: quite a send off.

Eventually reached area of 'hards'* and held up for some time whilst others loading. 12, 13, 14, 15 Troops finally loaded on same ship, an LST . . . USA.† Must have been midnight. Final sealing on board, and then bed. Comfortably housed in bunks. Believe we are due to sail in the morning, about 10 a.m. Managed to send letter to Jess just before leaving camp.

D +13 Monday 19.6.44

Reveille 6 a.m. – breakfast at 7 – excellent meal. American food. Still off Gosport. Day warm, but fresh breeze. Good to be on ship once again: everywhere clean: decent wash bowls: hot and cold water: showers: lavs. American crew: seem very free and easy. This ship has been in other campaigns – Algiers, Sicily, Salerno, and now the fifth trip to Normandy.

---

* A sloping stone or concrete foreshore built to facilitate access for craft to the water.
† Most of the Landing Ships (Tanks) were built in the USA.

A lorry disembarks from a landing ship on the Normandy beaches. Despite their huge size, the LSTs were designed to unload directly onto the shore. Photograph © IWM A23949.

Later: 2 p.m. Still here. Awaiting storm anchor: presume rest of unit have already gone this morning. Excellent lunch – pork cutlet, etc. – and real coffee. Notice the crew eating ice cream!

7 p.m. Tea – another good meal: if today's menu is typical, the US Navy is being better fed than the British Army. The food we have had today is probably in keeping with what the average civilian *thinks* we get normally. At tea meal we had 'hamburger', potatoes, etc., tinned fruit salad, jam, etc., coffee with brown sugar *ad lib*. Still no signs of moving.

11.30 p.m. We have moved at last – still without our storm anchor. Soon after 10 p.m., commenced journey to join convoy.

Gazing at the receding shoreline, an American sailor said 'have a good look at it while you can, buddy – it will be a long time before you see England again!' I felt resentful, but said nothing. The fellow could have been more tactful ... altho he couldn't be expected to know how much I was leaving behind.

Passed Nelson's *Victory* in the river. It only reminded me of the ghastly folly of mankind: that ship was in action 140 years ago ... and even then we were supposed to be civilised. A few minutes later passed close to the *Ramillies* in harbour. Her 15-inch guns were still uncovered and the muzzles black and sooty. Presume she had just returned from bombarding France. Lovely sunset as we sailed south from Portsmouth. Didn't feel so good: can't help thinking of Jess. Saw a huge collection of ships in the Solent, but we didn't join them. Shortly, another large group of ships became visible east of the Isle of Wight. Our convoy?

Later. Yes ... our convoy apparently: we took up a position to the south and dropped our forward anchor. Nearly midnight: believe the convoy is scheduled to sail at 1 a.m. Almost dark now: plenty of lights on buoys along Channel, and lots of 'winking' lights from signalling lamps. It all seems rather weird and terrifying.

It is difficult to believe that I am now en route for France – and action. Surely it cannot be possible that I may never see my love again. It is much more boisterous out here. The ship is rolling appreciably: nearly everyone is asleep.

Will we sail at 1 a.m.? I dread the thoughts – but I can do nothing ... nothing. May as well go to bed: expect we will be in mid Channel by reveille. Believe we are due at the beach 12 noon tomorrow. Have to wear Mae Wests now all the time. Supposed to sleep in it, but don't think I will.

D +14 Tuesday 20.6.44

Amazed to learn at reveille that we haven't moved during the night. What is the hitch this time? Went on deck before breakfast: can still see England to the north quite clearly ... and IoW to the west very close. Convoy still here too. Wind fairly high and ship rolling, but still anchored. Rumour that sailing prevented by rough weather out in Channel. Very much doubt this.*

Good breakfast: no sickness yet, but one or two felt a bit queer. Bright sunshine up on deck, but wind is quite strong and cold. Naval barge came alongside just now with another balloon for us. Our 'forrard' balloon broke away yesterday, but we still had one flying from stern. Two must be necessary. A bit of a job transferring the balloon, with barge rising and falling in swell – managed OK eventually. Seemed a hell of a lot of trouble just for a balloon. Don't think the crew have much faith in them. They *must* limit angle of fire of ships' AA guns.

Later: 3 p.m. No move yet: am told that 1 o'clock BBC news referred to heavy seas and difficult landing conditions on beaches. So weather may be the trouble after all. For the past hour or so, a small convoy of nine landing craft have been approaching from south. They are now close enough for us to see that they are fully laden with army vehicles, etc. Have they been turned back by weather? May be so. Lunch another good meal; asparagus for veg. this time.

Later. Many more landing craft, fully laden, have appeared from the south: counted at least 30: some seem to have

* In fact the storms disrupted the Allies' plans for three days, delaying the follow-up to the initial invasion and grounding air support.

joined in with our group. Surely they haven't *all* returned without unloading their vehicles. Perhaps they are assembling here from another port, awaiting escort.

This ship seems to be full of fumes. In the hold, petrol fumes from tanks: an hour at a stretch down there on guard is enough – feel half asphyxiated afterwards. On upper deck – diesel fumes. A diesel-driven dynamo is always working, and the exhaust fumes emerge from ship's side, about centre. That heavy poisonous smell seems to be everywhere. It is much worse when the main engines start. Here again, the exhaust is at the side. This seems bad designing to me. The exhaust fumes are comparatively dangerous, and would be better and more effectively swept clear of the ship via a funnel. Our sleeping quarters too are badly ventilated. There are no portholes for one thing. 'Feet-fumes' are almost unbearable at times. The air is always thick. Normally, neither fumes nor ventilation would matter much, because we would only spend about 12 hours on board. We have now been here almost 48 hours!

Later. A queer mixture for tea – sausage? – beans, sauerkraut, tomato ketchup, tomato chutney, mixed veg, piles of other seasoning: pineapple rice pudding, bread and butter, coffee – the latter too sweet! It is all excellent food (from tins) but I don't like these highly flavoured mixtures.

Half a dozen nurses from a nearby hospital ship were brought aboard at tea time by our small motor launch. Seemed a risky job for women transferring from tiny launch in this heavy swell. I think this was their only way of enjoying an evening out. They joined in some singing on deck later in evening. But the jokes . . . ! Nurses left about 11 p.m.

D +15 Wednesday 21.6.44

Still at anchor: sea still fairly high, but weather quite fine. No sign of moving. Mass of ships still with us. Half hour PT on deck this morning under troops. Good lunch ... ham, spinach, potatoes, gravy, lemon cheese tart – coffee: again too sweet!

Evening. Still here ... but now rumoured that we may sail about 2 a.m. Sea a little calmer this evening. Convoy seems to have grown: ships all around us and as far as horizon. Two cruisers arrived this afternoon: destroyers also chasing around. Is there another beachhead on the way? Have now been aboard three days – and travelled about 4 or 5 miles. Cigarettes are running low. Sleeping quarters becoming hard to bear: no ventilation at night: air foul and thick: partly oil and fume-laden, too. Rumoured this afternoon that we would move tonight, irrespective of weather: tanks have been shackled down by crew.

Haven't seen newspapers since Sunday ... and no wireless news. Hear vague rumours about war from crew, but nothing definite.

No mail: no word from Jess. Are her letters already over there? Presume they must be. Thank goodness there is something to look forward to. There must be at least half a dozen letters for me somewhere.

Good tea meal: steak, potatoes, mixed veg: tinned peaches – tea – bread and butter. Tea too sweet! I like sweet tea and coffee, but the Americans must like it sickly sweet. There is no shortage of sugar on this ship. Bowls full on tables for all meals. Later. Sailing midnight?

D +16 Thursday 22.6.44

Now about mid-Channel: weighed anchor midnight. Dull morning: low clouds but fairly good visibility. Convoy appears to be in extended formation – more or less in line, not in group. No sign of escort, but presume they are somewhere on flanks. All ship's AA guns fully manned. Believe there are nine of them. Ship rolling badly, altho sea not really rough – merely a slight swell. Not much activity among troops: most of them in bed. Has been some seasickness: cabin atmosphere now awful. Feel OK myself. Had a shower after breakfast. Been up on deck for fresh air, but diesel fumes seem to be everywhere, especially with main engines running. Spent half hour down in engine room. Awful noise. Two main engines 900 b.h.p. each – three auxiliary 150 b.h.p. each for power, etc. including de-gaussing.* All winches, etc. electrically driven: water electrically heated. But *fuel*-fired cooking ovens!

Slept in Mae Wests last night. All hatches and watertight doors closed: guard withdrawn from hold. Tanks shackled and now left . . . with all hatches, etc. closed and fastened. Believe there are subs about in 'wolf-packs' – but there were no alarms during the night. So far, everything OK this morning.

Later: 9.30 a.m. Just sighted land. Escorts on port . . . and minesweepers: dozens of them!

---

* A term first coined in the Second World War to describe the methods devised by British scientists to counter German magnetic mines. The *gauss* was a unit used by the Germans to measure the strength of their mines' magnetic field. 'Degaussing' is now common usage for the removal or lowering of magnetism from a device.

10.30 a.m. Land clearly visible. We seem to be preparing to anchor ... presumably in Seine Bay. Amazing collection of ships here: must be hundreds – several warships, including at least one battleship. Not a sign of the enemy either at sea or in the air.

2.30 p.m. Dropped anchor 12 p.m. after cruising around for some time: about 2 or 3 miles off shore. Courseulles-sur-Mer clearly visible: we appear to be on original landing beach near Caen. Dozens of ships here: many of them already beached, probably waiting for high tide, to withdraw. Believe we will go ashore at high tide (3.30 p.m.?) and disembark a couple of hours later. Heavy gunfire clearly audible on board here. Perhaps from Caen itself? Or has C fallen? Haven't seen any news since Sunday. Anyhow, the war is now damnably close, judging by that gunfire ... and I don't feel a bit thrilled! As I write, there are two or three dozen ships between this boat and the shore ... with Courseulles in the background. The latter seems undamaged through the glasses: appears to be a small town with gently rolling country to the right. Five church spires visible. Probably about 15 miles of coastline visible from here. It all seems very peaceful: gently sloping country, green and sunlit: not a lot of woodland.

3 p.m. We have just started moving again, this time towards the shore ... those beaches!! Few minutes ago, a lifebelted corpse floated past the ship: first tangible evidence of death ...

Later. Landed about 5.30 p.m. And what a sight! The beach looked like a ships' graveyard, altho most of the beached vessels were not really wrecks: they were merely high and dry awaiting next tide. But there certainly was some evidence of the last fortnight's fighting. One landing craft completely overturned . . . one steam tug holed and lying on her side . . . etc., etc. Looking back on the bay, there was an amazing mass of shipping, and the sky seemed literally full of balloons . . . local ones, and on more distant beaches. Cannot possibly describe the scene here.

Halted by the beach (we landed 'dry') and removed most of sealing: then drove inland to assembly area: Much evidence of the war en route: Fields still marked with Jerry 'skull and crossbones' and '*Minen*' [mines]. Our 'lanes' clearly marked and taped.* Country lanes already being widened and improved. Mass of wrecked vehicles by beach. Simple graves by roadside . . . bearing wooden crosses and steel helmets, etc. Terribly depressing sight. Army vehicles everywhere, and all troops look terribly dirty, but brown and cheerful. This entire region is just a huge army camp. God knows what all the vehicles are for: some weird-looking monsters. Saw a four-engine bomber lose a wing and dive to earth: eight of crew had baled out 10 minutes previously. Later drove on to congregation area: first of C to arrive. 'A' Echelon been here since Monday!

We are about 7 miles from front line. Terrific AA barrage over front as two groups of our bombers were returning. One bomber shot down. Seems a miracle they all weren't shot down. Worked on tank until dark, then dug long and wide shallow trench to sleep in. Ran tank over afterwards for 'roof' against shrapnel and Jerry anti-personnel bombs. Believe he comes over every night. A few Jerries been over already: met by heavy AA fire from our side. Took cover! Opened 24-hour packs for supper meal.

Saw a few of natives on today's journey thro villages and

---

* The Germans left lanes open for patrols and assault troops in their minefields, subsequently marked to allow safe passage.

fields. Seem almost a peasant type. Not much evidence of enthusiasm amongst them: just a few polite hand waves. Perhaps they resent our intrusion: can well understand this. Their former well tilled fields and lovely countryside is now a battleground. Not *all* crops and cattle destroyed, but there must have been much damage. Much material damage too in certain villages.

These people haven't seen war for generations, and now it has descended upon them *because* of the Allies. The Germans only occupied the country ... and seem to have behaved themselves at that. Local attitude probably inclined to 'a plague on both your houses'. Have seen a few Tricolours* hanging from bedroom windows nevertheless. A child of about four gave me an immaculate Nazi salute as we passed today. Probably thought it was correct greeting for *all* soldiers. Much evidence of local religious fervour. Even tiny hamlets seem to have imposing churches with tall spires. Also wayside shrines and Calvarys are quite frequent ... some very elaborately built. To bed about 1 a.m.

D +17 Friday 23.6.44

Fine day. Stood by, expecting to move nearer to front. Plenty of work on tank, preparing for action. Fed on 24-hour packs. Received details of our role in impending battle. Plenty of air cover all day. Haven't seen a Nazi plane yet, but much of our AA towards coast. Saw a burned-out Sherman: it received about four hits from 88s. Indescribable wreckage. Letters from home!! One from Jess: Also Kath and Plowman. Wrote Jess and Plowman. Also sent Jess my first field service card.

* The French flag: red, white and blue.

Cannot let her know I am here, but she will guess. K's letter included details of Bob's ordeals before his final flight. He went through hell alright ... and made no complaint to K. Something inspiring in K's story.* Felt better for reading it. Happy news from Jess about 'Poppet'. How *could* I carry on without her letters to look forward to? Feel terribly afraid when I think of immediate future: suffer awful depression ... but am better when I can switch my thoughts to home, Jess and Poppet ... and possible happiness in store for me.

The field service postcard which Trevor sent Jess on 23 June. Despite the instruction to write nothing other than the date and signature, he has added very faintly in pencil, 'I am in Caen'.
Photograph © The Trevor Greenwood Archive.

* Bob was shot down over Germany, and died in a POW camp. See Editor's Note for details of Trevor's family and friends.

Later. Now confirmed no move tonight. To bed once again in hole beneath tank. All tank crews doing guard throughout night. Bed midnight.

D +18 Saturday 24.6.44

Started feeding from 'compo' packs this morning. Beautiful morning, but cold at 6 a.m. Banged my head on tank bottom getting into bed last night ... just where grease had been slapped on for dump valve. Awful blob of grease stuck to my hair: slept with knotted hanky nightcap to keep grease off blanket. Had to wash my hair in petrol this morning.

Later. Boiling hot day and cloudless sky. No work ... just awaiting battle orders and eating and writing. Received further orders tea time. Moving nearer front at midnight. Don't feel so good about this: we appear to be destined for a fairly hot time during next 3 or 4 days. Can't imagine myself being 'bumped off': too much to live for.

Saw a newspaper today – last Wednesday's! The front doesn't seem to have shifted much around Caen. See what we can do about it! No incoming mail today so far. Wrote to Kath ... and sent official postcard to Jess notifying change of address to BWEF from today. Received further 3 days' food supply today. Don't know what the hell to do with it all. Am sure we could live for a month on present stocks: all tinned and 'ersatz' stuff, but reasonably good. Hard biscuits are main trouble ... no bread.

D +19 Sunday 25.6.44

Moved to new location late last night: only about 3 miles nearer front, but we spent about four hours en route. Awkward route ... probably for security. Conferences all day: all troop leaders doing little but studying maps. Our first action is now imminent and everyone is more serious. A and B doing one attack ... C another, and later in day.

We move out of harbour 7 a.m. Monday. I think we will have a hard task. Have spent all day trying to forget my jitters, but impossible. My stomach sinks to record low level when I think of facing barrage from Jerry 88s. Have seen their effect on a Sherman! Weather was bad, too ... rainy and gloomy. A really wretched day, all told. Two letters from Jess! Wrote to J.

D +20 Monday 26.6.44

Yesterday, I had grave doubts as to whether this page would ever be written. I felt as though I had been condemned to death. But it is obvious that I have survived. We left harbour at 7 a.m. for the front line, only about 3 miles away. Held up for an hour en route ... slap in the middle of a concentration of our artillery. And they had just started a barrage. What pandemonium! The earth itself shook noticeably. Jerry must have had a hell of a time.

Village of Cheux had only been taken by our troops that morning, and there was much evidence of the battle. The stench of dead cows in adjoining fields was awful. Several human corpses along route ... one, recognisable as a Jerry by torn bits of uniform, had been run over on the verge, and tanks subsequently passed over his body. It was just a pulpy mass of bloody flesh and bones. No one appeared to be bothered by it. Our own troops were too busy 'digging in' against possible counter attack to worry about dead bodies.

The village itself was a shambles ... just a mass of gaunt-looking walls and chimney pots, with a few remaining houses full of shell holes. Snipers were still busy in some of these houses. Kept my head down! Beyond village, every-thing was bustle and chaos. Enormous numbers of men and vehicles moving forward.

We took up our start position in a large field below crest of a hill: 5 p.m. Our infantry were in position too ... some hundreds of them. Had seen them on the way down. A sturdy looking crowd ... mostly Scotties* ... all smiling and cheerful. I think they were really glad to have our support. They asked us to swipe hell out of Jerry!

Had previously received our orders and were thoroughly conversant with plan of attack and ultimate objective. We also had a pretty good idea of where enemy's main anti tank guns were, from previous reconnaissance. Close to our zero hour, word came through that 60 Panthers had appeared within a few hundred yards of our line of advance. Hell's bells! Poor little C Squadron!

But very soon, and before we started, the Panthers advanced on our position and were engaged by some fairly heavy stuff ... 17-pounders, I think. After about an hour, Jerry must have retired: he certainly didn't get through! ... and we commenced our delayed start at 6.15 p.m. Infantry ahead, and rifles at the ready. Over the crest ... towards the woods where we knew there would be trouble. By 7 p.m. the battle

---

* The 9th Cameronians (Scottish Rifles), a battalion of the 15th Scottish Infantry Division.

was on. AT guns were firing like hell ... and so were we. Very soon, I saw one crew bale out, tank on fire. They crawled away in the long corn, avoiding Jerry snipers and MGs.

Advance proceeded: infantry kept 'going to ground' because of Jerry's MGs. We sprayed those woods with Besa ... tons of it ... and HE ... and AP ... and smoke. Impossible to see AT guns in woods. Could only fire at their 'flash'. Advance proceeded slowly: two or three Jerry tanks appeared and were engaged: they disappeared. More of ours were hit: some burning ... crews baling out.

Found myself behaving rationally and quite calm. Was really terrified just prior to 'going in'. Eventually we retired and waited ... it seemed hours to me. We were on the battlefield all the time. We should have left, but stayed in case infantry required more assistance. Good job we did. We had to advance a second time later on to help them out. Awful business. Major H* was grand. Picked up many men and some wounded – one stretcher case – and removed them to rear.

Were in action until it was too dark to see ... must have been 10.30 p.m. Our loss 8 vehicles ... all blazing away when we finally departed about 1 a.m.

Next had difficulty in returning to our lines. Front very fluid and we might have been shot up as enemy counter attack if not careful. RO went ahead to contact our forward troops. Eventually crawled into Cheux about 2 a.m. Lay quietly in Cheux: guard on each vehicle. Snipers still in ruined buildings: firing constantly. Left Cheux 4.30 a.m. ... only just in time: heard later that enemy counter-attacked Cheux soon after we left, using Tigers, etc. But our troops retained the village.

Eventually harboured couple of miles behind front

* Major Ronald (Ronnie) Holden, commander of C Squadron, who was to win both the MC and the DSO during the first six months of the campaign.

line ... and learned we were scheduled for another attack immediately! Thanks to Major's strong protest, we remained in harbour for rest, etc. Had no sleep for 2 nights, and no food for many hours. Even water was a godsend during the action. Vehicles also need attention ... those that remained! Disappointing result to our hard fight: no advance made at all. Infantry badly beaten up.

Opposition was far greater than anticipated. Where were our aircraft as promised? May have been weather. There was a terrible deluge during height of action. Periscopes almost useless: much water in vehicle: clothes soaked to saturation: infantry must have been half drowned. They had a bad time: survivors we picked up were thankful for our reappearance. Pity we couldn't have saved more of them: a grand lot of lads.

D +21 Tuesday 27.6.44

Major Holden managed to persuade the powers that be that we were unfit for further action, and so we remained in harbour for rest, sleep and food ... and to take stock of our remaining vehicles. Weather quite fine.

Several enemy snipers still lurking in woods 100 yds away. Four of them surrendered last night after our flame-throwers sprayed the trees. Enemy mortar fire falling around. Enemy fighters over this afternoon. Dived beneath tank when they machine-gunned us. One of our Auster OPs was shot down and fell a few yards away ... burst into flames immediately: no hope of saving pilot. Burned furiously for an hour. Sickening smell of burning flesh: ghastly business. Remains of charred body removed later.

Very few of our planes about ... very few. Jerry has been

over us several times today, greeted each time by a terrific barrage of every conceivable type of gun. Noise simply appalling. Meanwhile, our field guns – some very close by, others further back – are pounding Jerry ceaselessly. Impossible for speech during many of these artillery barrages. Our 25-pounders doing great work for lads in front line.

Keeble killed by sniper in Cheux today. Gotobed and Painter died of yesterday's wounds. Jim Chapman killed outright yesterday.* Terrible losses, but amazingly light considering the hammering we received. Expectation of life must be pretty low here. Every four seconds there is a chance of being hit by something ... apart from risks run in actual fighting.

Anticipate battering by HE tonight after Jerry's reconnaissance today. We have dug a huge sleeping hole beneath tank. Should be fairly safe. Strong guard on vehicles tonight: too many snipers about to run risks.

D +22 Wednesday 28.6.44

Still in harbour – our 'remnants'! A and B have done good work from all accounts, but met fairly light opposition. Their losses very slight. Major H said a few words to us this a.m. about our fight on Monday. Gather that the CO has now realised the size of our effort. Don't think they had any idea of the extent of opposition. We appear to have cleared the way for further advance next day (by much larger forces!)

---

* These four were the first casualties suffered by 9 RTR in the Second World War.

Later. This evening, a batch of about 20 refugees appeared: a frightful sight. Some had prams containing all their worldly goods: others had wheelbarrows. Two very old ladies were being wheeled in these things. Three tiny babies and a few children included. They seemed greatly relieved to have got away from the 'Bosch'. Some of them had been trekking for three weeks ... sleeping in fields at night. But most were from front-line villages nearby – Colleville and Grainville-sur-Odon, etc. In spite of official ban, much food was given them by the sqdn, and ciggies and money. They were with us until after midnight whilst arrangements were being made for their transfer elsewhere. Almost a carnival atmosphere in the camp for a couple of hours.

Many German prisoners came in during the evening: POW compound in adjoining field. Their troops are all youngsters, 17, 18, 19-year-olds: many *look* much younger. Hardly a fine-looking body of men, but almost without exception they have a very insolent bearing.* Some of them are snipers: they are lucky to be taken prisoners!

Later. The refugees were put up in a nearby field: Heaven knows where they will ultimately be sent: I suppose this will become a major problem before long.

D +23 Thursday 29.6.44

Left harbour 7 a.m. to relieve B ... defending forward position against counter attack ... and support for infantry at

* These were the 12th SS Panzer Division Hitlerjugend, recruited directly from the ranks of the Hitler Youth. Trevor wrote to Jess that 'they have been thoroughly Nazified since they were 6 or 8 years old. Fortunately their numbers are limited, otherwise I don't know where such fanaticism would lead us!'

Grainville if necessary. Arrived about 8 a.m. Remained static until afternoon, and then went in to attack near Grainville. Tigers reported approaching. Finally engaged a few Mark IVs, but they soon made off. Remained at alert until 1 a.m., and then back to harbour. Bed 2 a.m. I think we must have 'shook' Jerry today. We put up a tremendous barrage of AP and Besa. Only casualties were an NCO and OR: tank received direct hit from mortar and damaged. We were mortared mercilessly, almost from the moment of our arrival. Heavy mortar is a terrifying experience. Became quite adept at diving beneath tank. Several loads of mortar from 'Singing Sisters' or 'Moaning Minnies' [see Glossary]. They do at least give about 3 seconds warning by their weird wailing before exploding. The detonation is tremendous: sounds like nearby crack of thunder. These weapons have played hell with infantry.

And after only one day, I feel worn out. There is the constant physical effort of diving for safety, plus the awful mental strain of waiting for the explosion. At one period, we all had to take refuge inside the tank: it was too dangerous even to open hatches. Survival now seems to me more a matter of luck than anything: we are being fired at in the tanks by AP from ATs and tanks: machine gunned from the air: shelled by artillery: mortared: sniped at: machine gunned by ground forces . . . and then there are the countless mines and booby traps left behind by Jerry. He has left much equipment, especially personal kit, and many souvenirs have been collected. When rummaging around his dugouts, great care has to be taken because of booby traps. They are even hanging from the trees in places. There is a great deal of artful ingenuity in Jerry's efforts to exterminate us.

Saw many wounded today ... mostly infantry. There are German corpses about, too ... just hastily buried and often partly visible. Dead cattle too are quite common.

This is a beautiful countryside: gently undulating country with magnificent crops. The fields seem generally larger than in England. The farms too are larger and more solidly built and more prosperous-looking. Cattle that haven't been killed are just roaming about eating up fresh growing corn, beans, etc. They are literally living off the fat of the land. I suppose the farmers will ultimately return to organise things and reap the remnants of their crops. Haven't seen any civvies for ages ... apart from yesterday's refugees.

D +24 Friday 30.6.44

'Stand to' at 4.30 a.m. Jerry mortaring Grainville area heavily: seemed like prelude to further counter attack. We repelled him yesterday evening, and he may now have stronger forces. If he breaks through, our forward troops in salient will be isolated. Our area and Cheux seem likely places for onslaught.

Waited at alert for several hours, meanwhile keeping rigid lookout for enemy tanks. But nothing happened ... thank goodness. Our vehicle (and selves) were hardly prepared for heavy action after yesterday: petrol and ammo ... and sleep. We were relieved by 7th* early afternoon: seemed to be at least 2 squadrons! Was glad to see them. We retired to former base, behind Cheux and found B there: latter were on 'stand to'. Had a meal and wash ... and then sleep for hour or two. Unfortunately, this harbour

---

* The 7th Battalion, Royal Tank Regiment. 7 RTR were later to transfer, along with 9 RTR, from 31 Tank Brigade to 34 Tank Brigade.

is surrounded by many of our 25-pounders ... dozens of them. The nearest are less than 100 yds away, and firing towards us. They are firing ceaselessly, with frequent extra heavy barrages: noise indescribable: 'hell let loose' is too mild a term. In spite of this most of us have slept for an hour or two since returning from front line. We are still well within range of enemy mortars and still receiving attention. This mortaring is devastating to the nerves.

Don't know yet whether we will be required again today ... but B are still here: they will surely go before us, having had at least a day's rest.

Saw a remarkable sight this evening: tremendous procession of our four-engined bombers flew overhead, and dropped their loads just beyond front line (around Villers?) Must have been hundreds of planes, but all over in about 10 minutes. Seemed to be very little Jerry AA and didn't see a single plane destroyed. Shortly afterwards, a huge black cloud ascended and gradually spread towards us. Within an hour, we were literally in a fog: air became noticeably cooler and daylight partially obliterated, visibility about 200 yards. Fine dust particles settled everywhere. This 'fog' lasted for about 2 hours. Heaven knows what we hit, but it must have been a mighty bombardment.*

Believe enemy are grouping about 2 Panzer Divs in that area for heavy counter attack. Monty was here today and said 'they will be smashed'! Maybe the RAF have already smashed them. Hope so.

No move ... dug hole, and crept into it for sleep at midnight.

---

* This was the bombing of Villers Bocage, where there was a concentration of enemy tanks.

Avro Lancasters carpet bomb a road junction near Villers Bocage to prevent movement of German Panzer divisions. This was part of the 'mighty bombardment' that Trevor witnessed on 30 June.

Photograph © IWM CL344.

D +25 Saturday 1.7.44

Stand to at reveille . . . but nothing happened. Major Holden spoke to us all at 2.30. Gave resumé of present situation and our part in last day or two's fighting. We seem to have done good work . . . especially in repelling counter attack at Grainville. Reported that we smashed up two infantry battalions.

Grainville and Cheux now very important. Jerry anxious to recapture to break through our salient and eliminate bridgehead over river. So far, we have been largely instrumental in stopping him. Fighting has been bitter: Cameronians suffered fairly heavily.

A and B now officially 'standing to' to help 7th if necessary. C standing down. We appear to be regarded officially as temporarily played out. Not surprised to hear this!

After lunch, troop officer informed me he was sending me back to 'B' Echelon for rest ... Rather a shock to be so separated from the crew. But only for 2 days. Afterwards, I take his place whilst he rests. 'B' Echelon a few miles behind front ... away from these darned guns and mortaring. Will at least get some sleep.

Later. Left 'F' Echelon about five ... with all my kit. Felt a bit depressed about leaving those grand lads, but it wasn't good-bye. Will be with them again in a couple of days. Meanwhile, hope they keep out of trouble. Glasspool taking my place temporarily. He is in 15 Troop ... now non-existent. There were four of us. Lt Francis, and Tprs Moran and Cruickshanks. Former had to bale out twice, and latter once. These lads who have baled out on battlefield have suffered terribly. Sniped and mortared ceaselessly from moment of leaving tanks. Had to crawl for hours on bellies through cornfields, mud, etc. *And* they have seen some awful sights in their own vehicles.

Arrived 'B' Echelon about 7 ... at St-Gabriel-Brecy. Quiet and peaceful here. Village partly re-occupied. Many refugees here, too. Given plenty of grub: fixed up rough bivvy and had good supper, including milk and sugar in tea! How different is life in *this* army! Bed about 11 p.m.: raining heavily.

D +26 Sunday 2.7.44

Tea in bed at 10 a.m., thanks to Bert Cousins! And then breakfast: fried sausage, sweet tea, butter and biscuits. Rain ceased: morning bright and fresh. Slept without trousers last night for first time since leaving England! Changed under-clothing this morning. But still no chance of decent bath.

Letter from Jess this morning – dated 27th ult. She and Barry are well, thank goodness. Have done little writing myself for a few days. Cannot concentrate on letters: too busy dodging death, etc. But will write her today.

Later. Wrote to Jess. Done little but eat and sleep all after-noon. Went into village after tea. Must have been a charming little place formerly: signs of many ancient buildings. Most of houses and cottages still habitable, and damage nothing like as severe as at Cheux.

Lot of old people here ... mostly refugees. Plenty of babies and young children, too. The latter seem cheeky little devils: constantly begging ciggies ... and they smoke them, even nippers of about eight. Presume their fathers are all in German hands.

Seem to be plenty of our aircraft here ... probably defending beaches. We seem to have lacked air support at the front: perhaps due to weather. Ramshackle little café has opened up in the village: supposed to be serving some sort of French wine. Large crowd of our lads in the place: the three of us joined them and were served with a lukewarm drink – black coffee in appearance, but sweet water taste. Couldn't drink the stuff. Half tumblerful cost us 5 francs!

Returned to camp to hear 9 o'clock news. Learned that Normandy front had been quiet: Jerry withdrawing from certain positions. This seems surprising: a large counter attack had been expected.

Sausage for supper and sweet tea. Bed about eleven. Am sleeping in tarpaulin shelter built as lean-to against 3-ton lorry. Not very weather-proof, but better than nothing.

D +27 Monday 3.7.44

Slept little last night. Cup of tea in bed at 10 a.m.! Terrible morning. Raining heavily and misty. Usual visits from local youngsters with chunks of black bread: they barter this stuff for ciggies. Can't bear to look at it, let alone eat it. Am sticking to biscuits. Feel a bit better physically . . . but cannot forget that dreadful front, and keep imagining I can smell it . . . that sickly-sour ghastliness . . . what is it?

Saw burnt-out Jerry SP this evening. One of crew buried alongside: charred bones still visible. Visited Villiers-le-Sec – a small village en route from beaches. Tremendous amount of traffic through the place. Quite a few civilians living there . . . don't know whether they are residents or refugees, but their living conditions are appalling. Have never seen slums as bad in England. These people don't seem particularly pleased to see us. I always feel that they regard us as intruders. Children are becoming a nuisance . . . begging, etc. They hold out their hands automatically . . . not from want. There is an army cinema in Villiers: shows by allocation only. This is the first sign of 'entertainment' I have seen over here. No doubt it will be well used by the 'other army'.*

No incoming mail today. Wrote to Jess. Only evidence of

---

* The large numbers of support and supply troops behind the front lines.

war at this spot is aerial activity for the beachhead. Guns just audible in distance at the front.

D +28 Tuesday 4.7.44

Still resting with 'B' Echelon – eating and sleeping. Cannot concentrate on reading. Wrote to Jess. Weather showery: plenty of mud about: clothes and blankets caked in it.

Nothing happening at front. Probably preparing large offensive. Spent evening in camp: nothing to go out for. No incoming mail. Presume my letters are going up to 'F' Echelon. Bed about 11 p.m.

D +29 Wednesday 5.7.44

Little sleep last night. Much local AA fire: believe one raider was destroyed. Morning fine and sunny, but still plenty of mud everywhere.

Little sound of gunfire all day: lull on the front must be continuing. Many fighters overhead: seem to concentrate over the beachhead. Latter quite apparent from here by number of balloons 3 or 4 miles away.

Been reading a little today: also wrote to Jess. Still no incoming mail. No rain today for a change: quite pleasant this evening. A few of our lads are playing football with local French youngsters: all seem to be enjoying it. The youngsters are all wearing white blouses and blue overall trousers. This seems to be the uniform worn by pupils at the agricultural school here.

A few fresh vegetables have appeared lately – potatoes,

onions, etc. – suspect these youngsters are pinching them from the school. They are constantly arriving too with chunks of very brown bread tucked beneath their blouses. I suppose this is also pinched. Payment always in kind . . . either biscuits, chocs, sweets or ciggies. We derive some amusement from the language problem: some of the local children are even acting as tutors, altho they can't speak English.

D +30 Thursday 6.7.44

Received instructions at midnight last night that I and my colleagues Moran and Cruickshanks were to be on parade at 7.15 a.m. today with all kit in readiness to return to the squadron.

Departed about 8 a.m., and ultimately found the squadron some miles NW of their last harbour. We are now barely in the salient . . . and close to Bocage.

Had an easy day getting settled in again. Squadron moved here last night. They have done nothing since my departure, but were continually mortared in the former harbour. It is more peaceful here . . . but gunfire in near distance. No mortar, thank goodness. Probably Jerry doesn't know we are here: vehicle camouflage is excellent.

Weather beautiful today. Had a bath in a canvas bucket. Lovely surroundings. Grand trees, and magnificent crops. Two letters from Jess . . . wrote to Jess.

D +31 Friday 7.7.44

Still static. Letter from Jess. Wrote to Jess. Transferred to 15 Troop i/c 'Baker'.* Given vehicle from TDU. Spent much time stowing, etc. Heavy force of Lancasters passed over late this evening. Seemed to be a few hundred of them ... and their target may have been Caen area!

D +32 Saturday 8.7.44

Same harbour. Letter from Jess. Little sleep last night. A battery of 5.5s opened up about 2 a.m. and fired until about 5 a.m. Their location about 200 yards away. Terrific din: even the earth trembled violently ... and yet, at least one occupant of my bivvy snored through it all!

Learned that last night's bomber attack was NW of Caen. An attack has gone in there this morning. Last night's artillery was the prelude ... plus the bombing.

Received advance details of probable attack by us on Monday morning. Fine day ... with one or two light showers. Had a chat with Jimmy Aldcroft.

D +33 Sunday 9.7.44

Still static – just south of Brouay. Another bad night. Enemy aircraft spent some time hovering around last night. Queer variety of AA for some time.

Fine morning – stiff breeze. Had a chat with George

---

* Refers to the radio call sign of the tank, in this case 15B ('Baker') as opposed to 15A ('Able') or the troop leader's tank, which just had the call sign '15'.

Wright. Saw Ted Hinson last night. He has just been
attached to A from TDU. Bill Geary now with my troop
(15). Troop officers out this a.m. on recce.

Later. Now confirmed that we are definitely moving out
tonight for another action early tomorrow morning. C's
zero hour is 6.15 a.m. Letter from Jess.

Later. Left harbour 8 p.m., en route for laager just south of
Colleville. Only four- or five-mile journey but slow going.
Entire battalion was on the move, so hold-ups were to be
expected. Most of route through fields: rough cut roads
made by Bulldozers. Military vehicles and equipment everywhere. Every single tree and hedgerow seems to harbour
more vehicles and guns: even open fields are being used in
many places . . . there being insufficient hedgerows for cover.
    Eventually reached Cheux . . . scene of our first action:
the village was quiet and deserted apart from a few troops
and first aid post. A few of my colleagues buried here. There
are very few buildings left: mostly rubbish and ruin. But no
snipers now. Troop officer's vehicle had a breakdown in
village: he took mine and left me with the casualty about
10 p.m. Trouble due to broken bell crank in gear box . . . at
least two hours' work if fitters have necessary spare part.
Crew got busy . . . one man preparing brew. Fitters arrived . . .
no spare: BTO returned to base for spare: we waited.
    Much local activity, chiefly artillery . . . din incessant. Also
many queer lights in sky. Went inside nearby house – appalling sight inside. Owners must have left in great hurry. Most
of furniture wrecked: books everywhere: piano still fairly
good! Many personal letters about: some dated 19 May 44 . . .
probably a happy and peaceful middle-class home less than

two months ago. Now just a ruin: very depressing ... but only one of millions of wrecked houses in last four years.

Examined two Jerry Panthers in village. Fearsome looking tank, mainly due to enormous length of 88. Shocking smell ... dead crew still inside!

No sleep ... just waited for BTO's return and watched brilliant moon appear around midnight. But the beauty and peace of the evening was spoiled ... too many guns, and noise ... noise ... noise: it is terrifying at times. Many dead cattle still lying about: grotesque in moonlight.

D +34 Monday 10.7.44

Probably one of the worst days I will ever know ... BTO returned about 1 a.m., having had to return to St Gabriel for new part. Something of a feat to make return journey in darkness ... no lights, no roads, etc. Job finished about 2.30 a.m. and we moved off to find the squadron: only a hazy idea of their location, but we found them eventually ... about 3.30 a.m. Just in time to form up for march to Verson and FUP. It was a horrible journey. Cold, hunger, fear – terrible fear – these were only a part of the nightmare. I suppose the journey was about 3 miles, but it seemed longer. The territory was only newly occupied, and there were the usual obvious signs – visible even in the dark. Dead cattle, almost always lying with legs pointing upwards ... usually one or more legs blown off by blast or shrapnel: a horrible sight.

Vehicles, both ours and German, dumped in ditches along roadside: villages completely ruined and desolate: silent but for our noise. Sentries and guards standing at road junctions, etc., very much on the alert . . . waiting . . . listening . . . peering . . . snipers everywhere.

How I detest passing through these once beautiful little villages, especially at night. The destruction is heartbreaking. There is too that awful feeling of spiritual desolation which seems to become so real when in the presence of wrecked human houses and dwellings. Heaven knows where the people are: they have just gone, leaving everything, apart from their crops and cattle . . . many of the latter now dead. Our objective was just south of Verson – from where we were scheduled to launch an attack on Eterville, with 4th Dorsets:* zero hour for us 6.15 a.m. As we neared Verson, the noise became worse . . . terrifying. An enormous barrage was being laid down close by for B, who were going in further west at 5 a.m.

At Verson, ruins as usual . . . and we did more damage to walls and houses . . . unavoidable in the narrow lanes and darkness. Enemy only just cleared out of the place.

Later (a day later, I am writing). We were supposed to be holding Verson, but so difficult is it to completely clear out the enemy that it sometimes takes days to finally locate all their fox holes and snipers: in the village, the vehicle following mine was knocked out by a 50mm . . . broken track. But no one knew where the gun was located . . . probably still in the village! 15 Troop one tank short now – before battle commenced!

We were in Verson about 5.30 a.m., our FUP a field immediately south of village, just below hill crest. We were now able to see fairly well, but it was not fully daylight. As we manoeuvred into position, I noticed a

---

* The 4th Battalion, The Dorset Regiment.

tremendous barrage falling on our left flank, about a
quarter mile away. This was a grand sight: it was the
smoke screen promised – without it, our left flank would
have been completely exposed. Right flank was OK.
B had already 'gone in' there.

But the barrage was not the only activity. Jerry was sending over tons of mortar. It was falling around us, literally
plastering the cornfield. There was also much MG fire, both
coming and going: Jerry MGs were still only a few yards
ahead of us. Kept my head down as much as possible!

At 6 a.m. our infantry were in position, to our rear: the
mortar fire must have been terrible for them, but they seemed
unconcerned. I cannot describe my own reactions about this
time. I am always too much afraid for cohesive thought just
prior to action . . . mentally paralysed with fear, I suppose. But
my physical behaviour was quite normal. Up to now, I haven't
even experienced any trembling! Queer, that!

At 6.15, the major's order came over the air: 'advance'.
We commenced to move up the gentle slope . . . into what?
Eterville lay half a mile beyond the crest, in a shallow valley.

The air was very busy. B had been fighting for an hour on
our right, and seemed to have reached their objective: that
was some consolation. And on the left flank, we had our
white wall of smoke: I felt very secure from that quarter, and
I knew that this smoke would continue for four hours: I felt
very grateful for the artillery. By now, I had become quite
normal: deadly calm and unworried: it is not natural. Every
fibre of my being was concentrated upon the one thing . . .
enemy gun flashes. Miss them, and there may not be a
second chance. Most of my observation was done thro the
periscopes: too much MG over the top. Closed down occasionally when mortar became too concentrated around us.

We reached the crest ... and there were the enemy running for cover, towards Eterville and the trees ahead. Our Besas opened up ... every bush and shrub: every tree: every haystack: anything and everything that could hide a body was raked with MG.

Our infantry were now amongst and ahead of us ... and soon, prisoners started to come in: odd couples of Jerries popping up from the corn, hands raised ... scared to death.

At least three haystacks were now on fire from our incendiary MG. The smoke from them was a bit of a nuisance, blowing across our front. Ahead lay the trees immediately in front of Eterville: they were my worry. Jerry has a habit of concealing Tigers and Panthers in the woods. They usually open fire when we are too close to take evasive action – and *one* hit from an 88 at 400 yards ... !

Very soon, we opened up with HE on the village ... there were as yet no signs of any 88s.

The infantry kept steadily on ... walking warily through the deep corn, but always going forward ... forward. Our Besa fire passed over them, but it must have been uncomfortably close. Grand fellows those infantry lads: so brave and calm.

I felt terribly grateful towards them when I saw them amongst the trees: they would report any hidden AT guns and tanks. My vehicle was behaving well, and putting down smoke fire: crew worked splendidly: damned hard work too. And how we smoked cigarettes! Pedder solved the match problem by getting his lighter to work with gun buffer oil! And in the midst of an action! Mortars were still troublesome: as good as any air force to Jerry!

'The infantry kept steadily on...' The men of 15 (Scottish) Division advance through waist-high corn behind a Churchill tank of 9 RTR during Operation Epsom, the battle for Caen.
Photograph © IWM B5956.

Just as our lads reached the wood, I heard a couple of huge explosions and saw much earth and debris flying skywards by the wood. Bombers! God help those infantry lads! I saw what appeared to be an ME wheeling away overhead. There were no more bombs, however ... and then I learned over the air that they were our planes!! The infantry were appealing for them to be withdrawn ... but their attack had finished, thank heaven.

What sort of air support was this? If we are to have aerial assistance, why send it too late? And what on earth is the use of *two* bombs?

Time has no meaning during action: some time during the fight, Very lights* were seen from the village, and we knew the infantry were 'in': they had done a grand job and occupied the place with remarkable speed. We just remained

* Named after Edward Wilson Very (1847–1910), the American naval officer who developed the flare gun that fires them.

on the high ground, keeping on the alert for any armour . . . and a possible counter attack.

Meanwhile, the smoke was still literally pouring down on the left. B had done their job on the right, and now our front seemed reasonably safe: the tension was less acute . . . but always there was the mortar and snipers and the necessary vigil for lurking Tigers and Panthers.

Later, when the village had quietened down, we withdrew to original start point and replenished our depleted ammo racks . . . the SSM was there waiting for us.

Mortar was now quite regular and all around us, but we managed to replenish without trouble. All our vehicles were with us: we hadn't lost one in the action! Thank goodness it was over: we seemed to have been fighting for many hours . . . but it was only 10 a.m.

And now we had time for a 'brew' and a few biscuits and a little rest, in spite of continual mortaring. We were very exposed, in the middle of a large cornfield, but we couldn't withdraw further in case we were needed to repel a counter attack. The hours passed . . . maybe two or three . . . and we were all hoping for the order to withdraw. My crew in particular were dreadfully tired, having had no sleep the previous night owing to the breakdown. And the awful tension of the action had had its effect.

And then . . . the colonel's voice over the air to the major: another 'party' was being arranged for us: stand by for further action!! God! What dreadful depression!

Shortly, we learned about the 'party'.

A had passed through C and B to carry out a further attack to the south on Maltot . . . and things weren't going so well. It appeared that A had been hammered pretty badly. We were scheduled to launch a further attack on Maltot with fresh infantry. And we had been complimenting ourselves upon our neat little action in taking Eterville so quickly and without loss to ourselves. But now!?

Once again that terrible fear ... Well ... we went in, via scenes of recent action ... dreadful scenes. As with Eterville, we plastered the woods around Maltot with MG and plenty of HE. My gunner asked permission to have a go at the church spire, just visible above the hill crest: he was given permission, and got two lovely hits with HE. The steeple toppled. It *might* have harboured an enemy observer.

Once again, we were assisted by the artillery laying a grand smoke screen on our left flank. The infantry seemed to have little difficulty in entering the woods, and so down to the village. We did not follow: remaining on the high ground on the alert for enemy armour. We knew there were at least three Panthers in the village, or in the vicinity.

Occasional bursts of MG fire from enemy dugouts, and a few snipers, but we dealt with them. We must have passed an hour or two on that crest ... and then came the major's voice over the air appealing to the colonel for further assistance in the village for the infantry. Things seemed to happen rapidly: 3 SPs were promised ... but it seemed a poor response.

And then I noticed one of *our* tanks on fire. What on earth was happening? There were no signs of the enemy on the hill, and our infantry were in the woods and village. It seemed like a counter attack in force, judging by Major Holden's further appeal. He had somehow contacted the infantry commander.

Suddenly I heard some heavy gunfire ... and the swish of shells. Hells Bells! *My* tank was being fired at. Two misses! Darned if I could see any gun flashes or tanks. I peered frantically through the periscope: there seemed to be at least one more tank in difficulties, and several smaller vehicles on fire.

And then the major's voice ... *he* wanted help ... smoke. He got smoke ... all of us poured it out as fast as we could. In a matter of seconds, our former peaceful hill crest was pretty well littered with burning vehicles, and smoke ... a dense fog. I noticed one or two nearby vehicles moving away, but where to? Soon I couldn't see a thing but smoke, but gave the driver orders to advance: better go anywhere than stay and be shot up. Eventually found my way back to lower ground away from the danger zone ... but I was still hazy about the situation. All the same, I felt convinced that something pretty bad had happened.

Very soon, infantry appeared running towards us ... and away from Maltot. Were we withdrawing? Some sort of retreat seemed apparent. We were too far ahead to re-group and deploy for further action, so we withdrew to our laager north of Eterville, the latter being now well consolidated by the infantry.

And there we waited ... being fiercely mortared meanwhile. Ultimately, and without warning, we turned about and withdrew ... accompanied by terrific mortar: it seemed certain that we were under observation, so accurate was the mortaring.

Through Verson ... and fields and orchards and lanes to a point about 2 miles NW of Verson. A rather hectic journey and rather bewildering. Arrived after dark, in a field ... our final halt for the day.

My crew had been in the tank almost continuously for about 28 hours! And no meal in the period: but we had biscuits, and one 'brew up'. Heard alarming rumours about

casualties, etc., but things were too obscure to worry about.
Bed was imperative. Rolled myself in a couple of blankets,
and slept beneath tank.

D +35 Tuesday 11.7.44

Little sleep last night – bad dose of cramp: had it during
action yesterday. Felt lousy this morning. Much sorting out
today after yesterday's losses. C lost 2 tanks, and 3 or 4
damaged: few injuries, *viz.* Mr Drew, Mr Chapman, Cpl
Crowe. Sgt Purdy's vehicle burned out: he is missing with
two or three of his crew.

A had awful hammering. Only about 3 whole vehicles
left. Several casualties, including Major Ballantyne. About
17 missing. Ted Hinson wounded in arm. Fred Jackson
wounded. Jack Smith missing. George Wright OK . . . saw
him this a.m. SSM badly wounded . . . and several others.
Major Holden's vehicle was hit yesterday, but managed to
limp to safety. Think our smoke helped him out.*

B not so badly hit as A . . . only 1 or 2 vehicles out.
Something radically wrong with A's action yesterday.
Several new vehicles arrived from TDU. Almost full
strength again, after being about 50% down. We are still
being mortared: have moved vehicles to opposite side of
field for better cover. Several artillery batteries behind us.
Firing all last night.

Carpiquet aerodrome about a mile to east: hangars are
riddled with holes: had an awful battering. Caen quite visible couple of miles away. It *looks* alright from this distance,

---

* Of the 65 casualties sustained by 9 RTR, 41 were in A Squadron.

i.e. chimneys and spires still standing, but I believe the town has been badly battered. Presume we hold all of it now.

Much wreckage around here. Jerry Mk IV close by: two bodies still inside ... burned yellow-brown: awful smell. Typhoon in next field. Pilot buried close by. Two Tigers here ... both battered. This area is on the southern fringe of our first day's battle-ground. Twelve enemy ME 109s over today. Saw three shot down by our AA – two pilots baled out. We opened up with small arms: hell of a racket. Enemy mortar and our artillery firing all day. Not so good for nerves.

Some speculation about our next move. Will we be withdrawn? Or sent in again? We need some rest: everyone worn out, mentally and physically.

Definitely not moving today. Wrote to Jess. Brigadier and CO came around this morning: trying to cheer us up, I s'pose. Heard radio broadcast of our fight for Maltot. Actual recordings.*

D +36 Wednesday 12.7.44

Another bad night last night. Plenty of Jerry mortar, and our artillery shelling all night. More MEs over today: saw one hit. Attended conference by Major Holden. Our immediate future uncertain: we may relieve 7th who are standing by around Maltot against counter attacks: or we may 'go in' again south of Caen.

We are now more or less up to strength once again, but there are many new faces about. We have certainly been hammered since landing. All our actions have been in spearhead of salient

* The Second World War was the first conflict in which radio reporters and film-makers were able to record live reportage of military action.

SW of Caen. Seems to be strongly defended area with best German troops ... SS Panzer Grenadiers, etc. We have to attack everything: trees, shrubs, hedgerows, woods, haystacks, sheds, houses: all are strongly defended: held by an invisible enemy. Jerry certainly has the advantage in defending this area. Bad tank country ... too close and wooded.

Both padres went out today with stretchers. Removing dead from tanks and burying them. A terrible job. News tonight reveals that Maltot is still scene of heavy fighting. We move today.

D +37 Thursday 13.7.44

About 2 hours sleep last night. Much mortaring and two attacks by enemy bombers. But our artillery barrage was tremendous: seem to be more and heavier guns than ever. Heard a report that captured prisoners describe our artillery barrages as much worse than anything they experienced in Russia. Am not surprised to hear this.

We are moving later today ... a little further back away from mortar (to Les Saullets). Later: we are now a mile or so north of Cheux. Came here over our first battlefield, in reverse direction: dozens of enemy vehicles lying derelict in that area. Around one farmhouse saw at least 50 dead cattle. Major Veale, our 2 i/c, now CO of 7th.* Their colonel was killed on Monday. Several changes in this unit. SQMS David now SSM of A Sqdn. Captain Mockford now Major ... OC of A. Hope Major Holden remains with us. In spite of casualties, everyone seems remarkably cheerful.

---

* Later to return to 9 RTR as their commanding officer.

There was some amusement last night when a large percent-
age of the battalion turned out to catch a hare. The poor
creature wandered into our field and immediately caused a
hullabaloo. After five minutes hectic dashing about, it was
caught ... by about 10 pairs of hands simultaneously. It is
now being prepared for someone's meal. Later, a couple of
cows wandered amongst us, both obviously in need of milking. Once again there followed a terrific chase, some lads
even trying to use lassoos: but the cows refused to be
caught ... and we had no fresh milk.

Cattle are quite a problem: both alive and dead. No one
seems to bother about the latter. There must be thousands of
them in this sector alone ... grotesque creatures with fat
unnatural bodies and legs pointing skywards. The smell is
awful. The live cattle seem to be strangely morose: their eyes
seem almost lifeless. I suppose they are affected by the
constant noise of artillery and mortar: many also may be
wounded. They just wander about anywhere. The authorities
are gradually forming cattle compounds behind the front,
but we are usually too far ahead to see any signs of this
organisation.

The crops here are really fine: corn, wheat, barley, etc. ...
all healthy looking and very tall. Much of it has suffered
damage, but quite a lot remains. It has provided excellent
cover for German infantry and snipers. Our own lads too
are grateful for it when they have to bale out. In many places,
we now have 'main roads' running through corn fields: the
engineers are busy road making ... using bulldozers, etc.
For road foundations, the rubble and stone from wrecked
villages is being used.

We are now harboured in a cornfield using the corn for
camouflage ... and for bedding. The nearby village (Les

Saullets) is a shambles: houses and farms being totally wrecked. Depressing sight. May sleep better tonight: we are away from the mortaring, but there is plenty of artillery immediately behind us ... including batches of 5.5s and 7.9s. Our vehicles are harboured alongside a dirt 'road'. The dust is appalling. My laundry has been hanging out to dry, but is now yellow with dust. An RASC convoy pulled up beside us this evening. Several Lancashire lads with them ... almost like a family reunion!

D +38 Friday 14.7.44

There was a mild flap late last night, and we stood by for a move back to the front, but nothing happened, and we got down to bed. Another disturbed night for me: for one thing, the artillery blazed away all night ... these big guns make a hell of a noise, and we always seem to be harboured right in front of them. The blast can be felt as a series of 'puffs' on our own blankets.

Much traffic on the nearby road last night, too. Had a hell of a fright about 2 a.m. Felt a queer moving pressure beneath my leg: something alive was obviously trying to get through. A mole? I bashed the ground furiously through the blankets ... and then sat back, with a ciggy, and awaited a counter attack. It came five minutes later, this time beneath my thigh. Another bashing ... and another wait: Nothing happened, so lay down again ... and then it occurred again, this time beneath my shoulder. Gave it a further slamming, and had no further trouble. Presume its next emergence was beneath the tank tracks, just behind my head. Can't stand these wriggly things around my bed.

Believe we are moving 'in' again this evening: to relieve 7th who are standing by on Hill 112.* Troop officers out on recce this morning. Have done a recce myself, with Bill Geary. Neither of us is partial to 'rears' in full view of everyone. And our present lav. is about the worst we have had so far. We explored the ruined village . . . but too many troops about. Went as far as a wood half a mile away . . . but everywhere there are troops, hordes of them. Eventually, we had to swallow our pride, and perform very publicly. I was amused by the easygoing manner in which my crew solved the urinary problem on Monday during the action. We were several hours at a stretch inside the vehicle, and even back in the forward rally, it was really dangerous to leave the vehicle owing to mortar and snipers. The problem was solved by using a small empty oil tin, this being passed up to me for emptying through the hatch, at intervals.

At one of those forward rallies, I had a more urgent need, and simply had to leave the tank. I crawled beneath the rear with a spade and dug a hole. I felt fairly safe from mortar . . . but just as I was hitching up my pants, there came the ominous 'whining', followed by crashes dangerously near. I simply dived head first further beneath the tank . . . and stayed there, literally with my pants down!

We had a heavy shower last evening, but it is quite fine this morning, and warm. The dust is very bad: like being in a desert. All our food is covered with it. Pity we couldn't have harboured away from a busy road.

Ensa concert this afternoon: A very makeshift stage

---

* The Germans considered that 'he who controls Hill 112 controls Normandy'. A low elevation from which the entire valleys of the Orne and the Odon could be seen, the hill saw bitter fighting from 29 June to 23 July, when the 9th and 10th Panzer Divisions were finally driven from Maltot.

between two 3-ton lorries. It was held in the open in the midst of the wreckage of the village. Didn't attend myself, but believe it was a good effort, considering circumstances.

Announced at lunch time that we were moving forward about 5.30 p.m. to relieve 7th: defensive role against possible counter attack on our side Hill 112. Packed all kit and dismantled bivvy after lunch. Later announced that move postponed until 1 a.m. Later announced move cancelled. We remain here tomorrow, and work on vehicles: may even do some clothes washing.

Two or three groups of enemy fighters over today. Terrific AA fire locally. Plenty of Bren fire from our vehicle. Saw one plane crash: pilot baled out.

Two letters from Jess, and one from Johnny. Wrote to J. during afternoon. Learned yesterday of Jimmy Aldcroft's injury. His hand seems to have been badly burned, and face slightly, but definite information cannot be obtained. Hope he will be OK. He is one of many injured in Monday's action: cannot get full list, but there may be more of my friends for all I know. Several promotions today. Sammy Stubbs to Cpl. Johnny Havis [?] to Cpl. Cpl Hull to Sgt. Cpl Phillips to Sgt. Tpr Horner to Cpl. Self to Sgt. Reserve tank commanders are being prepared! Hope the moles leave me alone tonight: don't suppose the artillery will be silent, though. Sleeping in bivvy at side of tank in this harbour. No need for hole beneath tank: we are outside mortaring area.

D +39 Saturday 15.7.44

Little less disturbance last night. Artillery only spasmodic: two light bombing raids by Jerry. Seemed to be much air activity around 1 a.m. Several flares over front line, and much AA tracer. Slept from 3.00 until 7 a.m.

Vehicle maintenance all morning. No energy after lunch: felt lifeless. Lay in bivvy until tea time. First beer issue this evening. One pint per man @ 15 francs (1/6d). Seems rather dear to me. Sgts issued with 1 bottle whisky @ 8/6d. Dull and cloudy all day: no enemy air activity over here. Still harboured just north of Cheux. No further talk of moving. Presume we will sleep here again. Wrote to Jess, and Johnny. Another (second) bread issue this afternoon . . . one loaf per six men. White bread this time. Unable to obtain any news about wounded. Keep wondering how Ted Hinson and Jimmy Aldcroft are faring. Hope they are in England.

D +40 Sunday 16.7.44

At eleven last evening, instructions were received to be ready to move at 8 a.m. today. No orders, but assured that we would move forward and stand by in Hill 112 area to support 34 Brigade . . . the latter being scheduled for an attack on Esquay during last night and this morning.

Reveille 6.30 . . . all kit packed, bivvies stowed, etc., and at 8 a.m. revised orders: 'be ready to move at 9 a.m'. Finished breakfast more leisurely. Good deal of artillery last night. Probably heavy bombardment in support of our attack. We too were shelled during night . . . at 3 a.m.

HE awakened us, falling dangerously close. We dived from our bivvy and beneath tank in split second. Crawled out a few minutes later . . . dirty legs, etc. but unharmed. Bivvy was a shambles . . . blankets everywhere. Sorted ourselves out, and to sleep once again.

Later: 1 p.m. No move yet. Last night's action reported successful. Will we be needed? A few groups of prisoners have passed by this morning. Their bedraggled appearance is a natural consequence of the conditions on this front: it would be easy to misrepresent these men as a rabble. Nevertheless, they hardly looked like members of a 'master race'. Mostly small in build and dark in colouring: quite young too, most of them. They were being marched away to our rear.

Later. Latest information is that we are leaving here at 8 o'clock this evening, and moving up to relieve 7th. This harbour has become almost unendurable since this morning: will be glad to get away. The wind has shifted and the dust from the road is now blowing upon us. We are in a perpetual dust cloud: even the tanks are now thickly coated inside. Men's faces have become a dusty yellow colour... likewise our clothing. It is horrible.

Have just heard that our address is now 'BLA' (British Liberation Army): the change to become operative immediately. Nothing doing this afternoon: everyone resting and trying to avoid the dust.

D +41 Monday 17.7.44

Feel a bit confused after last night, but am thankful to be alive. Left Les Saullets to schedule, and arrived north side Hill 112 about 10 p.m. 'Seventh' seemed to be waiting for us: have no doubt they were darned thankful to be going. This new location is little more than a mile from enemy... and a happy hunting ground for his mortars. Very dusty journey: we looked like fiends, with blank faces, goggles, and mufflered necks. Was lucky enough to park my vehicle over a deep hole dug by 7th ... but we decided to enlarge it a little. Hadn't properly finished when fun commenced. Mortars, for a start. They just rained down upon us for a few minutes. All of us got well down in our holes. These mortars make a terrifying noise, and are very dangerous within small radius.

After this introductory barrage, I went along our line to see about the night guard. Was shocked to see a dead body in a trench: just killed by mortar. Another seriously wounded. Got back quickly to my own hole ... just in time to take cover against more mortar. Another respite of a few minutes ... and then came the bombers! First, two planes appeared and dropped flares – immediately above us. Darkness disappeared: felt horribly exposed. Few seconds later, bombs started dropping. We were obviously the target: no doubt our dust trail had been observed coming in. Cannot remember how many bombs were dropped ... nor how long the attack lasted: it seemed like hours during which we lay – probably half paralysed – in the bottom of our holes, with the tanks for overhead cover. A fairly safe retreat, but rather questionable if struck by a direct hit. Plenty of HE in the tanks!

I felt terribly afraid: mortars are comparatively gentle, at least: bombs are rather heavier ... and I know our vehicles are *mortar* proof, but bombs are a different matter. These were being aimed deliberately at us ... no haphazard affair. Strange how one attempts to sink into the earth during a raid.

To add to the confusion, our AA gunners put up a hell of a barrage: I had a fleeting glimpse of the sky literally brilliant with red tracer and other stuff criss-crossing in all directions. The din was appalling, but there was no mistaking the heavy crunch of the bombs: they made the earth tremble violently. Eventually the noise of aircraft faded and the AA gradually subsided, and we were able to rear our heads a little ... and breathe normally. There were shouts round about and some people running ... someone was calling for an ambulance: it was Bill Geary. He had somehow become a member of a rescue squad. A vehicle nearby had been damaged, and there were casualties.

About this time, just to complicate matters, our own artillery opened up with a terrific barrage. We were close to the guns and got the full benefit of their noise. Simultaneously, Jerry laid on the mortar ... and I guess my brain simply refused to function for a time.

Some time during the small hours, we wrapped ourselves in a blanket each, and got some sleep, about 2 hours.

Reveille 4.30 a.m. All kit packed and stowed and move at 5.15 ... just as daylight was approaching. Only a short journey, on to the northern flank of Hill 112 ... there to remain in readiness against a counter attack.

Mortar greeted us at the new location, but we remained in the vehicle. Eventually, about 9 a.m., got permission to dismount and prepare a brew.

All day we have been up here ... mortared almost continuously, and constantly diving beneath the vehicle for cover: a wearying business. On two occasions, we ourselves fired HE at his mortar positions, but it was indirect shooting and results cannot be guaranteed.

Tonight at 10 p.m., we leave the hill and return to last night's harbour. Am dreading it. Some enemy aerial activity today ... and a few of our Typhoons dive-bombing the front line. Wish we could see more of the RAF, particularly on enemy mortar positions.

In last night's nightmare, we lost about three killed ...

few wounded ... including colonel. Very much admired
Geary for his coolness and help to wounded during the raid.

Am writing this beneath tank, in a hole, with mortars falling uncomfortably close. We are quite exposed in large field
of long grass. Many cows around, dead ... vile smell. These
cattle are terribly mutilated. A few wounded cows are round
about ... gaping holes in their bodies, etc. Terribly depressing
sight. We ought to shoot them. Heavy smell of foul flesh in
last night's harbour: doesn't improve matters. But nothing
really matters there: except a deep hole for cover. Meals today
have been hasty snacks prepared in between mortaring: a hell
of a business. Have filled two flasks with tea for supper. Will
be very welcome in our hole later on.

D +42 Tuesday 18.7.44

Our vigil ceased at 10 o'clock last night, when we retired from
the hill to harbour. We worked very hastily on arrival, so as to be
well bedded down in our holes by 11 o'clock ... 'mortar time'.
Managed to have a wash, and tea from flask. Were all under
cover by 11 p.m. Soon afterwards a few mortars fell, but less than
previous night. These were followed by another bombing raid.
Quite a strong attack, but am not sure that we were target this
time: bombs not quite as close as last night ... but too near to be
comfortable. Artillery around us may have been objective. Several
of the planes came low, using their machine guns: didn't like this
at all. Our AA seemed very feeble. None of our aircraft about.
Doubt whether night fighters are operating over here.

Each crew kept one man on guard all night ... just for
safety. Jerry suicide squads are pretty desperate. Went to
sleep about midnight ... immediately after air attack. Only

spasmodic mortaring afterwards. On guard 2.30 to 3.30. Reveille 4.30 a.m., same as yesterday.

All bedding stowed, etc., and move off 5.15 to Hill 112. Not very restful sleep under these conditions. We remain fully clothed and merely wrap a blanket around our bodies and stretch out in our 'fox-hole'. Immediately after our arrival on hill, our bombers started to appear over a position south of Caen . . . about 6 miles to our east. It turned out to be the biggest air raid I have ever seen.* Sun was just rising as first bombers appeared . . . about 5.45 a.m. A beautiful morning: warm and clear.

Several hundred Lancasters and Halifaxes took part. They came over in swarms, circled over the target, and then headed for home. This must have continued for about an hour: bombs being literally poured down on some unfortunate Jerries. Very soon, a heavy mixture of smoke and cordite spread for miles and Caen was hidden from our view. We could smell the cordite very strongly at this distance.

Jerry AA fairly strong, but only saw three of our planes destroyed. Saw at least five bale out from one plane.

This attack had not finished before several Typhoons appeared immediately to our south. There followed half an hour's dive bombing with rockets and bombs. By now, the heavy bombers had finished, leaving an enormous cloud spreading towards us, and heaven knows what destruction. An hour later, the earth commenced to tremble again: more violently than before . . . and heavy rumbles could be heard further south of Caen. Seemed like a heavier raid still, but no bombers were visible. And then there appeared several

* 4,800 tons of high explosive bombs were dropped in the first wave of the bombing, destroying much of the town of Cagny and disabling large numbers of German tanks. Altogether three waves of bombers dropped over 6,600 tons of bombs.

groups of Liberators, wheeling round from the south. They continued to appear for an hour, causing really violent trembling of the earth. All loose instruments in the tank were affected by the vibration.

A very heartening three hours to those of us who have seen so many enemy planes . . . and so few of ours.

It is now 12 noon, and we haven't been mortared since the Typhoon attack . . . !

Later. Heard some very interesting news this afternoon about the present situation, and about our part during past three weeks. This morning's air raid comprised 4000 bombers, according to official report! Prelude to large attacks now in progress S of Caen. Double faux-pas by 53rd Div* rather amusing and highly successful too!

Very little mortaring since this morning's raid. The afternoon has been comparatively quiet, and have managed a couple of hours sleep beneath the tank. Some of the squadron have been busy towing dead cows into bomb-hole: the stink is now worse than ever. Have had some fresh potatoes lately: our lads are digging them up, contrary to orders . . . but orders can't always be obeyed!

This morning, Geary and Pestell went into the adjoining village hunting for chickens. They discovered two, but couldn't catch them. After cornering them in a shed, they flew over Geary's head and through the bombed roof! Geary says it was harder work than his whole 28 days in Fort Dadan!†

---

* The 53rd Welsh Infantry Division. It is not known what Trevor meant by the 'double faux-pas'.

† Fort Dadan remains unidentified. It may have been a nickname of some kind. It is clear from Trevor's letters home that Bill Geary was something of a character, who liked to drink when not on active service.

This evening, three of the crew have renewed the hen-hunt ... and have just returned with two. Plucking them at the moment. I believe we are having them boiled tomorrow! Can't spare any butter for roasting.

Letter from Jess this evening. Have not written for two days – mainly due to conditions here. It has been unsafe to sit outside writing, and not easy beneath tank. Have written this in several tiny instalments ... in between mortaring and air-bursts. The latter are HE shells which explode in the air above us. Jerry seems to mix them with his mortar fire.

Wrote to Jess this evening. Believe we are harbouring tonight as last night ... and tomorrow's programme may be same as today. We have sent a number of 95 HE* over Jerry today immediately to our south. About 2 miles range. Our two cows rounded up this evening. The lads are now milking them. Plenty of fun in this cow business! There are only one or two fellows who have ever milked a cow, but all seem anxious to have a go. The poor cows have to submit to some rough handling: lads literally tugging at their udders without success ...

D +43 Wednesday 19.7.44

Not as much enemy activity last night, altho there were several bombs dropped in a near-by area. Also some HE shells on our harbour. Not much sleep ... our artillery too active. They were firing practically all night. Our hole too is not very comfortable. Three of us slept abreast at one end, but the width is insufficient. This morning's programme as

* Two tanks from HQ Squadron 9 RTR were fitted with 95mm guns to fire high explosive shells only.

yesterday: reveille 4.30: Hill 112, 5.15 a.m.: now standing by. Our troops have advanced from Caen in three thrusts – one of them swinging right, across our front. This move started yesterday . . . and had made good progress last night. Presume it is bound to affect our position here.

Later. No change since this morning. We are now taking bearings, etc. to assist 7th with some indirect shooting, if necessary. Very little mortaring today: only two short barrages from 'Minnies'. Also a few air-bursts. Half a dozen Fw 190s came over this afternoon and machine-gunned us, without effect. Everyone somehow took cover in time. Nearby artillery have been shelling Jerry almost continuously since this morning. Very dull day with low-lying cloud: haven't seen one of our aircraft all day.

Boiled chicken for lunch: didn't have any myself. Have no stomach for local poultry or livestock. Everything seems diseased and lifeless, but this must be my imagination. My four colleagues really enjoyed the chicken . . . with boiled potatoes, grown locally. Most of the crews now seem to have a dead chicken hanging on their tanks. There are many more running wild in nearby village, also many tame rabbits. Know of at least one crew, in B, who have shot a young calf . . . and had veal!

Hate the sight of meat at the moment. There are too many dead cows lying around, some of them displaying all their entrails. An unborn calf fell away from one of them as it was being towed away yesterday. The smell of decaying flesh is everywhere: a disgusting smell: I often feel on the point of vomiting. Cannot understand the official indifference to this business. Some of these carcasses must have been here up to a fortnight, and nothing has been done about it. It cannot be healthy.

Unlucky accident yesterday morning. My fountain pen slipped from my pocket during one of my frequent dives for safety, and was broken in two when I ultimately found it. But am still using it.

D +44 Thursday 20.7.44

More disturbance last night ... enemy mortar and aircraft and our own artillery. Some heavy barrages by the latter. Enemy HE shells at 4.30 this a.m.: one of C injured by shrapnel.

Another day on north flank of Hill 112: no activity. Enemy mortaring now very infrequent. Possible that our right thrust from Caen is worrying them. No action by 7th yet: possibly tomorrow. We are remaining on Hill all night in readiness for early support. Dull morning, but warm and sunny at lunch time. Heavy shower late afternoon ... dull evening.

Hot bath in canvas bucket: four Jerry fighters appeared just as I had stripped naked ... but no machine-gunning this time. Did a spot of laundry. Wrote to Jess. Learned today that one man in B was killed by enemy aircraft yesterday.

A quiet day on the whole. Capt Link* arrived yesterday. Lt Col Veale now our CO. Soon back with us from 7th! Believe Col Everard now in England.† Letter from Jess this evening ... also a copy of today's *Daily Mail*. We are indebted to the air service for this: hope it continues. A very wet evening: but it is dry in our fox-hole beneath the tank ...

* Captain Sidney Link, second-in-command of C Squadron.
† Colonel Everard was the outgoing commanding officer.

D +45 Friday 21.7.44

Little trouble from enemy last night ... but very heavy downpour. Still raining hard this morning. Too wet to cook outside ... prepared breakfast in our 'hole'. We are now going to live in mud instead of dust.

Later. Rain subsided slightly about 3 p.m ... and then we were treated to a dose of mortar: a heavy dose: a counter attack was expected. Received 'stand to' order: meanwhile, our artillery and mortar opened up ... and for a couple of hours it was 'hell let loose'. To make matters worse, the deluge returned and we became soaked to the skin ... and literally plastered with mud. By tea time, the firing became more spasmodic, but still some mortaring ... and much MG just ahead. Presume the counter attack was repulsed: now 10 p.m. and we have not been over the crest.

Our living hole is quite dry in spite of the rain, but the mud is ankle deep immediately around. Conditions have become very bad in a few hours. Vehicular traffic is having a bad time in the mud. Heard reports over the air about trouble in Germany. Seems to have been some attempt on Hitler's life.* Hope something comes of it. No mail today – or newspapers. Can't expect normal services in such weather. All aircraft must be grounded.

B went forward today, slightly ahead of us, and had one or two minor casualties ... Maj W. injured. Sgt Tito injured† ... both by mortar.

---

* On 20 July Colonel Claus Schenk Graf von Stauffenburg had tried to assassinate Hitler with a bomb placed in a briefcase. Two generals, a colonel and a stenographer were killed, but the Führer survived.

† Major Bob Warren, shrapnel wounds, and Sergeant Michael Tito, wireless operator: right hand blown off and extensive shrapnel wounds.

Our artillery now warming up! Heavy barrage going down: batches of guns just to our rear. We certainly get plenty of noise. Expect there will be the usual Jerry mortaring around 11.30 p.m.: he is pretty punctual! Think our hole is pretty safe: we are beneath the tank, in a long hole 2 ft deep (5 ft wide x 12 ft long). Five of us sleep here. Have scrounged some straw for the floor. Plenty of insects and things, but they can't be seen in the dark ... fortunately! Now getting dark: not raining at the moment. Going to 'bed' ...

D +46 Saturday 22.7.44

Few hours sleep last night: cold and wet. Stand to all morning: large enemy concentration south of Hill 112: counter attack expected. Last night we had to withdraw from Esquay. All troop leaders out this a.m. on recce for possible attack by us tomorrow or Monday.

7th attacked today: we supported with usual HE from 5.30 to about 8 p.m. Believe our fire quite effective. 7th captured Maltot with infantry.

Later. Trouble seems to be expected for us. We are now on the alert – all kit packed and stowed, and ready for immediate action should Jerry appear over crest of Hill 112. May have to stand to all night. Little air activity today: weather dull. Jerry still mortaring.

Later. Slight relaxation of tension: we can now lie down from midnight until 5 a.m. ... but fully dressed, and without blankets: no kit to be unstowed. MG platoon digging in beside us to support small infantry attack during night.

No mail today. No opportunity to write Jess. We have now been on this flank of Hill 112 for almost a week. We are only a mile or so from enemy forward troops. Have been shelled and mortared continuously. Don't think I have averaged four hours sleep for last fortnight at least. Feel tired.

Our pressure here must be worrying Jerry: it is certainly giving encouragement to our forward infantry up on the ridge. Much bitter fighting up there during last fortnight. Summit is now more or less no-man's land.

D +47 Sunday 23.7.44

To bed about midnight last night ... but awakened 2.30 a.m. for 'stand to'. All crew in vehicle and ready for action in few minutes: horribly tired and cold. No development by 3 a.m., so we stood down again and crew tried to continue sleeping. Unable to sleep myself: colossal artillery barrage from our artillery just behind us. Entire hillside lit up by continuous vivid flashes from guns. Some MG fire coming over from Jerry ... and some HE shelling.

Had a hot drink with Vic Hewett 4 a.m. Very cold morning and damp. 5 a.m.... another stand to, but no move. My crew brewed up inside tank. Everyone tired out and rather miserable.

No development: stood down again 6 a.m. Carried on with breakfast: fried tinned sausages and biscuits ... and more tea. Believe an infantry attack last night not successful. Am not surprised! Two companies! Reminds me of the 3 divs from Caen after 4000-plane bombardment.

Later. No further orders re action. Still here on Hill 112 (by Gournay): keeping vigil against enemy counter attack. Little enemy activity in our locality during today, apart from early morning, and spasmodic mortar and air bursts this afternoon. Our artillery has been only spasmodic, since this morning's heavy barrage. Weather warmer this afternoon, but still misty with low-lying cloud. Have at last got my laundry hanging out to dry. Washed it on Thursday afternoon, and it started raining immediately afterwards – heavily. No option but to leave it outside. Rolled it in a bundle and stored it on a board beneath tank overnight. Someone kicked it . . . or wiped their feet on it. Couldn't touch it Friday owing to deluge. Re-washed it Saturday . . . but too much rain and damp for drying. Stored it in canvas bucket in tank overnight . . . still soaking wet. Have now hung it on a line in this afternoons fine spell: it may be fairly dry by tonight.

Later. Suddenly ordered to 'A' Echelon at St-Manvieu-Norrey (about 5 miles) with vehicle to have 75 [i.e. a 75mm gun] attended to. Were on the way in half hour. Via Colleville, Mouen, etc. These trips through once peaceful little villages are always horribly depressing. There is so little of them left – apart from piles of rubble, dead cattle and derelict vehicles of all kinds. Occasionally too a German sniper's body can be seen dangling from rafters in a ruined house . . . or from the branches of a tree.

Arrived 'A' in time for supper meal . . . and bed. Much more peaceful here: no mortar for one thing. There are guns (5.5s) nearby, but they are ours and cause no worry now that this noise has ceased to trouble us. Erected bivvy in the open . . . no hole tonight – we are fairly safe without. Am sleeping minus trousers tonight, for a change. No need to be prepared for sudden action with this 'army' at 'A'—!*

* 'A' Echelon – the supply echelon which carried the ammunition, petrol, tank spares, etc. – was normally positioned some way behind the front line, meaning that it was unlikely to come under fire.

D +48 Monday 24.7.44

Woke up at 10 a.m.! First good sleep for weeks. Quiet morning ... warm and sunny. Finished drying my laundry! REME working on gun.

Good lunch ... steak and kidney pudding, tinned peaches, tea, etc. Back to 'F' Ech. afternoon, accompanied by two of REME to test gun over Jerry's lines. Gun OK ... now back to usual routine on Hill. Sleep in hole tonight. Interesting raid by Typhoon rockets immediately south this evening. About 2 dozen planes involved ... all dive bombing. Few dozen Mitchells over Caen sector later. Seems to be fairly good evening for air operations. Wish we had more such weather. Three letters from Jess this evening. Grand! Finished yesterday's letter to Jess.

D +49 Tuesday 25.7.44

Another rough night. Several enemy bombers about and one or two local bombs. Plenty of mortar around midnight and later. Our artillery active most of night. As we are still at the alert all night, no bedding is allowed. Tried to sleep beneath overcoat, but too cold. Had an hour's sleep since breakfast. Quite warm this morning, but hazy. More Typhoons over enemy positions ahead. Received orders this morning to prepare to move some time today. We are leaving this damned hill at last. We will have been here 10 days this evening.

Later. Leaving this area midnight. Travelling during darkness to Fontenay-le-Pesnel ... NW from here. About 8-mile journey. Fairly quiet afternoon here ... but usual mortaring and a few air-bursts, also some enemy planes over. Our artillery fairly active.

Tea brewing now for night journey. We carry it in Thermos flasks: damned welcome about 3 a.m. Detest these night journeys out here. They are a strain at the best of times. But here there is a peculiar ghastliness about the country-side at night: there is the smell of dead cattle, and their grotesque shapes in the fields: the roads lined with derelict vehicles: the wrecked homesteads: ruined villages. The villages are the worst. Mere ghosts ... skeletons: no life ... no happiness. Occasional groups of graves at the roadside, with their small white crosses, don't improve matters.

D +50 Wednesday 26.7.44

Jerry gave us a parting farewell last evening. First of all, we were mortared ... followed by a bombing raid. We were partly under cover, by a hedgerow, when the bombers came over just before midnight: we remained very still and quiet ... and nervous! Several bombs whistled down ominously ... but not too close to us. Maybe their targets were the nearby artillery. It must have been a fairly extended raid because AA fire was visible all along the front, followed by dull red glowing on the clouds as fires broke out.

Our journey commenced midnight: pitch dark. Nearing the River Odon more mortars came over. Crossed the river at a ford, and then were allowed to use convoy lights ... a tiny rear glimmer which helped a lot.

The northern hillside of the Odon valley was an amazing sight. Several miles of it were visible to us as we left the river: visible because of the searchlights, and the long lines of artillery constantly blazing away. Shells screamed over our heads ... audible above the roar of our own vehicles. The entire hillside seemed to be alive, constantly spitting forth great long tongues of vivid white flame as each gun fired. The whole scene carried a background of leaping and waving searchlights, and red tracer AA, literally pouring upwards at the bombers. Personal precautions are impossible under such conditions. No question of keeping one's head down in the turret ... a commander simply *has* to observe the ground to help the driver in the darkness.

Half an hour later, we had left the valley, and headed west for our destination – Fontenay-le-Pesnel, via Marcelet. We travelled flat out ... away from the guns and bombers. A ridiculous speed, but fortunately the road was perfectly straight and fairly free from obstructions ... very few low-hanging telephone wires, etc.

Reached harbour 1.30 a.m. ... in a field: I expected we would have been at least 2 hours later. Most of the crews settled down for an hour or two's sleep inside the tanks. Few of us remained on guard. We are still fairly close to Jerry here ... about 2.5 miles. At 4.30 a.m., our forward MG units opened up with heavy fire ... about a mile south. And then Jerry replied with HE shells. Had to take cover.

Had an hour's sleep on gear-box hatch 6–7 a.m. Breakfast ... and then maintenance on vehicles and guns. They needed it. Infantry here are North and South Staffordshires: seem a decent lot of fellows. We are already indebted to them for potatoes, ciggies and tea. Have been out here a month – on Tilly sector and Caen area. Erected bivvy after lunch and had couple of hours' sleep: didn't feel so good. Some aerial activity here by RAF but nothing heavy today. Quite warm and sunny this afternoon and evening. My crew have already discovered a potato field and have collected a few pounds.

No hole beneath tank for bed tonight, but intend to bank-up bogies with soil ... protection against blast and shrapnel. Believe Jerry usually shells with HE around 11 p.m. daily. Understand that no more compo packs will be issued. We start on cooks' food from breakfast tomorrow. Everyone depressed about this: tomorrow will be 'black day' of 9th! Letter from Jess.

'The long lines of artillery blazing away...' A British 5.5-inch medium gun firing at night during the offensive in the Odon valley.

Photograph © IWM B7413.

D +51 Thursday 27.7.44

To bed about eleven last night ... beneath tank. Fell asleep immediately ... lulled t) sleep by heavy barrage by guns just to our rear!! Slept solidly until 7 a.m. Awakened just in time for breakfast, provided by cooks. Porridge, tinned bacon and beans, bread and butter and tea. Quite good. Bulk rations (cheese, jam, bread and butter, tea, sugar) being issued to troops for lunch . . . cooked meal tonight for dinner.

No excitement this morning. We appear to be here in supporting role for NS Regt.* Maybe against possible counter attack. Few Jerry graves round about . . . and two Panthers. Terrible tank country. Closely wooded, and a mass of hedgerows and orchards. Good for infantry . . . and Jerry booby traps and mines. Two officers and one sergeant killed yesterday on recce. S-mine. Mr Wolskel. Mr Smart, Sgt Nicholls. They appear to have wandered on to un-cleared road verge.

Received first pay since June 16th this morning – 200 francs (£1). Have needed little cash so far. Have spent a few francs on ciggies from Q. Given away some francs to refugees. Free issue of 60 ciggies from Q. Long letter from Jess this evening. Little enemy activity here during day.

D +52 Friday 28.7.44

Good sleep last night: believe there was much enemy mortaring during night . . . but I slept through it! No trouble from Jerry this morning. Maintenance on vehicles and guns. More ciggies from Q. for cash this time. 20 francs for 60.

* The North Staffordshires, who were part of 59 Infantry Division.

D +53 Saturday 29.7.44

Still static ... standing by against counter attack. Infantry about a mile ahead of us. Fine day ... fairly quiet. Bathed in nearby stream beneath artificial shower from water-fall ... jolly good ... but cold. Notified this morning of pending action ... cancelled later.

D +54 Sunday 30.7.44

Fairly quiet night ... good sleep. Heavy air attack by our four-engined bombers slightly SW from here: saw dozens – hundreds – of planes between 7.30 and 8 a.m. Some of the later ones turned back before reaching enemy lines. Fine day ... warm – large fleecy clouds.

Left harbour with 12 Troop about 1.30 p.m. ... dem. for benefit of N/K infantry unit* ... tactics for this close country, etc. Returned about 5 p.m. Same dem. tomorrow morning and afternoon ... presumably for benefit of brass hats.†

Seem to be constantly messing with rations: morning distribution of bulk supply for lunch: evening sorting out ration pack for tomorrow. We now seem to be on cooks' food on alternate days.

---

* The Norfolks. Probably the 7th Battalion, Royal Norfolk Regiment, who were part of 59 Division.

† High-ranking officers, so-called from the gold braid decoration on the peaks of their caps.

D +55 Monday 31.7.44

Quiet night . . . good sleep. Two dems. today . . . satisfactory, from all accounts. Fine day . . . hot and sunny. Good news from American sector. They appear to have reached Avranches. This may be the beginning of our emergence from this peninsula. Hope Jerry withdraws. Am dreading tank warfare in this close country: seems like suicide to me.

News from Caumont could be better. We appear to have met unexpected resistance . . . as at Caen. But this country is perfect for defence. Must be a Paradise for Jerry's AT gunners. Also excellent for booby traps, snipers, etc. It is terribly difficult for all attackers . . . especially infantry. Advances are literally made field by field, hedges and trees all being strongly defended.

We are too confined, and the country too close, for movement and deployment. My opinion that the Russians would simply encircle the whole area, and take it from the rear. Hope we have a similar plan. Saw dem. of 'Petards' this evening at Brigade. Went via Tilly. The latter has been almost wiped off the map – literally. Centre of village is now even clear of rubble. Only large open spaces remain . . . with roads being made everywhere.

Petard interesting . . . but don't believe it has any future here. Bulldozer very impressive. Plenty of Typhoons this evening. Letter from Jess – thank goodness. Artillery busy last night.

D +56 Tuesday 1.8.44

Cool morning . . . very misty . . . useless for aircraft. Everywhere quiet. Little activity all day. Letter from Jess.

We are scheduled for a dem. with the infantry at 3 a.m. tomorrow.

D +57 Wednesday 2.8.44

Reveille 2.15 a.m. 'Slept' in the open last night: just lay awake from midnight until called by guard 2.15 a.m. Some Jerry planes over meanwhile: fair amount of AA. Our artillery busy all night ... Maybe Jerry is pulling out in view of our breakthrough at Caumont. Artillery perhaps shelling his lines of retreat.

Tanks moved off 2.45 a.m. to area 2 m north. Dem. with infantry making use of artificial moonlight. Seemed quite successful to me. Back to harbour 6.30 a.m.... breakfast 7.15.

Saw a little of Fontenay-le-Pesnel on return journey. Just like most other villages ... almost entirely a mass of ruins ... with a few German tanks lying along roadsides. Free day for 14 and 15 Troops because of dem. Slept all afternoon. Wrote to J. during morning.

Shaved off moustache: can't stand it: prefer torture of lousy blades. Heard resumé of Churchill's speech, on radio. Turks have severed relations with Germany. More 'Jackals'?* Good news for us, anyhow. Americans making fine progress ... now in Brittany! Our push from Caumont making good progress too. Haven't seen a single Jerry plane since coming to this place. Fair number of ours operating every day ... especially Typhoons.

---

* Trevor had strong views about those countries which had initially allied themselves with Nazi Germany for reasons of political expediency. He likens them to the jackals that live off the leavings of larger predators.

D +58 Thursday 3.8.44

Usual routine ... but vehicles have to be ready for possible move. Something in the wind. Informed later that fairly large infantry attack went in this a.m., and we may be called upon for assistance if any stiff opposition develops. Received details of our possible area of action from Mr Francis: opposition expected close to Villers Bocage and east of the village. Saw another dem. by Petards after lunch. Inspected wrecked 'Panther' ... too many bits of humanity in it for my liking. But am now convinced that 'Churchill' is far superior* ... apart from that darned 88. Gun mantlet hollow! Further orders 4 p.m. We are moving further south at 6.30 p.m. Mr Francis and I LOB. Bill Geary in my place ... being tried out as commander. Much activity during next couple of hours: dismantling bivvies: packing kit: transferring my kit from tank: area clearing: tea, etc.

Tanks departed 6.15 p.m. for area nearer front. Possible action pending, but I suspect that Jerry will pull out. News seems excellent: our advance from Caumont going well. Americans have gone forward without opposition from Avranches: Nearing Rennes! This looks like a real collapse of Jerry's defence ... altho he is still strong around Caen.

Regretted having to bid farewell to my crew, but hope to get back to them. The most argumentative and 'ticking' crew in the whole unit, I imagine, but good blokes nevertheless ... 'Tiger' (Johnny) Boland, Ted Pestell, Derek Pedder, Bill Geary and self. Have been in every action so far, and am now going back to 'A' Echelon for rest.

Left harbour at Fontenay-le-Pesnel 6.30 p.m. in half-track.

* Its crews seem to have been remarkably loyal to the Churchill, even though it was outgunned by the heavier German tanks. The Churchill was tough, and could take a good deal of punishment.

Arrived Cristot ('A' and 'B' Ech.) about 7 p.m. Slight trouble with W and S.* Almost refused to go forward as co-driver! 'Mucked in' with Sid Shaw. Had best cup of tea since arriving in France! One or two resting colleagues here. Frank Hudson, Tom Phillips, Vic Crowe-Haynes: also Moran – Moran! He has just seen Psychiatrist.† Believe Pinkney has been sent forward again. George Banning [*uncertain*] in hospital at Bayeux. Bill Starkey now with TDU as wireless instructor!

Radio news tonight comprises capture of Rennes and Dinan‡ by Yanks: damned good. Hope Jerry's withdrawal is now too fast for Churchills ... especially in this country. It is suicide for tanks: paradise for AT gunners! Petards were going to help us, but they are useless for the job, in my opinion.§ Am bedding down beneath Shaw's lorry tonight. Not a sign or sound of a Churchill here ... seems like a holiday camp! Two letters from Jess. Poppet had his first 'dinner' on

Editor's note: The diary ends inexplicably here.

D +59 Friday 4.8.44

Awoke 8 a.m. ... too late for breakfast, but managed to scrounge some food from cooks. Another cup of real tea – marvellous! Sid dug out a tin of sausage. Breakfast at a table ... with newspaper 'cloth': also plate and knife and fork! What luxury!

---

* Unidentified, although the context implies a recalcitrant crew member.
† Moran was one of the troopers who had to bale out twice at Cheux. Clearly his terrible experiences in 9 RTR's first action had had a lasting effect.
‡ In Brittany.
§ Opinion seems to have been divided: other 9 RTR veterans have remarked on the effectiveness of the Petard.

Beautiful morning. Must write to Jess. Saw Noel Wright ... he was en route to 'F' Echelon from FDS. Received parcel from Jess ... including lighter.* Beautiful day: very hot and sunny. This echelon seems like a nudist colony: many semi-naked figures about, most of them very brown from frequent sunbathing. They are very lucky, being always pretty well out of harm's way. A very quiet day. Wrote to Jess and did some reading. To bed beneath 3-ton lorry with Shaw and Thompson.

D +60 Saturday 5.8.44

Some activity by local big guns last night ... probably 5.5s. We are too far back (Cristot) for 25-pounders. Am surprised that even 5.5s are here. Thought the front had moved out of their range even.

Jerry seems to be retreating rapidly. Our tanks did not go into action yesterday morning after all. Their anticipated attack on hill east of Villers Bocage became unnecessary as Jerry withdrew before they arrived. Don't know exact location of 'F' Echelon just now, but believe they are moving forward with our general advance.

Am now with 'B' Ech. at Cristot. 'A' have moved forward to Fontenay-le-Pesnel. Much card playing here: some heavy gambling. Noel Wright here at the moment – watching poker school. Seem to be thousands of francs lying about the 'table'.

Later. Believe 'F' Ech. are moving to new location east of Caen! Jerry must be withdrawing too rapidly for us on this sector. Quiet day here: have been reading – and writing to J.

---

* Trevor had asked Jess to send him a Utility lighter like hers. Instead she sent him her own, which he treasured for the rest of the war.

Moran going back to base tomorrow. Sgt Rathke out of tanks?* Sgt James now trooper! We are now prepared for quick move in this echelon. Believe we depart tomorrow a.m.

One of our principal irritants during last week or two have been wasps and flies . . . two varieties of the latter. The wasps are very persistent, especially when we have jam. They even cling to bread until it is almost inside our mouths. Can't get rid of them. Flies . . . we have domestic ones, and horse flies. God knows where the domestics come from: we find them in open country miles from anywhere. I suppose the dead cattle attract them, likewise bluebottles. The horse flies have caused several cases of severe swelling. Their bite is distinctly painful, and always leaves a minute blob of blood.

D +61 Sunday 6.8.44

Went to bed 10.30 last night, having spent some time organising a comfortable spot of earth: had a bad time night before with lumpy ground. Was dozing off about 11 o'clock when I heard my name mentioned close by. Soon learned the horrible truth. Mr Francis and I had to return to 'F' Ech. immediately: transport would pick us up in 15 minutes! I felt slightly amazed! So did Mr Francis. Mr Boden† and Sgt Debenham had turned up to take our places on 'B' Echelon. Damned cheek. We hadn't even been LOB – no battle had been fought! Crawled out of bed: Debenham seemed to take a delight in re-laying his bed in my warm spot.

---

* Sergeant Rathke, who provided the Greenwood family with many notes on Trevor's diary, suffered an infection that resulted in progressive deafness.
† Lieutenant Peter Boden, later awarded the Croix de Guerre.

Lieutenant Peter Boden (centre) led 14 Troop throughout the campaign and was one of only three 9 RTR troop leaders to survive the duration of the war with the same troop. Trevor is on the far left.

Photograph © The Trevor Greenwood Archive.

About an hour elapsed before we found all kit, etc. in the darkness. Departed in a jeep ... 'F' were harboured beyond Villers Bocage and the surrounding country was lousy with mines and booby traps: two of our 'B' vehicles were shattered day before by touching grass verges: one driver killed. About 5 miles south we entered newly won territory. It felt weird and unnatural: very quiet – very still – very smelly – very deserted.

Roads were quite narrow, and we knew all grass verges were still heavily mined, the engineers having had no time to attend to them. Passing oncoming traffic – especially large lorries – was a nightmare. Their drivers knew about the mines, and so did we ... but ours was only a jeep! We always had to veer over to the verge, and I just hung on and waited for the bang! Fortunately, it was a moonlit night, and we

managed to survive … but I don't recommend such journeys, especially for nervous cases.

All buildings and houses (barns, farms, cottages etc.) along
the route were railed off with white tapes indicating forbid-
den area: practically all of them are booby-trapped by Jerry
after he has looted them. One curious soul entered one of the
cottages … or tried to. The roof immediately went sky high,
and four walls partly collapsed. The place was a shambles
when I saw it. A neat white cross now records the whereabouts of the 'curious impertinent'. The entire countryside in
this newly captured area is similarly mined. Jerry 'sappers'
seem to spend their lives devising new and devilish methods
of slaughter. Even trees and bushes carry booby traps … an
egg-shaped grenade suspended inconspicuously. It explodes
upon the slightest touch. A new device is attached to a hori-
zontal wire about 10 ft above the road. Detonation takes
place when the vertical aerial rods of vehicle touch the hori-
zontal wire. I have heard too that he is leaving booby traps
beneath the bodies of his dead. This was done by Italians in
Libya, but have my doubts about Jerry stooping to this.
Anyhow, the mere existence of these deadly traps doesn't help
one's nerves … especially on night rides, in a jeep!

Reached the tanks 1.30 a.m.: all crews asleep. Spread my
own bedding on ground, and dozed off. Awakened 4.30 a.m.:
felt lousy: We managed some breakfast – tea and tinned
bacon – and departed 6 a.m. for area east of Caen … about
thirty-mile run: a new sector for us. Most of journey over
field tracks: dust appalling. Went via Cheux, Marcelet, and
skirted Caen to north. Reached assembly area 1 p.m. …
7 hours for 34 miles. Tank in shocking state … dust about
an inch deep everywhere: guns hopeless. Spent about three
hours tidying up.

Had a bath in canvas bucket: hell of a headache. Saw a few women today near Caen: first I have seen for weeks. Some houses here apparently undamaged ... and inhabited!

We are moving further forward at dusk ... nearer to Jerry. Believe we are scheduled to take part in heavy attack in few days' time. Intention to annihilate German armour? Will they wait for us?

Many Canadians around here: we will be supporting them. Saw much evidence today of road building: some fine wide roads under construction. Crossed Orne via RE bridge.

Farmers appear to be harvesting their corn, etc. around here. Fear the crops further west are now beyond recovery: the corn looks very much over-ripe, and is still unharvested.

Chips for supper! More loot from around Villers Bocage. The lads have collected a sackful in my absence. We carry it tied to front of wheels. Heavy RAF raid ... some bombs on our side!

D +62 Monday 7.8.44

Left yesterday's assembly point just south of Longueval [NE of Caen] at 10 p.m. ... destination open ground about 3 miles south of Demouville. Rotten journey: pitch dark, no lights ... and some activity from enemy guns and mortars. We are in an area which is still being heavily shelled. Jerry in Troarn, few miles on left flank ... and only about 2000 yds S of Demouville. He is also still on the coast, due N of our present locality. We are thus surrounded by enemy in northeast and south.

Passed through an artillery battery on journey. Not a pleasant experience: guns seemed to be firing all around the compass. Their vivid white flashes affected driver, rendering

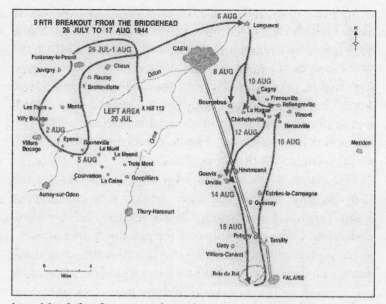

him blind for few seconds each time: coupled with the dust, this made convoy driving very difficult. Signals wires across roads are a darned nuisance too for night driving. A commander, whose head has to be above the cupola to assist driver, etc., needs to be perpetually on the alert. Even so, my beret was whipped off by one wire ... and another smashed two of Bill Geary's pipes. He was 'up' with me, and the wires caught him across his chest, smashing pipes in his breast pocket.

Arrived about midnight. Too dark to worry about 'digging in', in spite of proximity of enemy. Believe this area under constant mortar and HE fire. To bed beneath tank ... worn out – dirty – hungry – fed up! No letter from Jess for 2 or 3 days.

Reveille 5.15 a.m. 'Stand to' 5.30–6 a.m. No cooking of any sort until after 6.30. Spent about four hours in 'bed' last night ... and what a night! We discovered a new 'secret weapon'... mosquitoes! The bloody things almost ate us alive. Half the squadron have blistered faces this morning. Very few seem to have had much sleep. The major is in a bad way. No sleep at all last night, in spite of three almost sleepless nights previously. Believe the MO is trying to do something for us. Wasps and flies not so bad here ... yet! But prefer them to mosquitoes. Feel sure many nights like last will drive us all mad. Maybe the Orne (about 2 miles away) accounts for the mosquitoes.

Felt rotten this a.m.: had a brew of 'hot sweet'... and then 'digging in' after stand to. Breakfast by cooks about 9 a.m. Very misty in morning. Cleared up later and very warm and sunny. Officers out on recce for possible future action.

Jerry mortaring and shelling us this morning and afternoon – no damage to us. Still no letter from Jess ... Sent off green envelope [see Glossary]. Believe big attack imminent – tonight? Spent some time on maintenance today. Vehicle now ready for action. We are standing to all night tonight ... no bed! Probably pass the time slaughtering mosquitoes.

D +63 Tuesday 8.8.44

We were briefed about 10 o'clock by major. Big attack commencing with RAF raid on selected targets in many forward positions.* Had a good view of the raid. First signs of action came from artillery away on our right flank, sending over 'markers' on the targets. RAF arrived at 11 p.m.

---

* This was the start of Operation Totalise, part of a movement in which three Allied armies converged on Falaise from the south, west and north, encircling the German 7th Army and trapping 50,000 German forces in what came to be known as the Falaise Pocket.

exactly on time ... and then the bombs commenced to rain down. First target bombed for about 15 minutes ... and then came a lull whilst more markers lit up second target. More bombers arrived few minutes later ... more bombs. Certainly a very heavy raid: all over by 11.45.

Learned today that over 1000 Lancasters and Halifaxes did the job. *One* stick of bombs dropped in our lines ... in adjoining field to our harbour. I was at the rear of my vehicle and Geary on the turret. *He* arrived beneath tank with me! Some speed! This one stick of bombs gave us a hell of a scare. Can imagine Jerry's feelings ... he has to tolerate dozens of them.

By this morning, 1st Canadian Army were scheduled to have advanced about 4 miles ... a night advance towards Falaise, due south from Caen. This was done. Later, armoured divs are going through, including Polish Armoured Division. Official quarters believe this attack may mean the defeat of German Army in France. Thus, August 8th may become another 'Black Day' in German Army!

Another bad night last night: mosquitoes very troublesome. Half the squadron have swollen and blotchy faces and arms today. Some look very bad. Most of us wore 'turbans' over our heads and faces during night ... looked like a crowd of Arabs. Can't stand much more of this.

Last night's raid, and mosquitoes and guard, meant practically no sleep for third successive night. Felt ill this morning ... stomach trouble. Would give anything for a decent sleep.

At 12 noon we were ordered to prepare for immediate move. Went south and took up positions by place called 'Four' ... latter was in enemy hands yesterday. No infantry in the place: we have to hold it against counter attack until fresh infantry arrive.

Saw hundreds of Fortresses overhead about 1 p.m.,

bombing targets in forward area. Stood to at Four for a few hours ... then infantry arrived. Saw no sign of enemy meanwhile, but received much mortar and HE. Handed over command of vehicle to Geary: felt terrible. Feel I will be OK after sleep. Pulled out about 7 p.m. and harboured in orchard about a mile back. Believe we are scheduled for mopping up operations tomorrow. Have no interest in anything: no food all day. Received three letters from Jess tonight: a pleasant ending to a lousy day.

D +64 Wednesday 9.8.44

Feel much better this morning: slept from 11 p.m. until reveille ... 5.30 a.m. Tummy better: had bacon and beans for breakfast. Beautiful morning: We are scheduled to move out of this harbour at 12 noon to carry out mopping up on flanks of our salient: infantry will be with us.

Main attack appears to be going to plan. Canadians have advanced 5 miles towards Falaise ... but stiff opposition has been met. Have no news of progress of armoured divs.

Later. Damnably hot day. Left harbour about 8 p.m. ... sudden move. Anticipated move had been cancelled ... but came off nevertheless. Assembled at La Hogue, or what was left of it. The surrounding country is flat and sparsely wooded: visibility about a mile in any direction: good tank country. This is now probably the most devastated area in France: it is a barren wilderness of destruction, and resembles the battlefield of the last war. Most of the damage must have been caused by the bombers last night. Roads are unrecognisable, being covered with the debris from enormous bomb craters. The sub-soil here is chalk, and the landscape is now just a chalky patch-work, with a few gaunt trees standing up ... leafless, lifeless ... just reminders of what used to be. Three villages are easily visible in this area – each about a mile from the other, in an enormous triangle. There isn't a building left in any of them ... just a few walls and masses of grey rubble. The surrounding areas are honeycombed with bomb craters, some as deep as 20 feet. I have never before seen such destruction. No doubt it was necessary. These places, though only tiny hamlets, were heavily defended German strong points, and had to be blasted out of existence to enable our night attack to proceed.

It seems incredible that any living creature could have remained within a mile of the district, and yet ... a tiny live kitten greeted some of our fellows who went to explore Le Hogue. It is now a guest on their tank!

From La Hogue we proceeded last to the outskirts of Chicheboville to assist the infantry in occupying the place. It was getting late, almost dusk when we arrived, but we remained some time, blasting hell out of surrounding woods and ditches. It was dark by the time we finished, saturated in perspiration ... and dirt. Only a mile or two back to La Hogue, but a rotten experience. Pitch dark, dusty, narrow lanes, minefields ... and maybe snipers ... Eventually got back about midnight and harboured among the bomb-craters ... apparently in a minefield. But we were too tired to worry about these things. Very hot day.

D +65 Thursday 10.8.44

Reveille 5.15 – stand to until 6 a.m. Breakfast about eight, not improved by the sight of the surroundings: just a flat devastated wilderness . . . more gaunt and lifeless now in full daylight.

Moved out later to harbour nearer Chicheboville in lightly wooded area. Jerry must have seen us arrive: he greeted us with loads of mortar. Sgt Holding and Tpr Parks killed (both in 'A'). Had a couple of narrow escapes myself. Had lunch in spite of mortar. Remained couple of hours . . . and then sudden departure for Chicheboville again, apparently to assist 11 and 12 Troops.

Came under some mysterious shellfire, but couldn't locate source: seemed like 88 HE. Found three dummy Panthers! Remained until 9 p.m., and then back to former harbour. Very hot day.

D +66 Friday 11.8.44

Little sleep last night: mosquitoes still troublesome, and here we have millions of ants on the ground. Couldn't sleep on ground. Spent most of night doing troop guard with Geary: brewed up 3.30 a.m. Fell asleep 4.30 a.m. on engine hatches.

Issued with mosquito cream this morning. Two letters from Jess . . . one from Johnny. No signs of move this a.m. Maintenance on vehicle and guns: they need it. Had a bath in bucket: I needed it. First shave for two days . . . or is it three? We are now always dirty: dust here is terrible, and this hot weather doesn't improve matters. Unbearably hot this morning.

Later. No move today: terribly hot: No work since lunch time. Jerry quite close, but we have been undisturbed all day.

Kettle lost its spout! Tragedy. First, the lid disappeared, then the handle fell off . . . and now the spout. But we can still use it. The most useful implement on the tank. Must have brewed thousands of cups of 'hot sweet' thanks to that kettle.

Few more casualties yesterday: Sgt Holding, Sgt Phillips, Sgt Turner, Tpr Parks. All three sergeants were 'originals': all killed by mortar, former on his tank in this harbour, and the other two at 'A' Echelon. Phillips is a big loss to C: good fellow. Can't be many of us left now.

Enemy only left present locality a day or so before we arrived: His dug-outs are marvellously sound and well made. There are pine trees here and his dug-out roofs are of pine logs, four or more layers thick. One or two have 'curtains' across the entrances . . . probably to exclude mosquitoes. Jerry must have left here in a hurry: plenty of kit and ammo lying about: probably Tuesday's bombing raid scared him out.

Done very little today: feel too tired, and weather unpleasantly hot. Plenty of artillery fire day and night, but we seem to have got used to it.

D +67 Saturday 12.8.44

Another sunny day . . . very hot. Still awaiting further orders. Jerry must be keeping quiet around Vimont and Chicheboville, otherwise we would have had some activity. Still being mortared here . . . L/Cpl Miller wounded this a.m. by shrapnel.

Spent some time reading . . . and writing to Jess. Mobile showers arrived this evening: quite a nice change from buckets.

Believe we are having a 'party' tomorrow . . . helping infantry further east beyond Chichi. Two troop tanks (under Geary and Anderson) returned to Brigade this a.m. for repairs. My vehicle now attached to 2 in 11 under Mr Francis. Gin and cordial issued today . . . not free.

Our job here seems to be protecting and enlarging base of salient on Falaise. Vimont must be important point to justify such protection. Learned today that we are to have access to a rest camp on the beaches. One crew at a time will depart from squadron for four days 'rest'. Expect it will be weeks before the whole squadron is through this rest camp.

We are now back on compo packs . . . with fresh bread instead of biscuits. Haven't seen the cooks for about a fortnight. Have not missed them.

D +68 Sunday 13.8.44

Some disturbance last night. Several enormous 'crumps' sounded around midnight and for next hour. May have been bombs, but heard no aircraft. Probably air-bursts. Shrapnel buzzed around dangerously close. Transferred my bed from bivvy to beneath tank.

Reveille 6 a.m. Stowed and ready to move by 7 a.m. . . . scheduled to move to south of Chicheboville to help infantry push further east.

10.30 a.m. No move yet. Beautiful morning. Mosquitoes still busy . . . they are working hard this morning!

Later. Anticipated move cancelled. We are going instead towards Falaise: have to be ready to move any time after 6 p.m. The general situation, and rapid American encircling move S of Falaise, must have determined our plans. Presume the Allies will now go all-out to isolate the enemy in the pocket south and west of Falaise.

Heard this evening that Yanks are now 5 miles south of Falaise, and we and Canadians are 5 miles north.

Long letter from Jess today: interesting news about Barry. Now in his new cot!

Another minor casualty: Sgt Proctor shot through foot whilst cleaning his rifle! Sgt Hall now back in France: still with TDU. Believe he will return to his old troop – 15. I will no doubt be transferred to another troop.

D +69 Monday 14.8.44

Now harboured near Urville in a small orchard. Trees laden with small cider apples. Our journey here necessitated crossing the salient from east to west. Only about 2 miles from spearhead here.

Saw an amazing amount of war material and vehicles during journey last evening. Almost every field literally crowded with vehicles ... lorries parked as far as horizon, specially along main Caen–Falaise road. Several Polish units in this area, altho it appears to be mainly under control of Canadians.

Believe there is a big attack going in today about noon in an effort to close the gap and join up with the Americans south of Falaise. Our job will be defensive around St Croix [Saint-Croix-sur-Mer]. Much evidence of recent battle. Dozens of damaged Shermans ... Several minefields have had to be cleared too. We threaded our way through them yesterday.

Very few buildings left undamaged on main road. Fair amount of artillery last night, but had a good sleep.

Left harbour 12 noon: moved 2 or 3 miles E to defensive position. Our briefing included details of bombing programme for today. Three or four woods immediately south and east of our position were to be blasted from 2 p.m. until 4 p.m.

Reached our area at 2 p.m., just as RAF four-engined bombers commenced bombing wood 2000 yds to our front. What a sight! Horrible: terrifying ... and yet fascinating. The whole earth trembled: trees rocketed sky-high ... enormous fountains of earth shot upwards: smoke – fire – death. God help the Germans in that wood! Hundreds of bombs rained down in the first few minutes. We were thrilled by the RAF. This was direct support for us with a vengeance. Every one of us felt more cheerful. Knowing too that our very heavy attack had commenced at 12 noon and that the end of this campaign may not be far off.

And then came tragedy: terrible, heartbreaking despair.

It was about 2.30 p.m. Many waves of bombers had unloaded their bombs where we wanted them ... but suddenly, a stick of bombs fell on a point about a mile to our rear. Was it Jerry? No! There were two or three dozen Lancasters over the spot: one of them must have dropped his bombs accidentally over our own lines ... the damned fool! Hard luck on our lads, but an accident can't be helped.

More waves of bombers appeared, and most of these too dropped their bombs over our lines. The awful truth dawned: they were bombing the smoke-laden area indicated by that first stick ... even though it was 2 miles N of their most northerly target.

Why couldn't they be stopped? We endured hell, even though we were fairly safe from the bombs. What a contrast with our former jubilation! Half an hour later, more bombers dropped their loads over another area – slightly west – in our lines. The destruction behind us was now becoming greater than that ahead. And so it went on, with our own bombs murdering our own men, and dropping nearer to us as the afternoon wore on. We put out yellow smoke flares in a frantic effort to save ourselves. I saw bomb doors opening as the planes approached – and expected to be blown to hell any moment. They were quite low ... about 3 or 4 thousand feet. I saw Very lights being fired from the ground as signals to stop the bombing. I heard machine gunning in the air ... and was afterwards told that Spitfires had been trying to divert the bombers. I heard later too that a little Auster went up to try and stop this ghastly blunder. But it went on. I didn't know then that there was no liaison between our ground forces and the bombers. I could only wonder, at the time, and my heart wept. So much depended upon today's action: the war even may be shortened by its success. It had been planned carefully and secretly ... We had almost looked forward to it. And now ... this thing.

And we could do nothing about it – nothing. But we *did* do something: we watched the clock and anxiously waited for 4 o'clock. But by then, our hearts and minds were torn with black despair. Even the blindest fool would know that such fearful destruction must inevitably hinder, perhaps ruin, the day's action.

I learned later that the Poles suffered a lot. They were scheduled to move forward through our initial breakthrough. Their armoured div. was disorganised. The artillery suffered too: gunners had to leave their posts and run for their lives. But the full story must be terrible. I do not know it. I don't want to know it. I feel at one with my colleagues who are begging to be excused further 'assistance' from Bomber Command!*

* It is instructive to compare this account with a newspaper cutting which Trevor kept from the *Daily Mail* of 15 August. Their correspondent, Colin Bednall, had actually flown with the raid described above. His lengthy report is a glowing account of total success, with no mention of the disaster.

This thing has happened before, but not on the same scale. On the 6th, several bombs were dropped by our bombers south of Caen steel works ... in broad daylight. It happened on the night of the 7th in the next field to our harbour. It happened on 10.7.44 ... fighter bombers.

It happened on 18.7.44 S of Caen. But yesterday's error seems totally inexcusable. Fine day – perfect visibility: no enemy fighters, no enemy AA. Clear targets.

A main road (Caen–Falaise) dead straight for about 15 miles as target indicator: a chalk pit ¼ mile across, 1 ½ miles N of target as further indicator. This pit was bombed!!! Being used by Canadian echelons! We all hope that bombers will in future be confined to targets in Germany, where they can't harm our own troops ... and where their 'precision' bombing may do more good for the war effort. But we are grateful for Typhoons and fighters. They have contact with our ground forces. Maybe such liaison would be infradig for Bomber Command!

After the bombing fiasco, we kept vigil and waited for a possible counter attack. But it did not come. A few shells and mortars came over – one of B tanks was hit, our halftrack carrying red cross flag was hit and RC padre killed. A few wounded came in. At least one enemy tank was seen along edge of wood a mile away ... but no attack developed.

Had a meal about 10 p.m. ... and then bed. We remained on the ground, at alert, one man per crew on guard all night.

D +70 Tuesday 15.8.44

Enemy bombers raided area north last night ... probably
Caen. Quite exciting for an hour or so. Wireless reported
about 1000 bombers in yesterday's attack. They are alleged
to have bombed enemy targets to prevent counter attack!

Quiet morning ... still keeping vigil. Padre's body
brought in this morning.* Saw Dave Lubick last evening.
Still on Honeys, but expects to be on Churchills soon.

Later. Had lunch and then came sudden order to move. For
next 3 or 4 hours we seemed to be chasing all over Normandy.
Have no clear idea of whether we were seeking fleeing
enemy or just keeping up with our own advancing troops.
But understand we are now temporarily attached to
Canadian army to assist with final assault on Falaise. Saw
much evidence of day's fighting ... and some 'good'
Jerries ... all dead!

Finally harboured at Ussy, about 5 m NW of Falaise, at
dusk. Managed to brew up somehow ... and then bed.
Commenced to rain about midnight, but only a shower.
First rain I have seen for about a fortnight. About 3 hours'
sleep and 1 hour's guard.

Seems to be beautiful countryside: much agriculture,
orchards ... hills and valleys and woods, etc. War has not
caused heavy damage here: Germans must have been evacuated too quickly to necessitate heavy shelling.

---

* The Roman Catholic padre, Captain Patrick McMahon, was killed attempting
to rescue Canadian soldiers from a burned-out tank.

D +71 Wednesday 16.8.44

Reveille 5.15 a.m. No cooking until daylight ... but we moved off at dawn, so no breakfast. No definite orders, except that attack on Falaise going in this a.m., and we have to hold flanks against Jerry.

Hurried move to position 1 mile NW Falaise and stood to against wood, Bois du Roi. Managed to cook up a meal, but enemy fire rather troublesome. HE and mortar seem to be coming over from all directions. Plenty of activity in wood. Canadians are trying to clear it. Fine morning. Last night's rain only moistened ground: still plenty of dust. Much evidence of Jerry on run from Ussy this a.m. Several of his vehicles lying burned out on roadside ... some with dead crews still aboard.

Very few dead cattle around here: probably due to speed of enemy retreat rendering heavy artillery barrage impracticable. Snipers too now very rare. We must have wiped out his sniper battalion weeks ago.

D +72 Thursday 17.8.44

There was a sudden move yesterday. We spent the morning in a defensive role a mile or so from Falaise, close by Bois du Roi wood. There was heavy mortar and some HE and one or two bazookas: it seemed to come from E and W – so we deployed for 'all round' protection. Our 'B' tank hit by 88. Brewed up.

After lunch, we received sudden orders to move ... back to Chicheboville!!! It appears that the Canadians were making good progress and were able to dispense with us ... instead of supporting them through Falaise in the evening.

Well ... Chicheboville was a long way for a hurried tank march, but we had to do it. It was probably the worst tank journey we have done: dust, heat etc.: we did most of the journey (21 miles) across fields – mostly corn and wheat – to avoid the congested roads. The dust was unbelievable. It got so bad that the major could not see landmarks and we were temporarily lost ... so we had to stop to allow the dust to settle and reveal the surrounding country. My driver (Boland) said it was worse than being in the desert: he spent 2 years in North Africa.

Part of our journey lay through villages bombed by RAF – wreckage indescribable. Ultimately harboured near former area and had time for a meal ... and then bed. No water so we slept in our filth. Reveille 6.30 today, but slept until 8 a.m. Felt much better for it.

Maintenance all morning – sorting out, etc. Tanks very dusty: guns almost invisible! Had a bath ... portable showers. Two letters from Jess.

Geary rejoined us today: Sammy Stubbs returned to his own troop. Sorry to lose Sammy. We are moving tomorrow: southeast to Ouezy, nr. Mezidon – about 8 miles.

The east flank of the Falaise salient has shifted rapidly during last day or two. Jerry is now definitely on the retreat. Tonight's radio reports general withdrawal. Our landing in south will have important repercussions up here. It only commenced Tuesday, but appears to be making remarkable headway.

D +73 Friday 18.8.44

Left Chicheboville area about 8.30 a.m. Travelled via Vimont, and then southeast to Ouezy via main road.

Several civilians here: believe Mezidon is in fairly good condition and civvies have given our fellows a great welcome. Hope to see the place soon.

Harboured in orchard just off main road. Anticipated action now off. Believe we are not required in the 'bocage' country. Glad to hear this ... hope it is true.* Reported last night that we are joining up with 34 Brigade. Nothing definite yet. We are still being troubled by mosquitoes. Last night was hell. Many fellows had no sleep at all.

There is a pond and partly stagnant ditch in the grounds of the chateau here ... expect this will provide abundance of mosquitoes tonight. Had hoped that our move from Chicheboville would have freed us from this pest.

Worked on vehicle all afternoon, removing track plates. Beautiful day: warm and sunny. Very pleasant countryside: kind and gentle. Marvellous agricultural area: fertile soil: pleasantly undulating: fairly well wooded: many orchards, but mainly cider apples ... rather spongy and slightly bitter, but quite edible.

D +74 Saturday 19.8.44

Warned at midnight last night to be ready to move at 6.30 a.m. Reveille 5.30 a.m. Darned nuisance these sudden orders. This meant completely re-stowing the vehicle in the morning – before daylight – and without breakfast. We got away somehow. And we had a cup of tea. Had to drink the latter on the move. Not an easy matter.

Destination Mirbel ... just beyond Mezidon. Went

---

* The *bocage* country of hedges, ditches, high banks and sunken roads was extremely difficult terrain for tanks to negotiate.

through Canon . . . fairly battered, but not completely ruined. Then Mezidon. Largest place I have seen so far, though only a large village. Some good property and new houses quite undamaged, but the place has been knocked about a bit. Some civilians: they seemed generally pleased to see us, in spite of the early hour. Both river bridges blown, but REs have erected temporary crossings. Now harboured in orchard about a mile east of Mezidon on high ground. Hope we will have fewer mosquitoes up here, but have my doubts.

Several groups of refugees have passed by during the day: A pitiful sight. Children especially seem terribly under-nourished. These people have an amazing variety of vehicles for their transport . . . even those with cycles are usually towing small handcarts. Gave away a little food . . . sardines, etc.

No signs of any impending battle today. In any case, this type of country is totally unsuitable for our vehicles. Perhaps we will be reserved for later action. Plenty of apples here. Pestell tried stewing some, but he only ate a mouthful. No sugar! Plenty of our artillery to our rear – 5.5s – but no trouble from Jerry today. Not even a single mortar! He must be pulling out pretty rapidly. Monty is supposed to have announced 'battle of Normandy is won', according to radio. Some of the infantry here don't think so. Fifty of them, with three company commanders, wiped out last night on Vie River crossing. Jerry has left fairly strong rearguard of Spandaus, etc: Believe another similar action will take place tonight. Had a chat with officer of Leics. infantry unit.* He feels very strongly about non-combatant part of this army . . . Pleased to find someone with similar views to my own.†

* The 1st Battalion, The Leicestershire Regiment.
† Trevor's objection was that the noncombatants were living not only in conditions of greater safety but also in far greater comfort, and even luxury, than those

Heard some details the other day of a GHQ (Canadian) on this sector. The whole thing seems scandalous to me.

Artillery very busy tonight. Impossible to converse here whilst guns are firing: din is terrific. Shells seem to be whizzing past just over our heads. Guns must be very close to our rear. Rain this evening.

D +75 Sunday 20.8.44

Reveille 5.30. Lay in bed until 8 o'clock. Still raining: but soon cleared up. Had breakfast – and then sudden 'flap': 'Prepare to move immediately'—! Blast! Same old frantic rushing about and stowing kit, bedding rolls, etc. Storage is a problem. Originally, we packed most of our stuff inside the vehicle, but everything is gradually being tied on outside to leave the interior clear for action. When we move nowadays, we are more like travelling junk-shops than tanks.

My own vehicle, for instance. At the rear is a long roll about the size of two dustbins end on. This contains two bedding rolls, 2 or 3 overcoats and some waterproof clothing. The whole is enclosed in waterproof tank sheet and tied to rear with ropes, etc. Tied to this roll is a saucepan and a horse-hair chair. The latter a very useful piece of furniture. Three bedding rolls tied to exterior of turret. Food box tied on rear track cover. Pots, pans, water tins, kettle, spades and all sorts of scrap iron rest on engine hatches. Other vehicles have their own particular variants on this pattern. One tank always carries an improvised lavatory at the rear. This is a compo pack box with appropriate oval hole cut in one side—!

---

in the front line who were doing the fighting. His next comment concerning the GHQ (Canadian) more than likely also reflects this theme.

D +76 Monday 21.8.44

I have yesterday's story to finish. Our move commenced about 2 p.m. . . . roughly to the east after the retreating enemy. Over La Vie river, across RE bridge. This bridge had caused the infantry much trouble the day previous. From the bridge we went north, making for Crevecoeur-en-Auge . . . still in enemy hands. At a stop en route, several civilians paid their respects, shaking hands with all and sundry. The usual greeting: '*bonjour, mes amis.*' Drinks were provided . . . and we parted with a fair amount of tinned food.

This halt occurred a mile or two from Crevecoeur. Suddenly we received orders to move, with all guns prepared for action. The enemy had been reported leaving the village, but in fair strength on a fairly high hill just north of the village: heavily wooded on top. We had to clear the wood and help the infantry occupy it.

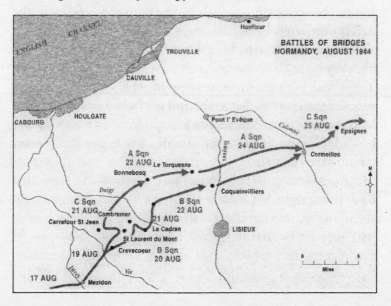

Our start point an orchard: the darned place was a mass of small orchards, and immediately ahead lay that hill, rising steeply for 3 or 4 hundred feet: quite a landmark, and a strong defensive position: but not a suitable attack for our vehicles.

Our troubles started almost immediately after the advance commenced. Firstly, it was impossible to fire our HE from the orchards, as contact with the trees would have exploded the shells over our own men. Also, each little orchard was surrounded by a deep ditch, making progress very difficult. In the first few minutes a few tanks were having track trouble ... mine included. I managed to limp towards a hedgerow, and took what cover I could. On inspection, I found the job would take at least 2 or 3 hours ... providing we could borrow suitable tools. That put me out of action, less than half an hour after it commenced.

Whilst inspecting my vehicle, I noticed another about 100 yds left, burning: it must have been hit. Meanwhile, the rest of the squadron were advancing painfully slowly up the hill. Immediately in front of me, a house was blazing fiercely: we had blasted it with HE: a terrible din, and uncomfortably close to me.

We had to make some attempt to repair my vehicle, so I ordered the crew to dismount and get busy, hoping we were sufficiently screened by the orchard in front to make the job possible. There was some enemy MG fire to our left, but we had to take the risk.

After working 10 minutes or so, an enemy HE exploded 6 yds to our right. We had no warning whatever. Immediately, we all rushed around the left of the vehicle ... not one of us had been hit by that first shell, altho the blast shook us. At the rear of the vehicle, two of the crew had scrambled beneath, when another shell exploded ahead of its predecessor. Again I felt the awful hot blast, and wondered why I hadn't been hit: it was only a few feet away. Beneath the tank, Geary said he had been hit in the arm. He had been just in front of me, and climbing beneath the vehicle, when the second explosion occurred.

He was bleeding profusely. I clambered out again to get the first aid kit from inside the tank. Fortunately, there was no third shot. By the time I found the FA kit, Geary had scrambled out, and was standing beside the vehicle, blood pouring from his left forearm. Nearby, there were infantry ambulance men taking cover in a house. I took him across, ignoring our own dressings, and left the other three members of the crew beneath the vehicle.

He was bandaged up, and a tourniquet applied, but already his colour was ashen, and I felt sure he was losing too much blood. The nearest ambulance, a jeep, was a quarter of a mile away in the village. He said he could walk alright and was already speaking of rejoining the crew! An ambulance man accompanied us to the village: en-route we had one 'rest' to take cover from mortar fire.

After saying good-bye to Bill, (he was still conscious, but looked very sick) I [*Editor's note: the first diary notebook ends at this point*] had a few words with the ambulance men. They were members of the H—shire regiment,* and struck me as being a poor lot. They seemed horrified when I told them we had already lost one tank. (I learned later that the co-driver, Bridgeman, was killed instantly, and the gunner badly wounded.)

My next job was to return to my vehicle, and I reached it

---

* The Hallamshire Battalion (not regiment), 49 (West Riding) Infantry Division. In fact the Hallams fought with distinction throughout the campaign, and one, Corporal J. W. Hooper, was posthumously awarded the Victoria Cross.

without harm . . . altho that darned Spandau MG seemed to be uncomfortably close.

To my amazement, my driver, Johnny Boland, now reported that he too had been hit by shrapnel . . . he had made the discovery in my absence with Geary. He seemed inclined to ignore the matter, as it was a very small wound on his shoulder blade . . . but I had to insist upon him having attention. And so, once again I returned to the village, via the orchards, etc. We heard the crack of a rifle en route, and I knew a sniper was busy in the vicinity. A few seconds later, we found Gilmore had been hit through the hand by this sniper. His presence made things a little more unpleasant.

Gilmore and Boland were both handed over to the ambulance men . . . and I haven't seen either of them since.

It was whilst making my second journey back from the village that I experienced what were probably my worst moments since coming over here. I had reached the first orchard, and a few feet to my rear was one of our vehicles, apparently in trouble. Some infantrymen had appeared and I was talking to one of them when an HE shell exploded without warning a few feet away. We all dropped to the ground instinctively and I and two of the infantry fellows crawled towards a log nearby for cover. I don't know how long I lay huddled up by that log. It was probably only for one or two minutes . . . but I will never forget them. The first explosion was the prelude to a 'stonk' [see Glossary] aimed perhaps at the tank. It was followed by 20 or 30 others . . . all within a few feet of us. Very soon, I heard a groan beside me . . . and one of the infantry lads said 'I've had it.' Soon there were more groans and the other infantry lad was hit. Meanwhile the shells came down relentlessly. I could feel the hot blast from each one: the air became thick with the acrid fumes of cordite. I knew I should have been blown to smithereens, by all the laws of explosives . . . but all the time I remained conscious of being alive. At one period, I realised that all the shells were landing on my side of the log, and wondered about changing to the other side . . . but there was insufficient pause between each explosion. So I just lay huddled up as small as possible, and hopĕd . . . and hoped.

I believe it is customary for a person to recall practically his entire lifetime when death seems imminent . . . but my case was different. I knew that I was constantly reminding myself that I still lived . . . and that I still had a chance to see Jess and Barry again. These thoughts must have crossed my mind after each explosion. I cannot say that I was aware of terror, but I know I was terrified . . . because my hands subsequently trembled for many hours. I must have become partly stupefied, because I remained on the ground for some time after the last round . . . until I heard some voices, in fact, and found the group of infantrymen helping their two wounded colleagues over the log. There had only been the three of us on my side of the log . . . and I alone had escaped uninjured. I cannot explain this.

Those on the other side of the log had been protected and were all safe. I made my way to a barn, collecting a Piat dropped by the infantry on the way. There I found the two wounded lads receiving attention. They seemed in a bad way.

But I had a vehicle . . . and I had to get back. I felt afraid of returning, being more conscious of death now: and that Spandau was about . . . and a sniper.

I took all possible precautions traversing the orchard . . . crouching by hedges etc., and eventually reached my vehicle and clambered inside. At last I felt reasonably safe. The two remaining members of my crew had wondered about my long absence, and had feared the worst after that stonk which they had seen. The tank that appeared to have attracted the enemy fire was un-hit. Its crew were inside with closed hatches. They knew I was outside in the midst of the shell-fire, and one of them seems to regard me as the luckiest man in the British army. Perhaps he is right.

Well . . . the three of us, Pestell, Pedder and self stayed in my vehicle for some time. The repair job seemed unimportant under the circumstances. We had water and dry biscuits for our lunch/tea meal, and just waited . . . and talked.

Meanwhile, the squadron were carrying out their job of scaling that crazy hill. By evening they had finished, successfully, and I heard the major over the wireless giving orders to return to a point near my own position. They appeared at dusk, and I then made contact with my troop officer and reported the wounding of two members of my crew. I needed other assistance to repair my vehicle but it could not be provided . . . so I borrowed some tools from other vehicles to attempt the job myself – with the major's blessing. Mr Francis also loaned me a member of his crew – Dawes – a remarkable worker. I was asked to try and make my way to harbour, about 1 mile south of the village, if I finished the job.

The squadron departed. It was almost dark. There was a burning house 70 yards in front: a burning Churchill enclosing a mutilated human body 100 yards to my right: to the left, a Spandau – if he hadn't been killed – and maybe a sniper or two.

I was afraid.

We set to work in this no man's land. The silence was awful, punctuated by crackling from the burning house . . . and occasional 'cracks' from the burning tank: the small arms ammo was exploding.

We worked until 11.30 p.m.: no more could be done as we needed more tools, and it was now pitch dark. I decided to spend the night in the vehicle, with my three colleagues, taking turns at guard in pairs. Too many Jerries in the neighbourhood to take risks. We informed HQ of this arrangement over the air, and settled down for our night's vigil. And now it started to rain ... like hell. Pedder and I in the turret, observing through the open hatches, were soon wet to the skin. Damned hungry too ... and tired, hellishly so. In between turns we slept, somehow ... and then came the dawn ... to my unutterable relief. Once again we radioed HQ for further assistance and were informed that help was already on the way: this was at 6.30 a.m.

At 7 a.m., no help had arrived ... but suddenly there was a vicious 'swish' outside, followed by a heavy explosion. God! What did it mean? We had wondered whether the enemy had really been driven far back, and now it seemed that he was shelling us ... the usual prelude to a counter attack. We closed all hatches, and waited ... and wondered ... Very soon came another heavy bang, and we heard the shrapnel slapping the side of the vehicle. Would we be hit? Or captured? Was it the end of everything? These were unspoken thoughts ... but looks were enough.

Personally, I felt pretty secure in the vehicle, after my experience in the open the previous afternoon. HE does not penetrate a Churchill ... but a direct hit could cause severe injuries. The shelling continued for half an hour. Each shot announced itself by a momentary 'swish' ... and then the explosion. Sometimes the vehicle shuddered ... sometimes the shrapnel clanged on something ... but we remained un-hit. After a time, I knew that we couldn't have been under observation. It was indirect shooting, otherwise we

would soon have been hit. But every shot seemed dangerously close and it was only a matter of time . . .

But the worst did not happen.

After half an hour, there came a pause, and our nerves
gradually slackened off: fear-haunted eyes became more
normal . . . But what about the repair job? We couldn't carry
on under such conditions. We attempted to radio HQ again,
to have the promised assistance withdrawn . . . but we
couldn't get a reply.

I decided to bale out and try and find our way back to the
unit. It seemed a more sensible plan than being shelled to
death or taken prisoner. We removed breech blocks and
strikers from the guns, and then hopped out and bolted for
the comparative shelter of a nearby orchard. Very soon I saw
some figures on a roadway, and they were wearing khaki . . .
not the grey-green of the enemy. Thank goodness for that:
the village was obviously still in our hands. A little further
on, we came to a roadway and there was one of our scout
cars. The driver had time to run us back to our squadron . . .
what blessed relief! It was still pouring with rain, but that
little journey, perched perilously on the top of that tiny
vehicle, was one of the pleasantest I have ever known.

We found the rest of the unit parked in an orchard, and
the men sheltering in various barns and sheds. Mr Francis
and his crew were having a meal . . . and we needed no
persuading to join them. How good was the taste of that hot
sweet! – the first I had had since breakfast the day before.
We were soaked and tired . . . but there was a remarkably
cheerful atmosphere as we swopped yarns and discussed the
previous day, in that crazy little barn with its mud walls and
musty smell, and general atmosphere of decay.

After our brief respite, news came through that the

squadron had to depart immediately for another attack . . . and so our colleagues left us for their vehicles, and we returned to ours, with more tools, to finish the job.

Meanwhile, our infantry were attacking, and so our position was now much safer. This infantry attack had been preceded by heavy shelling from our own artillery – and it occurred to us that our ordeal a couple of hours before may have been due to our own guns.

We walked back to our vehicle, still in the rain . . . and now had time to inspect the shell holes around our tank. There were dozens of them in a radius of 30 yards, some of them adjoining the tank, but not one direct hit. From rather obvious signs on the ground, we had to accept the sad truth . . . our own guns had shelled us! Perhaps we were too near the enemy.

We carried on with the repairs and completed the job by lunch time without further interruption. But the driving sprocket had been badly damaged and I felt sure a new one would have to be fitted before we went into action again. We returned to the squadron harbour . . . and there the BTO confirmed that a new sprocket would have to be fitted by Brigade. We had to remain where we were until further orders.

Spent the night in this harbour . . . beneath the vehicle. Meanwhile, the squadron were miles away to the north-east . . . chasing the retreating enemy.

D +77 Tuesday 22.8.44

The EME inspected the vehicle this a.m. and we have to move back a couple of miles to Brigade AWD to have the job done. Departed lunch time, and reached AWD shortly after. Had lunch, and then work on vehicle to prepare it for Br. fitters.

Later, had a bucket bath, and washed some clothes. Very hot day. Enemy must have retreated a long way: no sound of guns here. Tremendous amount of activity on roadway now: how different from the deathly stillness of Sunday when Jerry was still about, to welcome us in Crevecoeur! Commenced to rain about eleven p.m. Slept beneath vehicle.

D +78 Wednesday 23.8.44

Rained all night, but fine this morning. Blankets now hanging out to dry ... with my laundry. Br. still have the job in hand ... and it now looks as though we will spend another night here. Heaven knows where the squadron have got to. Radio news 1 p.m.: heard of the 'fall of Paris' ... occupied by patriot forces and civilians. Very good news. My crew seem to have enjoyed themselves last evening. Found a pub open in Crevecoeur and had some drink and singing with local civvies.*

Received letter from Jess ... and parcel of 1000 ciggies from Jess, Kath, Toddy, Dorothy. Have now enough to last for weeks. Heard of death of Woodfine ... by mortar. Another 'old boy' gone!

Later. Have received details of our location – when we move from here. We have to report to TDU near Repentigny ... about six miles NE. Hope we are not detained there. Repairs proceeding slowly: certain we can't move tonight.

---

* The French uprising had begun four days previously. The Free French and US forces entered the city on 24 August, and on 25 August the German garrison surrendered.

Trevor did not see liberated Paris until the war was over, when he attended
the British Army Exhibition in June 1945, where these photos were taken.
Above: Iron Duke was the CO's tank throughout the actions taken by
9 RTR, and was driven up the Champs Elysées in the Victory Parade.
Trevor is second left. Below: The turret is embossed with the unofficial
motto of 9 RTR: *Qui S'y Frotte, S'y Brûle* (Who touches me will burn).
Trevor is on the far left.
Photographs © The Trevor Greenwood Archive.

This location is on a main road ... roughly north–south to Crevecoeur-en-Auge ... and there has been much refugee traffic today. Large horse-drawn hay carts seem to be the most popular, and they are invariably stacked high with all kinds of household junk – beds, mattresses, wardrobes, pots and pans, etc. Usually, too, a few children are perched on top, and beneath the vehicle, wire mesh cages are suspended to carry the family poultry. Bicycles too are very popular, and they are made to carry an amazing amount of stuff. Sometimes, the refugees have no vehicle of any sort: they carry large suitcases and valises ... sometimes a rucksack as well. They certainly look weary. These refugees are travelling in both directions along this road: I don't know whether they are coming or going!

Raining hard this evening.

D +79 Thursday 24.8.44

Rained all night: blankets very wet this morning. Showery this morning, but fine intervals. Job should be finished this afternoon.

Later. Brigade fitters have now left: work finished about 3 p.m. Intend to depart for TDU about 5.30. Cpl Hodson's vehicle also with me: had some trouble. Heard radio news 1 p.m. Rumania have accepted armistice terms!* Good news. What about Bulgaria? Finland? Hungary? Marseilles occupied by patriots! How much longer? Have now been out of touch with the unit since Monday. Have no idea where they are. Hope to get back to them, particularly C, but have orders to report to TDU.

* Rumania discontinued military operations on 24 August and signed the Armistice on 12 September 1944.

Later. Arrived TDU 7 p.m. Had meal. Pleasant location:
orchards, etc.: well wooded valley near Repentigny and
south of Bonnebosq. Sleeping in bell-tent tonight ... with
'Geordie' Grant.

D +80 Friday 25.8.44

No rain last night, but very chilly this morning. Many
bombers overhead during night. Orders to proceed to unit
this a.m., but TDU fitters now working on vehicle and am
held up. Will be moving east this evening with TDU
column. About 15-mile journey.

No news of squadron: heaven knows where they have got
to. Will be glad to rejoin unit to get some mail: seems ages
since I heard from Jess. Beautiful day: hot and sunny:
managed to dry my blankets and laundry at last.

Cpl Hodson's vehicle back with Brigade again: sprocket job
not satisfactory. Expect I will move on tonight without him.

Had to give detail of date of birth, religion, etc. when report-
ing to TDU yesterday. For religion I stipulated 'Nil'. The NCO
(Sgt) clerk said 'that means nothing, and it won't do for the
army ... nor can you be an atheist'—! 'Is that so?' I replied.
'Well, put down atheist – that's official.' He entered the dreaded
word without further argument, adding 'that's the first time
I've ever heard of an atheist in the army.' This is not the first
time my non-belief has caused comment. But I always insist
upon a correct entry. Maybe I am regarded as a crank.

Fitters still working on vehicle when TDU squadron
departed at 7 p.m. Was therefore left behind once again. DR
being sent back to act as guide when we are able to move.

Later. Work finished, but too late to move tonight. Am sleeping here and moving on in the morning. Slade, Pestell, Pedder gone to Bonnebosq for evening.

D +81 Saturday 26.8.44

Mr Tindale returned at midnight with food and tea. DR also arrived soon after. Up at 8 a.m. . . . 2 hours later than intended. Moved off at 9 a.m., and eventually rejoined TDU about 11 a.m. . . . 19 miles journey further east. Yesterday was the first day since arriving in France that I heard no gunfire . . . not even the sound of distant artillery. Must have been many miles behind the front line. Even here – 19 miles nearer – it is very quiet and have not yet heard any artillery. Am now about eight miles NE of Lisieux. Another fine day: very hot.

Still no definite news of squadron, but a rumour that they are officially having a rest . . .

Many demonstrations of welcome by civvies on journey this morning. Most of the local menfolk raise their caps as we pass, giving the V sign with their hand.* I think the re-occupation of Paris will make us more welcome. Many of our bombers over here last night. Seemed to be passing overhead for several hours after dark.

Later. More vehicle trouble. We are now going *back* to Brigade AWD. Same final drive now leaking badly. Moving out with TDU again this evening and will harbour with AWD near TDU new location. We are at present near Le Ferroniese . . . high, flat country, fairly well wooded, but mainly agricultural.

* Churchill's famous 'V for victory' sign, made with the palm of the hand (not the back) facing outwards.

Another day without hearing any gunfire. Nerves will be reverting to normal at this rate! Am now with the 'other army' – of course! Still no letters. Can't understand why the unit don't make some effort to forward our mail.

Later. Tank now with AWD again – self and crew (less driver) with TDU close by. Locality now at Le Brevedent, about 1.5 miles SE of Blangy-le-Château. Pretty valley – well wooded and fairly high hills. Stream is a tributary of the Touques river. This place seems to have escaped the war. Farmers are working normally, crops have been cut, and the cows appear very healthy and are being milked regularly. Donkeys seem to be a part of the milking routine. They carry about half a dozen milk urns into the fields, and the cows are then rounded up and milked on the spot.

Have seen a 'yoke' in use . . . by a dairy maid carrying two pails. There are many picturesque details to this area, but much evidence of primitiveness. To bed in bell-tent . . . with four other sergeants.

D +82 Sunday 27.8.44

Fine morning but chilly. There seems to be a definite autumn nip in the air nowadays at reveille. Plenty of local noise at reveille . . . local 'ladies' out milking cows . . . complete with donkey, etc.

Later. Am now back with unit . . . 'A' Echelon. Have no vehicle, but expect to relieve one of C commanders. Am now about 8 miles NE of Cormeilles . . . and not far from Seine. Saw effect of Jerry bazooka on 14 Troop tank yesterday. Two hits – turret ring cracked – Tpr Button killed. Squadron appear to have had one action whilst I have been away.

Civilians here seem generally pleased to see us. Much hand-shaking, etc.: get a bit fed up with it all.

Bivvying tonight with Cpl Nunn. *Three* letters from Jess – thank goodness. Also one from Geary: he is progressing well in Bayeux hospital. Two snaps of Barry —!

D +83 Monday 28.8.44

Cool morning: good sleep. Saw MO orderly this a.m. – tummy trouble. Some prisoners just brought in by recce car. Nobody wants them.

Later. Have taken over my tank again. Left echelon to collect it @ LAD EME. Joining up with HQ Sqdn tomorrow . . . and C later in day.

D +84 Tuesday 29.8.44

Arrived HQ Sqdn early this a.m. . . . with four other tanks as reinforcements. All departed 2.30 to join up with C beyond River Risle . . . about 5 miles east. Went via Pont Audemer. This is the largest town we have seen so far: a fair-sized place situated in the Risle valley. Surrounded by beautiful country and quite high hills. It must be quite close to the Seine estuary . . . maybe 8 or 10 miles.

We approached the town from the west: a long gradual slope into the valley. Many orchards and houses . . . gardens are very colourful, particularly with dahlias. The town itself has been slightly damaged, but is mainly intact.

Our column was given a surprising welcome. Every house and shop seemed to be flying a Tricolour. The main street was lined with people: they looked genuinely pleased and happy. Everyone waved: in doorways, windows, gardens – roadside. Old men raised their hats: girls and boys threw flowers on our vehicles ... lovely coloured dahlias, mostly.

The old people looked bewildered ... as though waking from a dream. No wonder! Jerry was in the place only a day or so ago. There were a few gendarmes in the town, and many army MPs. Several shops were open – including cafés, tobacco shops and at least one chemist's. Queer how one reacts to these demonstrations. I *couldn't* keep that darned lump from my throat. There could be no doubt about the warmth and sincerity of these people. I felt glad to be helping to restore their happiness ... especially for the children's sake. Many of them looked ill and under-nourished: mere shadows of normal children. But they will no doubt be taken care of. Amgot [see Glossary] is already in the town and medical supplies are abundant.

I believe there is an army 'town major' too. He is preserving law and order. The Maquis need restraining ... already they have carried out a few executions without trial ... including some women. This is terrible in my opinion. Shaving heads is bad enough!*

The river bridge had been destroyed, but the REs have erected a new one. We passed over and up the eastern side of the valley: quite a long steep climb. Lots of cottages, mostly in orchards, lining the roadside. It is a gentle, peaceful countryside. Thank goodness it bears little trace of the war – apart from damaged buildings in the town itself.

---

* The Maquis were French resistance fighters, named after the brushwood thickets on the Mediterranean coast. Shaving the heads of collaborators and of women who had slept with the enemy was a traditional punishment.

We left the main road a mile or so east of the town ... and are harboured in a large tree-lined field. C had arrived earlier in the day. I joined my old troop – 15. Ahead of us is the Seine ... but a fairly large concentration of Jerries are still being rounded up in the forest of Brotonne. The infantry are dealing with them. We will cross the Seine after this local mopping up is completed. We may therefore remain here 2 or 3 days ... until a bridge is erected.

A passion truck has actually left the camp this evening – for the town! This is a treat indeed for the lads. A fair-sized town; a grateful populace: many girls ... pubs, wine ... *And* there was a pay parade this afternoon.

The weather has become cloudy and windy this evening: there have been one or two showers, but I believe we are scheduled for some heavy rain. Altho we are fairly close to the Seine – and Rouen – I have heard no artillery since arriving. This is unusual. But perhaps the infantry are better able to work alone in the dense woods in which the enemy is harbouring prior to attempting the perilous crossing of the river.

D +85 Wednesday 30.8.44

Little to report today. We are still in harbour, about a couple of miles from Pont Audemer ... with the Seine about 6 miles to the east. The fighting must by now be some distance away because we cannot hear a sound of gunfire.

We are still resting ... and another passion truck is going into town this evening. Received a letter from Jess. Sent home details about Jimmy Aldcroft's escape.*

* Jimmy Aldcroft was badly burned when his tank suffered a direct hit and the ammunition inside it exploded. His life was saved by two of his crew, the tank

D +86 Thursday 31.8.44

Heavy showers last night and again today. Also quite a high wind. Last night's news announced enemy withdrawal from Rouen – and the capture of Ploesti by Russians.*

I wonder what is happening at Le Havre. Presumably the REs will now go ahead with bridges to enable us to cross Seine without going to our bridgehead further south. It has been announced officially that we are in 34 Brigade from 12 noon today. And so we leave 31 Brigade ...

The 7th are also transferring with us. Also announced today that Major Holden and Captain Kidd have been awarded the MC. The former for the Cheux action – and the latter for [*indecipherable*] Nr Colleville.† Also an MM for Ken Virgo of B Squadron. These are the only awards to date, and it is considered a distinction for C to have gained the only MCs in the unit.

The colonel addressed the squadron this afternoon – urging continuance of our efforts. He took many bets 5 or 6 weeks ago that the war would be over by end of August owing to collapse of Germany. He now admits his error ... but seems convinced that he is only a fortnight out in his reckoning! He informed us of the tribute paid by the infantry (49 Div) for our assistance, especially in recent weeks. It seems to be generally admitted by authority that the speed of recent events is due in large measure to assistance of tanks.

---

commander Sergeant Jones and gunner Charlie Mansell, who dragged him unconscious from the burning tank.

* Ploesti in Rumania was the source of much of the oil required by the German war machine. Prior to their capture, the oil refineries had been extensively bombed by the US Air Force.

† Captain Kidd received his MC for outstanding reconnaissance service at Grainville.

Very heavy rain this afternoon. Almost impossible to keep dry: bivvies are all leaking and much of our clothing is now wet. Foot of my bed saturated last night: slept with my feet in pool of water. Too wet today for blanket drying. No signs of a move yet, but expect we will be joining up with 34 Brigade very soon. Ensa show here in open air yesterday afternoon.

D +87 Friday 1.9.44

September! Already the evenings and mornings are much colder – particularly the latter. Getting up is something of a problem. No rain last night, and quite fine today, but cooler than of late.

We have done quite well for food lately ... thanks to the lads scrounging food from people in Pont Audemer. Fortunately, there is much garden produce just now. We have had a few eggs, and plenty of tomatoes. Also lettuce, onions, potatoes. This morning we had tinned bacon, with fried egg and tomatoes for breakfast. Cigarettes are in great demand by local civvies. They were allowed 40 per month by the Germans. Our fellows are using them for bartering. Pestell brought back a full bottle of cognac the other day ... genuine stuff ... And a bottle of *vin rouge* last night. There seems to be little shortage of wine and spirits here – but maybe present supplies have been kept hidden from the Germans since 1940.

Children seem to delight in visiting this harbour. There must be a couple of dozen here just now. They seem to enjoy fooling with the tank crews. Their language is impossible to follow: they talk too quickly. Rather amusing to watch an argument between a little girl of say, eight years, with one of our fellows – both speaking their own language.

Latest information is that we are going to move about 30 or 40 miles to join up with the rest of our new brigade. But where? And when? Judging by the radio news, the enemy must be a long way from us now . . . unless there is a strong pocket at Le Havre. Last night's news announced a 65-mile thrust from the Seine to Amiens in 48 hrs by members of the 2nd Army. And today, the Canadians are nearing Dieppe. Americans 5 miles from Belgium! Can't help wondering what our next role will be. Present pace is certainly too fast for us. Maybe we will have to do some 'mopping up'.

Heard today that Geary is now in England . . . in Preston! Leyshon [*uncertain*] has returned: he remained at Bayeux hospital: self-inflicted hand wound. Mail now coming through OK from Jess . . .

How long since I heard artillery? Must be days. Remarkably peaceful here. We don't see many aircraft either . . . There has been some speculation about Burma! Even rumours that we will be re-fitted and sent out there!

Later. We are moving in the morning . . . depart 6.40 a.m. Destination a forest, about 30 miles distant, further up the Seine. Apparently, bridging is impracticable here as the river is tidal, so we are moving inland to cross. Believe we may be used for assault on Le Havre . . . if it doesn't fall meanwhile.

We have orders to carry out a 'salute' to our late brigadier en route tomorrow. He will be standing at a certain point on the route, and as each tank passes the turret will be traversed and gun dipped. A typical piece of army baloney this, but it may look very effective.

Presume there will be some farewells in Pont Audemer this evening. Some of the inhabitants have been very kind to our lads. Issue of vitamin tablets today.

D +88 Saturday 2.9.44

Reveille 5.00 a.m. Depart 6.40 a.m.: battalion march. Back to Pont Audemer, and then SE up the Risle valley. Lovely countryside . . . very green and fertile and well wooded.

Brigadier supposed to be at Les Ruelles . . . but he wasn't, so there was no 'salute'. Must be a reason for his absence. Through Corneville (Les Cloches). Just beyond were some enormous caves running into the hillside on the left: narrow gauge rail lines: heavy camouflage. Fields on opposite side too were heavily camouflaged, and evidence of heavy excavations, etc. May have been flying bomb site.

Appeville . . . a small village, but badly damaged. There must have been some resistance here. Likewise Montfort-sur-Risle: badly battered, but quite a few civilians about. Usual greetings and hand-waving, etc. Turned left, away from valley, just beyond Montfort – and up through the forest. Beautiful morning: grand scenery. Some evidence of battle on the high ground. British and German tanks burned out . . . Into harbour (orchard!) just beyond Boissey-le-Châtel. Arrived about 8.30. This was supposed to be a temporary halt for breakfast. The cooks had arrived night before and the meal was ready . . . and so were we!

Later. Not moving on today: we have to remain parked away in this place. Meanwhile, the war is moving swiftly away to the east. Le Havre still holding out, but no one seems to be bothered about that. Shouldn't be surprised if we *don't* carry on to our intended destination at 2195.* This is in the Foret Domaniale de Bord: nearest town Louviers, about 4 miles south. We are still 20 miles away.

* Almost certainly a map reference.

Everyone in high spirits about war news. It seems possible that the war will soon be over – possible! I hope the colonel's forecast is correct. But my mind simply refuses to grasp the real significance of what is happening. I daren't allow myself to become too optimistic. Another vitamin tablet per man!

D +89 Sunday 3.9.44

Hell of a night: high wind and heavy rain. Slept beneath tank, but nearly got blown away. Fortunately, we were issued with clean blankets yesterday, and I obtained another one (three all told) and was much warmer. Wind had dropped this morning: surprising change: sunny and mild.

Breakfast 8.45 a.m.! Vitamin tablets at breakfast ... ! Heard 10 a.m. news. Finland now seeking armistice terms ... again! Our troops on the Moselle!

Later. We are moving in the morning – about 35 miles SE and over Seine. On arrival, it is hoped to put us in *civvy* billets! Now with 8th Corps* ... they are fighting [*Editor's note: the diary entry is seemingly unfinished here.*]

D +90 Monday 4.9.44

One or two false alarms, but we eventually got away from harbour about noon. Carried out the ceremonial salute to

---

* The US Army VIII Corps. However, VIII Corps were in Brittany in August and September. Possibly Trevor had broken off writing in order to verify which corps 9 RTR were with, and never returned to his correction. Unusually, the 9 RTR War Diary is blank from 27 August to 9 September, so it cannot help to clarify this entry.

Brigadier en route. Eventually crossed the Seine at Pont de L'Arche and harboured close by beyond Igoville. Mr Francis's vehicle developed trouble en route – changed places, and eventually harboured about 10 p.m. Believe we will be moving to Le Havre to assist in clearing German garrison still holding out. They are being shelled and bombed until Sept 8th, and then our assault, if they haven't surrendered meanwhile.

Today's journey revealed much evidence of the RAF attacks on German transport. Several roads literally lined with burned-out vehicles. A Panther on roadside had been hit by Typhoon: engine had completely disintegrated.

Saw several Dakotas today . . . Transport planes evidently taking urgent supplies to our forward units . . . Heaven knows where *they* are. Saw also convoy of Scammells with tank transporters loaded with compo packs! All heading east. A new use for transporters!

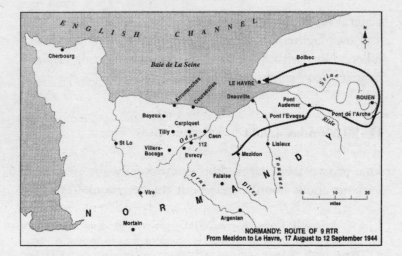

NORMANDY: ROUTE OF 9 RTR
From Mezidon to Le Havre, 17 August to 12 September 1944

D +91 Tuesday 5.9.44

Another move, this time to Yvetot, en route for Le Havre (first hop ... about 35 miles). Mr Francis's vehicle still troublesome ... new gearbox being fitted. Am left behind until job is finished. Will follow squadron later ... probably first thing in the morning ... via Rouen. Hope to catch them up at Yvetot, but they may have moved on. Managed to barter a few ciggies, etc. for eggs and tomatoes for tea. Crowd of refugee children around this evening. About 50 of them, all under five ... in charge of two teachers. The latter knew about as much English as we French. Rather amusing half hour. Children all from Rouen. Sweets caused a minor sensation ... and chocolate! We were cleaned out. Also parted with some ciggies. Other refugees have been round. Pitiful wrecks, some of them. They had to endure much of our bombing of Rouen. M&V* seemed to please them a lot. No mail.

D +92 Wednesday 6.9.44

All work on vehicle finished by 12 noon, and we departed, intending to have lunch in Rouen. Learned that the squadron were leaving Yvetot at 3 p.m. for another 25-mile hop of the journey to Le Havre. We would either overtake them, or sleep somewhere en route. Arrived Rouen about 1 o'clock. Tremendous amount of traffic on roads.

Great welcome in Rouen: everyone seemed utterly relieved and cheerful. Seeing so much apparent happiness made me feel more light-hearted than I have felt since

* Meat and veg (tinned) from the compo packs.

coming over here. Such spontaneous gaiety is certainly infectious. Entered the city by the dock road along the river. All property between cathedral and river is demolished. Cathedral too is damaged but not irreparably so. The fantastic lace-like spire seems to be unharmed. We pulled up on the riverside, amidst the wreckage of one of the bridges, and there we 'brewed up', with an audience of dozens around ... some just curious ... others begging food ... ciggies, chocolate. We dined on top of the vehicle: unwise to tempt the half-starving beggars too much. One of the bridges already patched up by the REs and in use.

All these bridges were bombed by the RAF just prior to D-Day. Much damage to surrounding property by near misses. Saw many smartly dressed and sophisticated girls ... quite a change from the country maidens of Normandy.

On the move again about three ... more cheers and hand-waving and salutes. Along the entire length of the city there were people waving: we had to return their greetings ... it became a most embarrassing business. Much begging for cigarettes.

Yvetot ... more greetings ... flowers, apples, tomatoes showered upon us: one of the latter splashed on operator's hatch and covered three of us with tomato juice! Squadron had departed, so we carried on along the route. Had lunch just outside Yvetot ... and then on to Bolbec. Bolbec! A small town, apparently untouched by the war. Here the people seemed frantic with joy. We had caught up with the main column just before reaching the town – and were the last of the Churchills.

At Bolbec I saw absolutely unrestrained enthusiasm ... at times it even seemed like hysteria, particularly amongst some of the girls. We were showered with fruit and flowers.

Even along the narrow main cobbled street of the town, there were large crowds, apparently unafraid of our vehicles.

Fortunately there were no accidents, but *I* felt nervous: my vehicle was difficult on the steering ... slipping sideways a good deal on the cobbles. Our pace became slower after Bolbec: we were now in convoy.

Goderville: more crowds and cheering and hand-waving ... and so to harbour, in the region of St Sauveur-d'Emalleville about 10 miles NE of Le Havre. It had been a long run for my vehicle and crew. We clocked 62 miles for the day! The unit had done the journey in two days. The major said it was an achievement ... a 'bloody miracle'!

We harboured about 9 p.m., in a field beneath some large beech trees ... not an orchard this time! It commenced to rain immediately, and we just had time to erect our bivvies before the deluge. Today's journey revealed little evidence of enemy occupation, apart from the damage in Rouen and the ruined railway viaduct at Barentin. Here, the main Paris–Le Havre line passes over a high viaduct across the valley. This had been dynamited in two places ... one of them leaving a 50-yard gap, across which the steel rails still sagged. French engineers were already on the job of clearing the mess, but it will be a long job repairing that viaduct.

D +93 Thursday 7.9.44

What a night! The rain poured down all night and the wind blew with gale force. Bivvies had only been hastily erected last night, and so everyone is wet this morning. But blanket-drying impossible: the rain is still pouring down.

Later. A brief respite in the rain at lunch time: blankets and other clothing quickly hung out to dry . . . but not for long. After an hour, the rain started again, with a terrific wind. Everywhere – everything – is wet. The entire harbour is now a sea of mud. Feel very miserable: wet clothes: wet bedding: cold – no means of getting warm, or dry.

Later. Another respite at tea time. Partially dried my blankets in the air outlet from the engine. Much hot air from a running engine! Laid out my bed beneath tank. Driver has sealed up one or two of the leaks, may be fairly dry tonight.

Later. Still raining heavily: will probably continue all night . . . nothing to do but try bed: may be a bit warmer there. Mail this evening . . . at last! Two letters from Jess.

D +94 Friday 8.9.44

Rain again all last night, but the wind is less severe this morning. Fewer wet blankets because of precautions taken yesterday. But what a wretched life! The rain is bad enough . . . but the mud, and wet clothes . . . wet feet! Even cooking is a major problem. And writing letters is almost impossible.

Learned this morning that we may attack Le Havre tomorrow. The place was again heavily bombed this morning, but it appears that the enemy commandant has rejected our ultimatum. He is reported to be Von Kluge's brother. Maybe he is determined to avenge the latter's suicide.* We seem to be preparing a very heavy assault.

---

* Field Marshal Gunther von Kluge was Oberbefehlshaber (supreme field commander) of the German forces in the west. While not actively involved in the failed attempt to assassinate Hitler on 20 July, he was known to be sympathetic to the conspirators and, recalled to Berlin on 17 August, he took cyanide rather than face arrest and trial.

D +95 Saturday 9.9.44

Another deluge last night, and still very showery this morning. Managed to cook a breakfast during a fine spell around 10 a.m. Not much chance of drying clothes and blankets under these conditions.

No further orders regarding Le Havre . . . but officers are out on recce this a.m., so expect some news later in the day. Many transport planes – Dakotas – have passed over during last few days. They seem to be defying this awful weather. No mails yesterday, but expect some today. It is almost a week since we saw a newspaper. Maybe the brigade transfer has caused some confusion.

Noticed local farmers yesterday removing 'anti aircraft' wooden pylons in their fields . . . a sign of the times! I imagine the war is now as good as over to these people . . . They are lucky. Some of our fellows went to Bolbec last evening to an Ensa concert, and a cinema show the night before.

Later. Sudden move at 7.30 p.m. . . . nearer Le Havre. Presume sudden favourable change in weather has affected the situation . . . otherwise we were to have remained in harbour until tomorrow.

D +96 Sunday 10.9.44

We only travelled about 8 miles last evening, to a harbour about 2 miles from Jerry's forward defences and due east of the town . . . but it was a hell of a dash. A hold-up at the outset resulted in most of the run being done in the dark. Travelling flat out along country lanes and through small

villages is a bit of a thrill in the dark. I noticed many dim
figures waving to us from the roadside as we passed through
the village. And even our own troops waved at certain places!
Everyone must have known the purpose of our mission.

Harboured in a narrow lane, and slept in the adjoining
field, beneath the stars. The weather has changed remarkably in a few hours. A brilliant moonlit sky ... not even a
speck of cloud. Went to sleep counting shooting stars. But
beforehand, I again heard the sound of massed artillery –
unpleasantly close. They were hammering at Le Havre. The
place has also been heavily bombed for the last two or three
days, but still no sign of surrender. It looks like a tough
proposition ... maybe another Brest ...* Altho I believe we
are more intent upon capturing Le Havre as a supply base.
Our attack will doubtless be a determined one.

Up at 6.30 this morning: damnably cold: soon had a brew
on the way! During the morning the entire population from
the nearby village (St-Martin-du-Manoir) must have been
around here. It has been like a Sunday parade in an English
park. As usual, the youngsters have been driving us dotty for
ciggies, 'bon-bons', chocolate and biscuits. The grown ups
too have cadged many ciggies – and a few bottles of *'essence'*
[petrol]. But we have got a few tomatoes in return.

A few rounds of Jerry HE fell quite close during the
morning. We are on high ground here ... and so is Jerry, to
the west, across an intervening valley. We must be quite
visible with binoculars. Recced the area of our first phase
this a.m. The enemy certainly has some formidable defences
judging by our maps and 'information'. We are scheduled to

* Hitler had ordered the Brittany ports to be defended 'to the last man'. The US
VIII Corps had reached the city on 7 August, but it took five weeks of fighting
street by street before it fell.

do a 'shoot' this evening. No incoming mail as yet, but managed to send a note to Jess.

Later. Carried out 'shoot' and returned to same harbour in time to prepare supper before dark.* Only one casualty (Sgt Hewett) – due to Besa 'blow-back', not enemy action. We fired heavily on German defences for 45 minutes. Artillery also busy all the time. Soon after finish of our shoot, and before we returned to harbour, witnessed a raid by Bomber Command on same defence area. The result defies description. We were about 3000 yds from the area, so felt *fairly* safe (Bomber Command!). But this time, all the bombs were dead on the target.

The planes came over in endless succession for about an hour . . . literally pouring out their bombs. I could actually see the bombs leaving the planes through my binoculars. It was a terrifying sight, but horribly fascinating. The target area was blasted in an orderly manner, with sticks of bombs falling further and further over the area. Meanwhile, there were showers of green and red 'stars' falling through the dense volumes of smoke and debris. These seemed like phosphorous incendiaries. The whole spectacle made our shoot seem puny and utterly useless. Five thousand tons of bombs were dropped, by heaven knows how many hundred bombers . . . mostly Lancasters. I suppose it would take us months to 'shoot' the same amount of HE!

All the same, the mere sight of our ground vehicles must give Jerry food for thought. Apart from our efforts and the bombs, there were many Typhoons over during the day – firing their deadly rockets on selected targets.

---

* The 9 RTR War Diary reports: 'The high explosive and machine gun fire was accurate, heavy and well controlled, and did much to soften and harass the defences for the attack on the following day.'

They are doing a grand job in this war. We all pay tribute to the Typhoon pilots.

Fortunately, there has been little AA fire and I haven't seen one of our planes destroyed. It would certainly appear that we are determined to secure Le Havre, judging by today's activities, and the number of troops employed in this assault ... including the 51 Hd Div and 49 Div.*

To bed again tonight beneath the stars: fortunately, the weather looks like remaining fine, altho cold at night. Another 'casualty' among my crew this evening. Co-driver, Slade, violently sick in vehicle due to Besa fumes. He had to cease fire. Presumed he would be OK in the open air later, but has been sick again tonight. Leaving him behind tomorrow: have fixed up relief for him.

Reveille 4.30 a.m. tomorrow ... we have another shoot at 5.40 a.m. to assist A. Not so good shooting in the dark.

D +97 Monday 11.9.44

About 10 p.m. last night – just going to bed – the artillery opened up ... plus searchlights. This was another amazing sight ... hard to describe. The searchlights, about a dozen of them, were all directed towards the town at a low angle ... thus providing artificial moonlight. The guns seemed to completely cover the unlimited horizon ... there must be many dozens, maybe hundreds, of them in an arc of a few miles. There are 25-pounders, but also many larger guns ... 5.5s, 9.9s and 9.5s. They opened up simultaneously ... and the whole region seemed to rock with the noise. For several minutes, the sky

* The 51st Highland Infantry Division, and the 49th West Riding Infantry Division, known as the Polar Bears.

seemed aglow with gun flashes ... far too rapid to count. The searchlights meanwhile just remained stationary – piercing the darkness with their long beams. The heavy barrage ceased, but I went to sleep still hearing artillery fire.

Reveille 4.30 a.m. ... and how damnably cold it was! We moved off at 5.15, but in spite of having bed-rolls to re-fold and re-stow, etc., we managed a brew of 'hot sweet' before departing. We were lucky in having *real* moonlight as well: the searchlights were *still* shining.

Fired several belts of Besa before daylight, and then stood by on the hillside, watching A's action across the adjoining valley ... we also had a running commentary over the air. We managed a brew-up, and later breakfast of bacon and fried tomatoes ... still standing by for action, and within sight of the enemy! Also collected some carrots for lunch.

And later still, the SSM came to our rear with yesterday's mail ... in a jeep. Good work! Soon after daylight, another heavy force of Lancasters appeared, and dropped their loads a little further west than last evening, so it was not such a thrilling spectacle by comparison. But God help those Jerries!

Watched A for some hours: a slow job, clearing a well dug-in enemy from wooded areas, etc. Flails were brought in too to clear way through minefields. Rather an interesting show, but wasn't sorry to return to harbour about lunch time, and soon had another meal on the way, including carrots – and spuds!

My co-driver, Slade, still poorly, but may be OK in a day or two. Much heavy artillery shelling today ... and more Typhoons.

Some *very* heavy explosions from the harbour area this afternoon: they may indicate demolitions ... One o'clock news announced that battleship *Warspite*, and monitor

Erebus are also shelling the port... 15-inch guns! We certainly mean to take Le Havre!

Churchill flame-throwers were used by A in today's attack, and these finally brought out the remnants of the enemy. They had been ordered to hold the woods at all costs and had put up a hard fight from their well prepared positions. Our Koylis* suffered fairly heavily against heavy MG fire. But Jerry had not bargained for the flame-throwers!

Later. Today's programme has been modified due to highly successful advance from northern forces... so we are not going in again today, through B, as intended. But we may be required for final assault on the town area in the morning. Moving tonight about 2 m south... close to main road leading into Le Havre via Harfleur.

Churchill Crocodile flame-thrower in action. A fully fuelled Crocodile was a deadly weapon against dug-in infantry in bunkers or blockhouses: it could fire up to 80 one-second bursts of flame up to 120 yards.

Photograph © IWM H37930.

* The King's Own Yorkshire Light Infantry.

D +98 Tuesday 12.9.44

The whole village (St-Martin-du-Manoir) turned out to say good-bye as we moved off last evening. We soon arrived at the new harbour on the high ground above and east of Harfleur.

This morning, before daylight, three troops departed for the final assault on the town ... 13 and 14 and HQ. We remained in harbour with 11 and 12 and listened to progress over the air. We were in reserve. C Sqdn's task was to clear the enemy from a stretch of territory between the main dock road and the Canal de Tancarville, ending at the Bassin Bellot – i.e. an area about 500 yds wide and 4000 yds long. It was mainly a built-up area, consisting of high blocks of workers' flats, warehouses, docks, and repair shops.

Over the air, we learned that opposition had been met, and about mid morning, we reserve troops were requested by the major to join him immediately.

We proceeded through Harfleur, where there were many of the Maquis still snooping around for Jerries, and eventually joined up with the major who was waiting about half way to the final objective. We had passed over roads heavily damaged by bombing and by mines. To our right lay the high ground overlooking the town: its eastern end had been literally blasted to smithereens by the RAF. Up there too I could clearly see the slits of the enemy fortifications running along the ridge. There were guns up there: I presumed they had been silenced.

Crowds of people welcomed us into the town along the roadsides. It seemed extraordinary, and totally unreal, to find civilians mixed up like this on what was really a battleground, but they seemed unaware of any danger and persisted in waving and cheering and throwing flowers upon our vehicles. We

reached the major at a point where a barbed-wire roadblock
straddled the road. On our side of it, there was a mass of
humanity, including some Maquis running about excitedly.
They kept gesticulating and pointing down the long straight
road ahead of us. Beyond the roadblock it was entirely deserted:
not even a cat being visible ... and at the far end were two
ominous shapes, concrete 'domes', evidently harbouring guns.
They were almost 2000 yds distant, and I presumed they would
open fire when we got nearer. Well, it was our job to secure that
road, and I wasn't surprised when the major announced that he
was going forward ... 15 Troop to go with him. And so, the
four tanks moved forward, leaving the crowd behind ... but
not the Maquis. *They* came with us ... and I must here pay
tribute to the work of those dozen or so Frenchmen. They
seemed utterly fearless, and ran along with us, darting into
buildings and doorways and generally looking for snipers or
small pockets of enemy. Their enthusiasm was terrific: they
were armed, some with rifles – German! – some with pistols –
small protection against machine-gun fire. All wore the Maquis
armband,* and some had steel helmets. All were poorly dressed,
and obviously belonged to the working classes.

There ought to have been some British infantry with us,
but there wasn't ... the Maquis accompanied us instead and
seemed glad and proud of their job. This was my first experience of street fighting, and I felt very uncomfortable. It is
bad enough having one's head protruding from the turret in
country fighting, but here it was worse. We were grand
targets for snipers in the upper windows of the houses ...
and for hand grenades, and infantry bazookas.

---

* Fighting alongside the Allies after D-Day, the Maquis wore armbands to iden-
tify themselves as legitimate combatants. This meant – in theory if not in practice
– that if captured, they were subject to the Geneva Convention.

The Maquis certainly gave me confidence, but even they hadn't time to thoroughly examine all buildings along the route. I think *they* knew that the Germans were in strength at the *end* of the road, and they seemed anxious to get there ... perhaps to wipe out a few old scores! They kept running ahead, waving us to follow.

When we had reached a point about 1000 yards from the pillboxes, Mr Francis fired one round of HE and hit the main gun. There was no answering fire ... just silence and complete absence of any sign of life. It seemed strange. Was there an ambush somewhere ahead? We advanced still further, the major leading, and suddenly I noticed the Maquis yelling with delight and holding their hands above their heads. They were telling us that the enemy had surrendered ... and there, sure enough, right at the end of the road, half a mile away, a white flag was fluttering by the roadside.

We surged ahead at full speed ... the Maquis chasing along behind. It was like a scene from some fantastic story by Sabatini.* The deserted street – the wreckage of earlier RAF attacks – the tanks – the burned-out vehicles and smashed guns at street corners. The charred remnants of warehouses down by the docks ... and the wildly careering Maquis. My God, they were in terrific spirits ... and how delirious with joy. I wondered what had happened to our infantry, but it seemed now that they wouldn't be necessary.

The major was the first to reach the German with the white flag ... a lonely figure by the roadside. He was quickly

---

* Rafael Sabatini was a popular writer of swashbuckling adventure novels whose many books included *Scaramouche* and *Captain Blood*. *The Sea Hawk* was filmed starring Errol Flynn in 1940 and *The Black Swan* starring Tyrone Power and Maureen O'Hara in 1942.

joined by Mr Francis, myself and Sgt Hall . . . and the Maquis were there almost as quick. In a few moments, a long stream of Germans started to emerge from a huge blockhouse in the open square at the end of the dock road. They all seemed tidily dressed, and were carrying valises . . . and some even had suitcases! They had evidently prepared in advance for this surrender. The Maquis quickly had them lined up in threes and started searching them for weapons, etc. What a great moment it must have been for those French workers. There were 120 Germans in this particular batch and it seemed to me only a matter of a few minutes before they were all rounded up and being marched off. Mr Francis and Dicky and I had dismounted, with revolvers ready cocked, to assist with the rounding up. The major meanwhile was busy running around snooping in pill-boxes, etc.

Very soon, he ordered me to take my vehicle to guard the entrance to a bridge running across one of the dock basins. There were a couple of blockhouses at the side of the bridge, but the Maquis soon explored them and found them empty.

I manoeuvred my vehicle into a suitable position, and kept observation down into the docks . . . and then I noticed a number of large steel canisters lying lengthwise across the bridge immediately in front: they were all connected with electrical cables – about nine canisters in all. I had wondered why this particular bridge had not been blown . . . and here was the answer. There was enough explosive in those canisters to destroy a village, let alone a bridge . . . and there they were – about 20 feet from the nose of my vehicle! Fortunately, the rest of the crew appeared to attach no significance to them . . . I had a suspicion that they were either connected to a 'time' mechanism, or to some detonating point in the town. I hoped for the best, and waited – keeping observation for possible snipers along the docks.

Meanwhile, more tanks had arrived, and a general orgy of looting had commenced. The German blockhouses produced a fair amount of stuff, including binoculars, pistols, etc., but the major had the first choice as he was ahead of the others.

A Maquis appeared by my vehicle: he had found eight Mauser rifles and was staggering beneath the load. He was given permission to sit on my vehicle, and we gave him ciggies, etc. He seemed very happy . . . Some of his colleagues arrived soon after and started sorting out the rifles . . . firing them on the spot to test them! A crazy business this: our nerves were on tenterhooks, and unexpected rifle shots were rather frightening. But these fellows didn't care a damn . . . and we couldn't argue with them in French. I was glad when they had departed, in search of more Jerries . . . and loot!

After about forty minutes, small parties of our own infantry arrived . . . they were the H—shires (Crevecoeur!)* Later, I breathed a sigh of relief when they started to cross the bridge into the docks beyond . . . And I felt positively light hearted when they asked us for some wire cutters to attend to the explosives on the bridge. One of their fellows seemed quite conversant with these obstacles, and after a *very* careful scrutiny, he cut the wires. I was darned thankful!

We had been in the area for about an hour and no-one seemed to be bothering about orders. The major himself, and most of the tank crews were too busy looting to worry about the war! As the infantry had arrived, my crew were allowed to dismount and join in the looting: we also started preparing a

---

* The Hallams distinguished themselves in Le Havre, capturing over 1,000 prisoners, three flying boats and a submarine.

brew.* By this time, civilians had appeared on the scene, and the formerly deserted roadway was already coming to life. There were people running about, darting into buildings, wheeling handcarts, prams – any mortal thing with wheels. Whether they were returning to their homes with belongings, or merely looting, I cannot say. We had other things to think about, and nobody bothered. One interesting item of news came over the air . . . the garrison commandant had been captured by the 7th in another part of the town. We felt certain that the fight for Le Havre was almost over.

In the midst of the excitement, the colonel of the infantry appeared, and asked for our assistance at a bridge in the dock area. The enemy were still holding out and inflicting casualties. So the major detailed Mr Francis and his troop for the job. We departed, but the enemy had surrendered before we arrived . . . to my relief! A nearby tavern opened up, and the hostess asked us to join her in drinks: we did. We were all dry and thirsty and hot. The tavern soon filled up with French people. How excited they were! We weren't allowed to pay, but ciggies were not refused. They never are over here.

Eventually, orders were issued to return to harbour. The job was over. Le Havre had been liberated. The final clearing up was somebody else's job. Our departure was something like a triumphal procession. Crowds of people had appeared as if by magic . . . probably from cellars and other places of safety. There were young and old . . . mostly poor and badly dressed. But their enthusiasm was terrific. Flags too were now flying from scores of windows, lending some colour to a very drab neighbourhood.

* It should be noted that the looting in this instance was of German blockhouses, not of civilian homes. Nonetheless, it is striking how often Trevor refers to looting by Allied troops, and the apparent extent to which it was sanctioned.

Mostly, the people cheered and waved frantically as we passed. Some were even in tears, whether of sorrow or joy I cannot say. Certain it is that the joy of Le Havre must be mingled with much sorrow. The brutality of the Germans was not their only ordeal. Our bombers caused indescribable wreckage, and killed 6000 civilians. '*C'est la Guerre*' was all we could say by way of consolation ... to which they usually agreed with '*Oui – c'est terrible ...*'

A word about the Maquis. From my observations throughout this campaign, I am of the opinion that they belong mostly to a low order of society. Their behaviour has been suggestive of mob rule and I have deplored their habit of shaving the heads of female *collaborateurs*. It has seemed to me that in the Maquis, with their weapons and ruthlessness, the French people may find themselves with a miniature Nazi party upon their hands when the war is over. And I have wondered whether they may prove more a curse than a blessing. But after today, I must acknowledge their courage and their usefulness to us. Their behaviour was grand: an inspiration.

But I still think they may prove a problem to the future government unless they are handled wisely. They are working men, so I believe, and they may take the law into their own hands. I hope I am wrong. I hope the future government of France will see that these men are treated with decency worthy of their courage and suffering.

We returned to our harbour of the morning, but were quickly transferred to another place for the night, close to St-Martin-du-Manoir. En route we saw many hundreds of prisoners being marched off to cages.

Some of the long column were headed by officers ... typical arrogant looking Germans – at least one wearing a monocle. The German soldiers on the other hand seemed an ordinary lot: and they looked very pleased with life! Some were laughing and joking.

Just before our departure from Le Havre, and about three hundred yards away, I witnessed the largest explosion I have ever seen. It occurred on the dock-side. There was a most God Almighty roar, accompanied by heavy blast and breaking of windows, and then an enormous black cloud ascended skywards. The flash from the explosion soared well above the warehouses and must have reached at least a hundred feet. Sailing gently upwards in the huge volume of smoke were bits of masonry, and two complete huts ... one with a metal chimney stack still protruding from the roof. They went up to about 400 feet, and then seemed to remain stationary, before slowly coming down. A most amazing sight. I believe a magazine had been blown up, but none of our troops were in the vicinity at the time.

Later. It has been announced that over 8000 prisoners were taken today – Our casualties being just over 400 killed and wounded! The number of German dead during the three days of our assault has not been revealed.

D +99 Wednesday 13.9.44

Another move today ... back to the former harbour area near Emalleville ... about 10 miles from Le Havre. In an orchard once again: the usual mess of apples, etc. in the vehicles.

Passion truck this evening to Goderville and Bolbec. Letters from Jess ... Jim Aldcroft, Haydn, Stan Smith.

D +100 Thursday 14.9.44

Reveille 8.00 a.m.! A leisurely day. Learned this morning that we may shortly go into civvy billets as our immediate future is uncertain. MT of the unit already taken over by RASC. Believe they are being used for carrying prisoners from Le Havre to Dieppe.

Official figures now 10,500 prisoners, and 50 British killed. Tonight's radio describes the Le Havre assault as a model of its kind . . . brilliantly planned and executed. And confirms that earlier reports of the surrender of the garrison were misleading. The enemy only surrendered when he had no option . . . almost at the point of the bayonet. There was no official surrender. I omitted to mention earlier that my booty from Le Havre was a white surrender flag. Saw today translations of several interesting documents captured. Many 'orders of the day' by the commandant. Also some propaganda instructions from Goebbels. Also details of enemy plans to combat the Normandy landings. Direct orders from Hitler on June 6th to ensure that our forces were annihilated on the day!

Two letters from Jess – one from Kath.

D +101 Friday 15.9.44

Parade 8.30 a.m. Major announced that further changes in plans for our future are possible. Meanwhile we remain here. Work on vehicle this morning.

D +102 Saturday 16.9.44

We are moving tomorrow to Dieppe area. Nothing to report today. Local farmers here gave us a roasted chicken this evening ... a bit of barter. Will come in useful for lunch tomorrow.

Spent most of today writing letters – Haydn, Marjorie, Kath, Stan Smith, and Jess. Clocks go back one hour tonight.

D +103 Sunday 17.9.44

Commenced today's journey 10 a.m.: a battalion move. Via Goderville, Fauville, Yvetot, Yerville, Totes, and then due north to harbour near village of Gonneville ... about 11 miles south of Dieppe. Total run about 48 miles. Drove about 30 miles myself ... change from commanding, but felt damned tired afterwards. Usual waving crowds en route ... and showers of apples! Had to park en route to allow passage of 49 Div ... About 3 hours delay. Ultimately harboured about 8 p.m.... pitch dark: first day of revised time. Sleeping in bivvies tonight, but understand we are moving into billets tomorrow morning. Appear to be staying here for a little while. News tonight announced latest figures for prisoners at Le Havre: 11,309 ... not a bad 'bag'. Also learned tonight of today's airborne invasion of Holland. Must have been a huge effort.

D +104 Monday 18.9.44

Spent this morning transferring all kit, etc. to billets. We are harboured in the grounds of a 'chateau' ... a rambling old house, with farm buildings all around it. The men are sleeping in the latter ... in stables, hen sheds, barns, lofts, disused cottages, etc. Officers and sergeants sleeping in the 'chateau'. We are, as usual, buried away in the country, but presume passion trucks will be laid on ... if we can get petrol!? Men's quarters could be better, but they are at least under cover. My troop sleeping on floor of stable ... using plenty of straw. A dirty-looking hole, but dry. Been raining all day, so we are here just in time to prevent further soaking. Sgts are on top (3rd floor) of house. Occupying two dilapidated rooms with tiled floors. First time I have been under a roof since coming to France. Scrounged some timbers, etc. left by Jerry, and have erected a bed well above the floor. Electric light may be laid on, if supply can be found. House already wired up. Sgts' mess starting tomorrow morning. Don't know what all this means. But the fighting front is now many miles to the east, apart from 'pockets' at Calais, Dunkirk and Boulogne – they are now being liquidated ... especially the latter. It is obvious that we will not see further action for some little time. Presume the vehicles will now get real overhaul. They need it ... having done about 600 miles since landing without any real maintenance. A marvellous performance.

D +105 Tuesday 19.9.44

Breakfast in the 'mess' this morning. Spent the day working on vehicles. Still no light: no option but to go to bed early. Major announced at lunch time that he is not satisfied with billets – men's in particular. Seeking permission from Brigade to change to better accommodation in village about 1.5 miles away.

Later. Confirmed that we are moving to new billets tomorrow morning.

D +106 Wednesday 20.9.44

Transferred to new billets in village of Beaunay this morning. The squadron seems to be very scattered, but the accommodation seems better – on the whole. Two troops (14) are in a private house – the remainder in cowsheds and stables in three different farms. This time, the sheds seem to all have concrete floors – instead of the former earth floors – and they look cleaner. But it is really dreadful accommodation for human beings. Little attempt has been made to make the places habitable – altho there is now little evidence of animal excreta. The men are spreading straw on the floors lavishly: it makes the 'rooms' look cleaner, and is certainly softer and warmer than bare concrete for sleeping.

I and the other sgts of the sqdn are housed in a small village hall – the 'hall' itself being the mess, and the sleeping quarters up above in the loft – via a narrow 'cat' ladder. A dusty and cobwebby bedroom – hardly fit to sleep in, but a palace by comparison with the mens' quarters. Most of us have erected beds of some sort to keep us off the floor.

Have found a German palliasse – and will be sleeping on a straw 'mattress' tonight for first time since leaving England. The men's quarters are better than the sgts' in one respect – they have electric light, whereas we have none. But we have rigged up some batteries and vehicle bulbs, and will at least have a little light. Two letters from J. tonight and one from Geary.

D +107 Thursday 21.9.44

Late last evening we discovered that our 'bedroom' is a home for bats. The darned things flutter in and out through the eaves, ad lib. Prefer bats to rats and mice!

A hullabaloo this morning about 12 and 15 Troop's quarters. They are in the same farm – and their 'bedroom' came to life late last night. The walls appear to be infested with woodlice – and other things. Also, those sleeping in the loft above complained of rats and mice. Most of the men seem to have packed up and transferred to the tanks during the night. Inspection by colonel this afternoon: believe some attempt is being made to disinfect the place. Work on vehicles all day: Also hot showers. On guard tonight.

SSM and one or two others arranging sgts' dance for Sat evening – in sgts' mess, on concrete floor! None of them can speak French!

D +108 Friday 22.9.44

Orderly sergeant today – SSM's errand boy, in other words. Visit by brigadier this a.m.: caused usual tidying up, etc. 'FFI' inspection* this a.m. also by MO. Nothing to report today. Weather fine and warm: very pleasant little village this (Beaunay). Local people seem anxious to help and are very obliging. Three of the sergeants are sleeping out in civvy quarters. Officers in local chateau: owner in residence. They appear to have been invited there. Interesting news on

* Free From Infection. Not to be confused with the FFI, the French Forces of the Interior.

radio this evening about revised pay from September 3rd – and plans for demobilisation.

D +109 Saturday 23.9.44

Sudden change in weather. Heavy rain during night: misty and drizzly this morning. Major announced on morning parade that we are having an official ceremony at local church in the morning: sqdn is providing and laying a wreath on war memorial in church. Not much work on vehicle this a.m. – rained off! Holiday this afternoon: liberty truck to Dieppe – sgts' mess dance this evening. Two letters from Jess.

D +110 Sunday 24.9.44

Queer dance last evening. Invitations had been sent out to local people – composed by someone who knew French language. No one knew how many people were likely to turn up. I became voluntary sandwich-maker in kitchens. Fair amount of food, sweets and cakes. Looked very well on table. We also had coffee (French liquid variety), cider and gin – and tea.

First arrivals about 8.30 p.m.: two old ladies, very decrepit, dirty and poor. Accompanied by old man – more decrepit – and dirty: wearing farm labourers' clothes and clogs and battered trilby: he wore the latter all evening. They just sat down – and watched the antics of some sergeants dancing together. The band had already commenced – drums, violin, accordion, guitar and piano … the latter borrowed locally during the day.

A girl accompanied the dirty trio . . . probably a dairy maid. She was soon trying to dance . . . The SSM went for his young lady from his billets. Bob Anderson went hunting for girls with a torch – without success. Likewise Jack Tomney.

Ultimately, three more girls arrived . . . two of them with their fiancés – the latter wearing blue overalls. They were politely told they weren't wanted – but their girls were dragged inside. The disappointed swains lingered outside – gazing in through the window!

The girls couldn't dance: they all seemed flat footed and completely wooden . . . probably through wearing clogs. The SSM tried hard with his girl, but had little luck at first: she wouldn't even tolerate his right arm around her waist, knocking it away each time he moved. Finally, she went with him into the kitchen for 'exercise' in private!

At supper, the dirty trio seemed to become my especial charge. How they ate! And drank! I lost count of the number of coffees – they just poured it down – likewise sandwiches and sweets. There weren't a dozen outsiders present, but fortunately they had good appetites. They must have eaten food sufficient for two or three times their number. It may have been our white bread. Sugar, too was plentiful. Ciggies were much in demand. Each time I passed my case to the trio, the old ladies usually took 2 each – handing them immediately to the old man!

Supper over: more 'dancing'! Dicky Hall disappeared with the two girls whose beaus were still waiting outside. He returned half an hour later – with the girls, but without their men! He had shaken them off somehow. Eight of the sergeants did a Scottish jig – an amusing performance. I suppose the local civvies thought we were mad – men dancing with men.

Conversation was very limited, needless to say. Even dictionaries weren't much help ... As a dance, the whole business was really a farce, but our fellows seemed to enjoy themselves – especially dancing with each other.

Jock Wilson says the SSM really messed up the attendance. He appears to have seen a few people in the village – and said '*oui*' to everything they said. He knows little more French! His '*oui*' must have acknowledged several refusals without him knowing it!

Another thing – we heard during the afternoon that the local '*maire*' and '*mairess*' (of the chateau) had expressed disapproval, to the major, of our method of issuing invitations. The *mairess* said there were 'some not very nice girls' in the village. Presumably, she and her husband should have been consulted beforehand. These local '*maires*' – every village seems to have them – appear to be local oracles or something. Maybe our particular specimen banned the dance to all the 'nice' girls as a measure of his disapproval. He was supposed to appear at the dance, but didn't ... Well, it was a queer performance – but provided a diversion, and plenty of fun.

This morning's wreath-laying ceremony is at present in progress. I have missed the parade – clothes not fit. The weather is cool, and very showery.

D +111 Monday 25.9.44

Terrible weather. No work on vehicles. Did a bit of washing. Concert this evening in mess. Officers doing a sketch – and a few turns by others. Tom Hamnett conjuring.

News from Holland not too good. Must be some ghastly fighting around Arnhem.* Think the situation is more critical than generally realised. Most of airborne army may be lost in next few days. Perhaps weather will improve and give Typhoons a chance to help. Rumour that we are moving in few days time – to Holland! Three hundred miles by road! Ten days' journey being planned.

D +112 Tuesday 26.9.44

Another wet morning. Holy Communion at 11 a.m. – in 15 Troop billet. Work on vehicles this afternoon. My tank going to LAD tomorrow for new engine. Successful concert last evening. Eight local civvies attended. Good job they don't understand English – fair amount of rich language!

News from Holland a little better this morning but situation must still be critical.

D +113 Wednesday 27.9.44

Nothing to report. My vehicle left for LAD this morning with driver and co-driver. Radio announced withdrawal of airborne force from Arnhem. Horrible news – but it relieves the awful suspense.

* The loss of the British First Airborne Division at Arnhem dealt a significant blow to the Allies' plans of invading Germany before the end of 1944.

D +114 Thursday 28.9.44

Announced suddenly this morning that we are leaving this area tomorrow morning. Hell of a flap. Three-day journey, 150 miles: somewhere in Dunkirk area. Confirmed at midnight that the remainder of my crew have to go to LAD and remain with vehicle. Letters from Jess (two), Jim Aldcroft, Ernest Bland.

D +115 Friday 29.9.44

Arrived LAD about 1.30 a.m. – fitters also: working on vehicle all night and until job is finished. Slept in tarpaulin for about three hours.

Later. We have to report to TDU with vehicle this evening – ready to move with TDU convoy at 8 a.m. tomorrow. Now 6 p.m. – job still not finished. Hate this TDU business: it causes a lot of unnecessary bother. Wrote to Jess and Wilf.

D +116 Saturday 30.9.44

Work finished about 11 p.m. last night: we then departed for TDU in area of Auffay – about 7 miles. Stopped Auffay midnight: had coffee. Lucky to find café open.

Arrived TDU 1 a.m. – with serious oil leak! Cannot now move in morning with convoy. Luckily two squadron fitters still with us. Convoy departed 9 a.m. – leaving us behind, with fitters still working on vehicle: several hours work ahead: may even have to remain overnight. Don't mind following on alone: have maps and route, etc. Horrible morning: cloudy and wet.

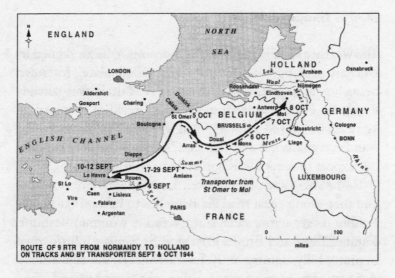

ROUTE OF 9 RTR FROM NORMANDY TO HOLLAND
ON TRACKS AND BY TRANSPORTER SEPT & OCT 1944

Later. Oil leak has rendered steering brakes useless. Fitted
new ones – now too late to move tonight. Intend to proceed
tomorrow morning: Will need full day for 60 mile journey
to Pende, near St Valery on the Somme. Met Boland: now
with TDU. He was not sent home after all. At present doing
odd jobs – and on TDU rear party. He hasn't altered at all—!
Seems to have done much travelling since I last saw him.
He was even sent to Brussels in search of the unit!

Been raining intermittently all day. Sleeping tonight in
nearby stables. Some bartering this evening. Slade came in
late with two chickens – one dead, one alive – the former
ready for cooking. We had been led to understand that both
were already roasted when making the deal. Damn the
French language! We have now also about 2 dozen eggs and
much butter – and milk. Tied up the live chicken in the
barn with about 6 ft of string. It scrambled over the face of
Jewer, sleeping peacefully – but he did not wake up.

D +117 Sunday 1.10.44

The weather seems brighter this morning. Was awakened by chicken pecking biscuits from enamelled plate! Intended being up at 6 a.m. for early start ... but it was already 8 o'clock! No use worrying. We had breakfast – sorted all kit, etc.: re-stowed vehicle: filled up with petrol, water, etc. – and eventually got away 11 a.m. No news of rest of column, but expect to meet a DR somewhere en route.

Route: St Saens: Neufchatel: Londinieres: Fresnoy: Eu: and then along coast road via Brutelles to harbour at Pende. A hilly route, across valleys of rivers La Varenne: Bethune, Eaulne, Yeres, and Bresle. First stop St Saens – a little town in pretty hilly country on R. La Varenne. Brake adjustment! Adjourned to restaurant for coffee – Everyone served when I arrived – 'No grub in this joint?' Pedder said something to a waitress – and she later appeared with plate of potatoes! God! They were serving us with dinner!

Another course arrived – meat and peas – and then lettuce – and bread ... We had to tell her to stop. Our available cash was very low. We asked for the bill apprehensively – 200 francs (£1). We just managed to scrape it together.

Meanwhile, the seventh member of the party had been invited by a lady to lunch – all seven of us! A free lunch too! The lads really enjoyed it this time – no financial worries! Could only manage coffee myself – with much cognac in it. Decent old couple. The husband carried many scars of last war. Several people outside gave us food – cake, fruit, etc. No payment asked – no begging. How different from Normandy.

Stayed too long in Saint Saens, so had to make up lost time. Next stop for food at Brutelles – after long tiring run. Very cold on high ground between valleys. Saw English

Channel soon after leaving Eu. The English Channel! Am nearer home now than for a long time – Ah, Jess . . .*

Reached Brutelles about 5 p.m. Pulled up on roadside – and immediately surrounded by dozens of youngsters, all over the vehicle. Chicken released on string – caused some fun. Corn was provided for it! Brewed up and had bread and jam, and then off once again – only a few miles to go to Pende. But soon had to pull up again – this time it was a group of people standing in the roadway waving baskets. They must have had news of our arrival, and had grub all ready for us. Bread, fruit, eggs, cakes! How very kind these people were! One woman even gave us some ciggies – we were very short by now. Through Lancheres and more fruit and tomatoes and finally to Pende – where the village turned out *en bloc*.

We harboured about 7 p.m. A long run and tiring day, but very interesting. Much more fun travelling alone than with a squadron! TDU convoy had left Pende in morning for next harbour – but Geordie Grant was there with a burned-out engine. Erected bivvies – and then back to village to a dance, after washing, etc. The dance was in the local inn – one concertina for band – and several young people swishing around a tiny board floor. What a medley! 'Life' in a French village! Amusing to watch Geordie's reactions to a girl of about ten drinking beer . . .

Back to harbour at ten and a brew. But rest of fellows had disappeared from the dance. Went to bed beneath vehicle – cold, but dry.

---

* Trevor wrote to Jess: 'It made me feel terribly homesick. I might just as well have been thousands of miles away: there was no chance of seeing my love . . . no chance at all.'

Trevor records frequent encounters with French children, usually cadging
bon-bons or 'cigarettes for Papa'. Here three boys are contemplating
a knocked-out German Panther tank.
Photograph © IWM B9665.

D +118 Monday 2.10.44

My colleagues returned during small hours. They had
walked to farm near Brutelles where food had been given us.
Some sort of 'date' seems to have been made at the time,
unknown to me. The lads kept the date – but it cost them a
long walk. They brought back more eggs, etc.

Had a good breakfast – and soon after, presents started
arriving from villagers – more food! The lads have been in
the village again, and we now have rather too much food.
One lady here is even roasting our dead chicken for dinner.

The other still lives – and is now contentedly ambling around the vehicle, freed from its string. It seems to be more tame after yesterday's journey. Pity we can't remain here, but I must leave after lunch. Next hop is only 24 miles, across the Somme. Presume the TDU will be in another harbour further on when I arrive this evening. But hope they have left fuel, etc. for my vehicle, otherwise I cannot proceed. No mail . . . seems ages since I heard from Jess. But there must be some letters for me with the squadron.

Later. 8.30 p.m. Am writing this in a bivvy by the side of the tank. I have a good light – an electric spot-light connected to the vehicle battery. It is a brilliant moonlit night – cold, but not damp or raining. My crew are out – as usual. Already they are keeping a date, altho' we only arrived here 2 hours ago.

Our location is now in the village of Nampont, about 8 miles south of Montreuil. We left Pende at 3.30 p.m., travelling via St-Valery-sur-Somme, then over the Somme, and through Noyelles, Nouvion, up the west side of the Forest of Crécy, and Vron – about 24 miles in all. And here we have caught up with the TDU. They have not departed for a new harbour.

I am a bit bewildered by events in the last 24 hours. It seems almost as though a chapter of *Don Quixote* has suddenly come to life. But I must proceed in order.

Our roast chicken arrived at lunch time – beautifully cooked. Our kind benefactor had earlier invited all of us to eat our dinner in her home, but I had to refuse the offer. So she sent plates for us, and potatoes (enough for 20 men!) and 6 large bottles of cider with 7 glasses – one for each of us.

After dinner, more villagers arrived with more food – eggs and apples and pears. It was simply overwhelming. And then a fellow came along with a camera, and we all had to pose for him on the tank – with the flags of Britain, France and USA prominently displayed. Unfortunately, time was passing quickly: I had to get a move on.

Pedder and Slade returned to the village with the plates, etc. . . . Quinn disappeared – he had a date somewhere! We started re-stowing the tank. By 3.30 we were ready to go . . . and then Pedder and Slade returned. Slade said Pedder had some bad news for me. Bad news? Yes – the daughter who had been responsible for much of our generous reception was going to St Valery, and she wanted to come *with* us – on the tank! Why did I ever tell Pedder we were passing through St Valery? How could I refuse? I had to agree – on condition that they smuggled her into the turret – out of sight. I would drop her *this* side of the village. But then Pedder appeared – would I mind the two youngsters coming as well? First the daughter – aged about 18. And now two youngsters, a girl of about 12, and a tiny lad of about 3. I didn't mind carrying the latter outside, but where on earth could the other girl ride? Slade offered his co-driver's seat and I agreed, again providing this girl also kept well out of sight. That made a total of ten of us, including the fitters, L/c Quinn and Tpr Jewer . . . not to mention the hen! We managed to smuggle the girls inside – after the elder had given me, '*pour le commandant de tank*', a bag containing six more eggs, and dozens of apples. A bribe? But where on earth to put the darned things? We stowed them somehow. There must have been dozens of eggs on the vehicle somewhere.

Just before we were due to move off, I heard guffaws of laughter from Slade and Pedder. They were talking to another girl of about 18. She was waving her arms – and looked almost frantic. What did *she* want? By a 'coincidence', she too *had* to go to St Valery – and she had to go with us, inside the tank! This girl had very fair hair, and blue eyes – I couldn't refuse . . . Somehow, God knows how, she was bundled into the co-driver's seat with the other girl . . . By now I felt desperately anxious to get going before we had more passengers.

We got going – and then I found that we had *two* little boys on top of the turret: I only expected one. I don't know even now where the other came from. But I didn't mind the youngsters: they were a different proposition, especially in the eyes of 'authority'! And so we had five passengers, and a 'crew' of seven, on a five-man tank – to say nothing of containers and tins and buckets and boxes crammed with food hung on anywhere outside. *And* we had a live chicken, still in her box at the front and surprisingly quite happy.

The top of the turret was crammed with loose apples – just an overflow. I noticed the fellows get rid of them when we had passed through St Valery – somewhere by the Somme. In St Valery, a quaint little village, there were the usual greetings and people waving frantically and shouting: how thrilling for the two youngsters. They waved themselves to a standstill.

It was in St Valery that the Canadians suffered many casualties in 1940. They re-took the place a few weeks ago – and there is still much evidence of heavy fighting. But life seems to be returning to normal in the town. We reached a quiet stretch of road after crossing the second Somme bridge, and I pulled up, determined this time to unload the passengers. They all dismounted – except the fair-haired one! I told Slade to tell her that the vehicle remained where it was until she got out. And then there started an argument which lasted 20 minutes. We all had a go at that girl: but she simply stuck in that seat – wedged down securely near the floor. To lift her out was almost impossible. Eventually she commenced to cry: she cried a lot. Her father was in Germany: her mother was cruel to her: she was leaving home: she was coming with us: no matter where we went, she would stay with us: she would not get out . . .

Well: it looked as though she wanted to be abducted. And I had no stomach for the role of abductor. One or two of the lads suggested using force, but this seemed wrong: besides, I did not want a public scene with a hysterical French girl. Eventually, and to my great relief, she agreed to leave us – and I was more pleased than I can say to see her slowly hauling herself from that tiny seat. We shook hands all round and said good-bye – And then we drove off across the low-lying ground of the Somme estuary: I hadn't the heart to look back at those people . . .

From this point, our journey was fairly uneventful and we reached Nampont in the evening just before dusk – and in time for a meal. I reported our arrival . . . and learned that we would be expected to depart for our unit in the morning. After tea, the lads disappeared again – on the scrounge as usual. They returned just now with more eggs, bread and butter. And now we have 36 eggs on board!

D +119 Tuesday 3.10.44

Ready to move 8.15 a.m. Heavy rain last night, but we remained dry – thanks to Slade having purloined extra bivvy and waterproofs. We were part of convoy of six vehicles re-joining various units.

Route: Montreuil, Maninghem, Fauquembergues, Arques, Wizernes, outskirts of St Omer – and on to this harbour with the 9th – Renescure. They only arrived a few minutes ahead of us. And so we are now in the Pas-de-Calais area – about 30 miles from Calais and Dunkirk. Saw some evidence today of our bombing of 'flying bomb' sites. One place in particular, Wizernes, was a terrible shambles. There is hardly an undamaged building in the town. And yet the people were able to smile and cheer as we passed through! This town had the misfortune to be situated at the foot of some high ground on which the Germans had built a flying bomb base.

Reached harbour in daylight – 37-mile journey – and re-joined the troop. The local village appears to have some attractions, and most of the lads are out this evening. Sleeping in a large wooden building erected by Jerry as emergency hospital for casualties from Calais and Dunkirk – he expected us to invade there—! He required 7 more days to complete this place . . . but it is an excellent billet, in spite of being not quite completed. Three letters from Jess – thank goodness.

D +120 Wednesday 4.10.44

Heavy rain last night. Maintenance on vehicle all day. Depart tomorrow – on transporters. Lined up 9 a.m. at local aerodrome. Very cold this evening. Lads all out again. Wrote to Jess.

Saw a train today – moving under own steam!* First since leaving England. Quite an event. Tomorrow's journey to Arras. Next day to Brussels, Third day to Ghent – close to the base of our salient into Holland.

Editor's note: the second diary notebook ends at this point.

D +121 Thursday 5.10.44

Start delayed this morning about 2 hours, but we eventually left harbour about 11 a.m. Short drive to concrete runways on local aerodrome where transporters were parked: loaded and shackled vehicles soon after. And then followed a long wait ... until 3 p.m., when we ultimately started – crew on tank, self in transporter driving cab.

Just as we were moving off, I noticed Mr Wintle running towards his vehicle which was moving slowly into position: A few seconds later there was a commotion round about, and we pulled up. A few yards to our rear, I saw a mass of torn rags dark red in colour, and some pieces of a body – two feet in particular. This unrecognisable mass lying on the concrete was the remains of Mr Wintle. He had attempted to board his vehicle via the towing bar and slipped – the trailer, carrying the tank, passed over his

---

* A rare sight in war-torn France. Trevor wrote home: 'We have become used to seeing railway lines rusty with neglect: railway bridges blown up: steel rails blasted and bombed into chunks of twisted iron: occasional coaches overturned and burned out ... never, throughout several hundred miles of travelling and fighting have we before seen a sign of movement on a railway track. That is why we all stared in amazement when we saw this strange monster moving through the countryside.'

body. The three axles, each carrying 8 wheels, had completely mutilated him. A sad business this. He was very young – and had been through most of our actions without harm. How very fragile is this nebulous thread we call life!*

The day's journey was quite uneventful. We passed through Aire, Lillers, Bethune, and pulled up on the roadside about 3 km before Arras – about 45 mile trip. A cold journey, especially for the lads on the tank, but we had a little rain.

This area seems to be fairly well industrialised –. especially around Bethune, where the horizon is marred by many coal slag heaps, and overhead conveyors. All the mines appear to be working, thanks, I believe, to the vigilance of the workers and the FFI.† It would no doubt have pleased Jerry to destroy them all, altho his retreat in this area was somewhat hasty.

Today, too, I have seen some evidence of the last war – A number of war memorials, and three enormous cemeteries. Two of them, British, contained many hundreds of graves laid out in neat straight rows, each grave bearing a white gravestone. The third cemetery, and largest, contained German dead. There must have been thousands of them – each grave bearing a wooden cross. I wonder whether this depressing sight had any effect upon the modern version of

---

* Leslie Wintle was a lieutenant in A Squadron. This terrible accident deeply affected those who saw it happen, as is attested by accounts on the 9 RTR website and in *Tank Tracks* by Peter Beale.

† FFI here refers to the French Forces of the Interior, the name given to the French resistance fighters as they became a more organised fighting force in the later part of the war. From October 1944, with most of France liberated, the FFI units became part of the regular French army.

the Herrenvolk* who have but recently departed. No doubt the French landscape will shortly be littered with additional cemeteries – monuments to our incredible madness. Will they bear the usual legend 'To the Glory of God'? It seems an expensive way of glorifying any god, to me ...

Vimy Ridge is quite close somewhere, but it was invisible in today's mist. I am told there is a bigger cemetery still there. This evening, we are sleeping in our bivvies on the grass verge by the roadside. Tomorrow evening, we halt at Brussels.

---

* A key concept of Nazi ideology, the supposed ideal of a pure Nordic master race.

Part Two

Belgium
and
Holland

Hazards of driving tanks across country. The weight of this Sherman has collapsed a bridge, plunging it into a stream. Three recovery vehicles are hauling it out.

Photograph © IWM BU4162.

D +122 Friday 6.10.44

A long day on the transporter. Route: Douai and then into Belgium – Rumes, Tournai, Ath, Enghien, Brussels ... harbour about 6 miles east of Brussels, on aerodrome. We crossed the border at 11 a.m., and there was an immediate difference in the appearance of our surroundings. Firstly, the Tricolour was superseded by the Black–Yellow–Red of the Belgian flag ... Practically every house was adorned with some evidence of the national colours. And then, the homes of the people – neater, tidier, more modern. The air of dilapidation, so evident in France, was far less noticeable.

The people everywhere gave us a grand welcome. There seemed to be no end to the showers of fruit, including peaches, grapes, tomatoes, pears, apples. Our vehicles were littered with the stuff. Passing through Tournai, I saw an ice-cream vendor on the roadside selling 'wafers'! At Tournai too the trams were running as well as the railways. It is a large town, and seems to have suffered little material damage.

Our journey into Belgium was an interesting experience. I felt that, here, we were really welcome ... But at Brussels—! It is difficult to describe the scene. It may have been a royal procession, so great was the acclamation. We passed through some of the principal streets of the city at a time when there were many business people about – 6 p.m. ... and what a contrast with France! Here there were well-dressed civilians, fine shops, cleanliness, order – and intelligent looking people. And the girls! There were so many – so clean and healthy – fine looking. What a sight for our lads—! The city was a blaze of colour: every shop, every house, every window carried a flag. And many civilians too were wearing colours.

Our convoy was a very large one, and attracted great

crowds. And once again we were bombarded with fruit and flowers – on a greater scale than ever. One lady handed me a huge bouquet of dahlias – beautiful flowers: she had bought them specially! Perhaps it is strange for grimy and coarse looking soldiers to be given flowers in this manner … but maybe it was the only way these people could demonstrate what was in their hearts. The German occupation – four weary years – has caused indescribable misery and depression amongst the majority of the population. And now their gratitude knows no bounds.

There can be no doubt that the Germans have left behind memories which will remain, perhaps for ever, in the mind of the Belgian people. They have learned to hate – really hate … Brussels seems to have suffered little, if any, material damage. It is a fine city, and very modern. After our rather hectic journey through the city, we proceeded east for about 6 miles, and finally harboured by an aerodrome – sleeping in our bivvies. A windswept place, and very cold.

D +123 Saturday 7.10.44

The last day of our journey by transporter. Route: Haacht, Aarschot, Herselt, Westerlo, Geel, Mol. Another journey through flag-bedecked towns and villages, past waving crowds … and more fruit! The transporters left us at Herselt, and we travelled unaided the remaining 12 miles to Mol – the latter a small country town.

We arrived early in the afternoon, and to our amazement learned that we were harbouring in the town itself – by the roadside in a residential area. Before we had really dismounted, the neighbours came alongside the vehicles with offers of beds and hospitality. Many of them spoke English – a decided change from France, where very few people could talk to us.

The kindness of these people is overwhelming. Within a few minutes of arriving, myself and crew were seated in a house drinking champagne liqueur, and coffee – the latter ersatz. They implored us to dine with them – to sleep with them – to stay as long as possible, so that they could demonstrate something of their gratitude to the 'British soldiers'. They put their houses completely at our disposal – and their attentions became an embarrassment.

During the afternoon, the major announced that we were to spend the night in civvy billets, but all accommodation would be provided through the police authorities. This news was accepted sadly by our kind neighbours. They had so wanted us to stay with them. All crews were the same – and all had to sleep in houses some distance from the vehicles. But we dined with our neighbours – in my case Mr Alphonse Theeuws, a one-armed veteran of the last war. And we had supper in the evening – and talked. I learned something of the meaning of Nazi occupation, and I began to understand why the Germans are hated over here. Also, I heard many first-hand accounts of the treachery of *collaborateurs*. They will get their deserts – in Belgium, at any rate.

This evening, we learned with regret that we are departing in the morning, at 7 a.m. . . . I think our Belgian friends are more sorry than we are.

D +124 Sunday 8.10.44

Reveille 5.30 a.m., ready to move 7 a.m., and soon on the way – to Eindhoven in Holland. Route: Lommel, Luyksgestel, Bergeijk, Westerhoven, Steensel – and then round the western suburbs to the north side of the town. We crossed the Dutch border at 9 a.m., and once again the houses and buildings were displaying red, white and blue flags – this time the Dutch flag. Our welcome through the Dutch villages was at least as warm and enthusiastic as in Belgium – but this time there was less fruit.

Near Stausch, Mr Francis commandeered my vehicle – his own having developed bogey trouble. So once again I became a one-vehicle convoy – the EME ordering us to proceed to harbour very slowly. Had a brew before moving off – and the first civvy who came along spoke fluent English. We chatted for an hour. He had left his own village, and studies, 14 months before, and had since been in hiding on a farm to avoid deportation to Germany with the labour conscripts. He told us of the smuggling of British pilots across the border to Belgium – a first-hand account of something we only dimly believed before. Passing through Eindhoven, we stopped two or three times to confirm the route – and always there were people around who could speak English.

We found the unit parked by the roadside on the main road north of the town – once again in a residential area, and with the usual crowds gathered around. But the people were well dressed – maybe because it was Sunday. There were groups around every tank – all speaking English. Once again, invitations were issued liberally, and we all hoped to stay the night.

This is a fairly large town, and seemingly fairly prosperous, due probably to the huge works of Philips – one of the largest and most modern factories I have ever seen. It was captured by us intact, after having produced ⅔ of the German radio valve requirements for about three years.

We are all much impressed by the Dutch people. They obviously have a high educational standard and seem very progressive. The houses too are neat and tidy and everywhere seems spotlessly clean. But their hatred of the Germans! It is too deep for words. Everyone I have spoken to has the same unutterable loathing of the 'swines'.

Later. The squadron have moved off north to a point about four miles away – it is the front line of the base of our Arnhem salient. Our job at present is to protect the flanks from counter attack. The scene before they moved off was totally unreal – crowds of well dressed civilians, some with prams, or dogs, or cycles, all enjoying friendly conversation with our lads. It was a typical Sunday afternoon crowd – just out for a walk . . . And yet – only five or six miles away were the Germans, and our lads were going out to fight them, leaving this peaceful atmosphere – for what? In Normandy, any point five miles behind the front line was usually a shambles, and subject to artillery fire – with the dreadful smell of death everywhere . . . But here—! It is obvious that Jerry has no big weapons in the locality, otherwise there would be a different story. Already he has tried to bomb the Philips works since our occupation, but he failed.

I am remaining in Eindhoven for the night. The tank has to be repaired here, and not forward where there may be enemy artillery. The crew have already got accommodation – and have had to refuse at least a dozen offers. I am sleeping in the house of Mr Slaats and the other four in two nearby houses. We are having meals with Mr Cornelese – a member of the local underground group. Everyone here is anxious to help: we are literally embarrassed by their kindness.

Mr Cornelese has been speaking to us about life under the Nazis – an incredible story. The underground movement of which he was an active member, seems to have operated on the same lines as in France – with a 'leader' at the head, and several subordinates, all again with their subordinates – a sort of pyramid. Most members used 'nommes de plume' – and a subordinate did not usually know his superior. The activities of the organisation included smuggling airmen over the frontiers, printing and distributing underground newspapers, obtaining food, and hindering the Nazis wherever possible. Mr C. was glad to have been of assistance to a few of our airmen. 'Dangerous, but it was good,' he said.

The food situation here strikes me as having been much worse than we in England ever realised. And the black market, encouraged by the Nazis, was scandalous. Even Dutch farmers expected £2 per lb for butter, 2/– each for eggs, etc. Each person was issued 1 small tablet of ersatz soap per month! Coffee – all ersatz – made from acorns, or wheat or tulip bulbs ... Bread – largely sawdust ... Tea, either in tablet form (1 tablet for ½ litre of tea) or made from leaves of hawthorn and blackberry. Milk – a minute ration, always skimmed. Vegetables – practically non-existent unless home grown, or bought via black market. It is a wretched story. The Germans too were never loath to use torture when it suited them ... What these people have suffered will be doubted in England – even disbelieved.

Their hatred of the Germans will not be understood – so it seems to me. I hope I am wrong.

D +125 Monday 9.10.44

A good sleep last night in a civilised bed ... Had an interesting chat before bed with Mr Slaats. He is very well informed politically. Fitters working on vehicle. Job more difficult than anticipated. May be here a day or two yet ... Good!

All meals with Mr Cornelese and family. His daughter, Thea, very charming and intelligent schoolgirl. Also little Willy, aged 2. A very religious family. I believe everyone is religious in this part of Holland. Grace is said before and after every meal. Many religious pictures in the house. Also a small figure of Christ on a wall bracket, and small neon cross always burning. Pastor visited the house this evening. Chatted with Mr Cornelese and family all evening. Also heard 9 o'clock news. Radio is only used for news bulletins owing to rationing of electricity – 125W per day is limit: meters checked every second day.

D +126 Tuesday 10.10.44

Rained very hard all day – a steady downpour. Glad to be indoors here at Mr Cornelese's house, but feel sorry for crews away in front line. A few tanks have been out today – they captured 40 prisoners. Fitters working under difficulties with the rain. Tank on fire through welding, but soon extinguished. Definitely not moving today. Writing most of day – to Jess.

With the Cornelese family in Eindhoven. Left to right: Mr Cornelese, Cpl
Johnny Davis, Trevor, Thea Cornelese, Alf 'Titch' Mead holding Willy
Cornelese, Jimmy Smith, Mrs J. P. Cornelese, Freddy Glasspool.

Photograph © The Trevor Greenwood Archive.

The Cornelese family is overwhelming us with kindness:
they seem unable to do too much for us. Fitters also being
cared for today – drying clothes, etc. Marvellously clean
people – always seem to be working in the house.

Talked much with Mr Slaats again this evening. He
pays great tribute to us soldiers – maintaining that the
activities of their underground workers was nothing by
comparison with our job. He is almost scornful of his
fellow countrymen who speak proudly of their underground work. It was nothing, he says. But how he hates the
Germans!

How like us these Dutch people seem to be – much more
so than the French. They have their problems of

government – almost identical with ours. Very pleasant to have intelligent conversation with an enlightened foreigner. I have spoken with a few local families and always it is the husband who speaks English – not the wife.

The Germans seem to have robbed these Dutch people of every conceivable thing – even to the extent of shipping away in barges huge quantities of rich soil from the tulip bulb-growing areas. It will take about 10 years for the Dutch to replace this valuable soil. To bed again in Mr Slaats's house.

D +127 Wednesday 11.10.44

A fine morning – thank goodness. But a bad day for us: we will have to move up to the squadron at lunch time – dinner will be our last meal with Mr Cornelese, for the time being, at any rate. He is taking a photo of the crew before we depart. No heavy activity at the front – we seem to be carrying out 'nuisance' raids on the enemy.

Later. Here I am back with the sqdn. We are in a defensive position about 4 miles N of Eindhoven. Our billet is a small, but new and well built cottage. It must have been vacated hurriedly because it is fully furnished, with drawers etc. full of clothing. There is a canary – still living – some puppies, a large rabbit – and a clock in working order. Presumably the owners departed 3 or 4 weeks ago when our airborne troops landed. The house has probably been used since by our troops. The electric light has been disconnected, so we have improvised electric lighting from the tank parked in the front garden. Fortunately, the house is equipped with

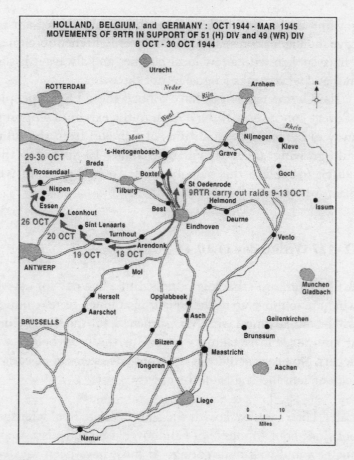

excellent black-outs* – Jerry is only a mile or so from here across the nearby railway line.

Today, I have heard artillery and mortar fire for the first time for some weeks. We are located between our mortars and the enemy, and have now to re-accustom myself to mortars – ours have been whining overhead all afternoon.

* Windows were fitted with blackout curtains to prevent any lights being visible at night.

Said good-bye to Mr Cornelese after lunch. The three days spent with him were probably the best I have known since leaving England – decent people, cleanliness, food nicely served, a comfortable house – and the overwhelming kindness of the family.

Mr Slaats too has been extremely decent: our talks were especially interesting. He seems much more politically alive than Cornelese. The latter took our photo at lunch time . . . In both houses I was aware of the appalling scarcity of food. Bread and potatoes appear to be their only regular food. We helped a little with our tinned foods.

The lads are playing cards in this room – the only room with a light. There are fourteen of us in a tiny living room – it is rather overcrowded, but palatial by comparison with our bivvies. Dicky Hall is nursing a puppy, after feeding it with milk. It was howling terribly an hour ago, but now appears to be asleep.

Today has been quite fine – I hope it remains so. There is gaping hole in one of the walls of this house, and half the tiles are missing from the roof: it is hardly waterproof. In spite of this area being in the front line, there are still many civilians living in the neighbourhood in scattered cottages. I think they are foolish; there is a fair amount of mortar and shell fire about. Also, the air is laden with the familiar smell of decaying flesh. There are several dead cattle lying about the fields – reminiscent of Normandy.

D +128 Thursday 12.10.44

On guard last night, but it was uneventful. We have to be keenly on the alert here, as enemy patrols have been active and there has been some infiltration through our forward infantry positions. The tiny puppy has been whining this morning. The general verdict is that it is bunged-up. It has been given a powdered bile bean (there are plenty in the house) – with satisfactory results! Mr Francis brought along another small dog – bomb-happy like most of the animals still living in front line areas. It is terrified – and trembles violently all the time. We can but feed it and hope for the best.

The canary has chirped today! We are not going out today: 14 Troop are moving into enemy lines this afternoon. Received three letters from Jess.

Have been exploring a few of the local houses: all must have been hurriedly vacated – there are personal belongings and furniture in all of them. Am amazed by the number of religious knick-knacks in all houses here. In one house nearby, there is a small room containing 15 images of Jesus and the Virgin Mary; 7 religious pictures on the walls (last supper, etc.) and 21 bibles and prayer books. Other rooms in the same house were also liberally supplied with this lumber. What a profitable industry for the church ... There is not even any beauty in this stuff. Most of it is very crude, especially the pictures. And the Virgin Mary is always represented as an insipid female with long lean features and a shiny neck. She was probably a semi-barbaric hag – but we have to allow for 'artistic licence!'

One thing here surprises me very much. These Dutch people are spotlessly clean in their habits and homes – and yet I have not yet found a single house containing a bath! And I have been in some quite new houses. Even Mr Cornelese and Mr Slaats – comfortable middle-class people living in houses less than 20 years old – had no baths or bathrooms! Also, I have not yet seen a WC. The newer houses have closets, but no water flush. A bucket of water has to suffice.

Fair amount of gun fire and mortar all day – shells whizzing overhead seem damnably close.

D +129 Friday 13.10.44

Guard last night: not very pleasant in this front line area. Some bursts of Spandau alarmingly close near midnight – and a few enemy HE shells close by. Our artillery fairly busy too. Gun flashes visible along whole of northern horizon.

Twelve Troop going out today – hoping to bring in more prisoners. 'Snowy' Fisher badly hurt by shell in Eindhoven last night. Shells too dropping dangerously close to nearby bridge over canal. Many Typhoons about today – also Spitfires.

Picture show this afternoon. Slade brought in more chickens this morning. He has now collected half a dozen: they are penned up in the garden here. Two rabbits for lunch. Have a suspicion they were tame ones. The lads say they 'caught' them yesterday. After lunch, most of troop went to pictures. Slade and Pestell disappeared elsewhere. They returned an hour later triumphantly escorting a goat. 'It's a milker,' proudly proclaimed Slade. We have tied it to a post in the garden. Pestell has tried milking it, and it works! We now have fresh milk for the puppy.

Later. Had a visit from two Dutch Maquis. They brought us a couple of oil lamps. Slade and Pestell again disappeared at tea time. Returned an hour later in a jeep – with two

20-gallon barrels of beer, a sack of sugar, bottles of liquids, and other odds and ends! One of the barrels was immediately opened by chiselling open the plug – and our kitchen was sprayed with froth. For the next ten minutes, there was a mass of struggling humanity around the barrel – some trying to stop the flow, others trying to prevent wastage of the precious fluid by drinking what came out. Some hullabaloo! The sugar will be very useful. Pestell has milked the goat – successfully. And the puppy gobbled most of the milk. The canary is now singing lustily.

We did some spring cleaning today – and dug a hole to bury the debris, tin cans, etc. But the hole had hardly been commenced when a large tin appeared: it contained many skeins of gaily coloured silk wool. More digging revealed a carefully covered dustbin. This was later examined, and found to be full of good linen tablecloths, clothing, jewellery, pre-war Dutch currency, watches, etc.! The absent tenants had buried their valuables before fleeing, and we had accidentally stumbled upon the hiding place. We intend to replace everything exactly as found.

D +130 Saturday 14.10.44

Little doing today, apart from usual routine work on tanks – preceded by daily stand to from 6.15–6.45am. We re-buried the household valuables this morning.

Another visit from our friendly Dutch Maquis. They had an early lunch with us. Very large force of four-engined bombers flew eastwards up the salient this morning. Is this a prelude to another big offensive?

Yesterday's newspapers arrived here at lunch time today.

This is a change for the better. It is a long time now since we received newspapers less than a week old. I learn today that the King and Monty were in Eindhoven yesterday – only four miles away, but we knew nothing about the visit.[*]

The bridge immediately in our rear over the Wilhelmina Canal was hit by Jerry artillery last evening. It is now graded class 25 – so we are temporarily cut off, as our vehicles require class 40 at least.[†] Usual mortar and shell fire whining overhead all day.

Saw a copy of a translation of a remarkable German Army document today. It was published originally last August, and addressed to the Wehrmacht Officer Corps and endorsed 'Top Secret – not to fall into enemy hands'! The purpose of the document was to emphasise the present low morale of the German troops and to instruct officers how to combat the situation. The question of surrender was dealt with – and an extract by Ludendorff[‡] defining the meaning of the word was reproduced verbatim in order to illustrate some hidden meaning discovered by the Nazis. Ludendorff acknowledges the necessity of surrender whenever conditions seem hopeless: better, he argues, to save one's life for future service to the Fatherland, than to die needlessly. But the Nazis impress upon the Officer Corps the fact that Ludendorff makes no mention of who decides the surrender. They argue that it is up to the higher command to decide, not the

[*] King George VI spent three days with the British Second Army during a brief tour of the headquarters and units of the 21st Army Group in October 1944.

[†] Bridges were graded according to the weight they could support. Heavy tanks such as the Churchill (38 tons) were limited in the bridges they could cross.

[‡] Erich Ludendorff was a German general and military theorist who published his theory of Total War in 1935. He died in 1937.

individual soldier or junior officer – the latter must always fight on and never consider surrender – unless permitted by higher authority. It would appear that Ludendorff's writings are 'gospel' to the Wehrmacht, and this is an attempt to distort his meaning for the benefit of the Nazi hierarchy. It is a very crude attempt – there can be no mistaking the literal meaning of Ludendorff's words. But the worst of this document was its beastly cynicism – and apparent contempt for the soldier in the ranks. Officers were reminded of their own importance, and ordered to leave their men, if necessary, to avoid capture – contrary to 'some junior officers who think they should always fight on with their men'.

Instructions are given to officers for dealing with recalcitrant or rebellious soldiers – especially those who spread the argument etc. of 'Soldier Councils' (whatever they may be). Firstly, officers are ordered to send such men into the forward areas of the front line, 'where experience shows they rarely come back'! But don't allow opportunities for desertion.

A second instruction on this subject seems to be a repetition of an old formula – *viz.* inform the soldier that his people at home have been 'bombed out', and grant him immediate compassionate leave. At the same time taking care to inform the Gestapo or Military Police, so that he can be arrested at a suitable place, en route. By this means, the troublesome soldier is liquidated, without his comrades, and possible sympathisers, being any the wiser.

But the most revealing portion of this strange document is that dealing with the next war! Officers are reminded of the failure of their army to obtain world domination in the 1914–18 war . . . They are told that success in this direction in this second attempt seemed probable until recently – but this possibility (of failure) 'was foreseen'. Therefore, it is up to them, a duty to the Fatherland, to ensure their own survival, in order to prepare for the third attempt! The document becomes almost lyrical – 'we can look forward with good heart and high spirits to this third attempt'!!!

In the midst of this, the ghastliest and bloodiest war in history, when already millions of their own men have been slaughtered, and are being slaughtered, the 'gentlemen' of the German army can actually speak, almost with longing, of the next war, their next attempt to obtain mastery of the world! Has history any record of such fiendishness?

It is the numbers of the 'Officer Corps' to whom the message is addressed. It is upon them, and their efforts, that success will depend next time 'especially in the technical aspects of war'! The question of manpower is dismissed as almost irrelevant: the absence of any past shortage in this direction is emphasised. 'Cannon fodder' is expected to be plentiful for the next war – as in all wars!

I see no reason to doubt the authenticity of this document. Our copy was circulated officially from the HQ of the 34th Tank Brigade. It is even possible that Mr Eden's recent statement in the Commons, in which he assured the house that the government had irrefutable evidence of present German preparations for the next war, was based upon this, or some similar document. No doubt the original is already in London. To me it seems absolutely incredible that anyone professing to belong to a civilised nation can envisage another war, particularly after the slaughter of the last few months . . . but apparently I do not understand the German mind.*

Informed this afternoon that we are leaving here on Monday, and going to a new area near Antwerp. Back to Belgium! And we were only paid yesterday – in Dutch currency! Tomorrow, 11 Troop are going out: we remain here.

D +131 Sunday 15.10.44

Stand to 6.15–6.45 as usual, then breakfast, followed by an hour or so on first tank parade. Large numbers of planes flying eastward about 9 a.m. Great height, practically invisible, but each one created a vapour trail. An almost cloudless blue sky soon became filled with long fluffy white clouds.

Fair amount of HE and mortar flying around today. Saw a burst from a Nebelwerfer explode in Best village: hell of a bang and much dense black smoke. Some weeks since I heard one of these beastly things.

A few of the lads turned up with small motor bikes this morning – and have been playing with them all day! More loot! Received three letters from Jess . . .

Eleven Troop went out today, but only saw three Jerries: no excitement. We leave here at 3 p.m. tomorrow, and spend the night in Eindhoven – a journey of about 4 miles. Move

---

* In his earlier limited edition of the diary, Barry Greenwood observes that Trevor would not have known about Germany's race to produce an atomic bomb, 'hence his bafflement at the optimistic tone of this document, its hinting at "technical aspects" and its disregard for manpower. With hindsight, it seems likely that the "third attempt" envisaged in the document was to be a push-button atomic war – with German officers pushing the buttons.'

to Antwerp area on Tuesday. Animals all seem OK: three chickens for dinner. Passion truck to Eindhoven this evening. Heavy rain since dusk – guard tonight.

D +132 Monday 16.10.44

Cold and dull this morning, but rain has ceased. Usual stand to until 6.45 a.m. Spent some time stowing kit, etc. and cleaning up the house in preparation for our departure.

Left Best area 2 p.m. and harboured Strijp (pronounced 'Stripe') about 3 o'clock – 3 km west of Eindhoven. After tea, decided to visit Mr Cornelese and Mr Slaats with a few items of food and ciggies. About 6 km walk – but must have walked 8 miles! Eindhoven is world's worst town for getting lost. Eventually reached Slaats 8 p.m. – set out 5.30! Two sergeants from HQ with Slaats, so left very soon. Was glad I took a few items of food and coffee across to Cornelese – much fuss – coffee and supper, etc. Photos not ready, but will be forwarded. Said good-bye to family about 9.45 – having got details of 'short cut' back to tanks. Short cut! I should have been in bed by 11 p.m. – but eventually found the harbour at 12.30 a.m. Found myself going due south somehow – miles out of my way. Lucky to meet a Dutchman about 11 o'clock who spoke a little English. He insisted on accompanying me until I reached harbour. And thanks to his enquiries, I did get back. All my fault really because I did not know the name of the harbour area. Am damned if I can remember some of these long Dutch words and place names.

My guide was very kind indeed. He said it was a privilege for him to be able to help an English soldier. Every Dutchman was deeply grateful to England, etc., etc. This is the usual attitude towards us in Holland. So different from France . . .

We left our animals behind today at Best. But relieving troops arrived just as we departed and we left instructions for them. At least three of the motorcycles came with us – duly painted and camouflaged!

D +133 Tuesday 17.10.44

Back to Belgium today. Left Eindhoven (Strijp) about 9 a.m. Route via Arendonk to Turnhout. Harboured in small village 3 miles west of Turnhout.

Crossed frontier about 11 a.m. And now we have another language problem. In Holland we managed quite well because so many of the people speak at least some English. But here the people are mostly of the peasant type and only speak 'Flams'* – Flemish. We are in Flanders. This language seems to resemble Dutch more than anything else. It is useless trying to use French words – it is an unknown tongue with most of the villagers. Luckily, there is an old lady who knows French and she has been very helpful as interpreter. Our arrival during the afternoon caused some commotion, and we had little difficulty in finding civvy billets for ourselves. We all seem to be housed very close to our vehicles which are parked at the side of the main street: this is very handy. We were originally ordered to find accommodation in barns, stables, etc. – but the people won't allow this. And so we are in their houses – but heaven knows how they are managing. The houses are quite small, altho they appear

---

* The correct word is Vlaams. Flemish differs from Dutch only in incidentals of pronunciation and spelling, much as American differs from British English.

fairly large externally: this is because every house has a cow-shed attached to it.

I think the people must be peasant farmers – each having a small plot of ground, and a cow or two, and maybe pigs and horses. The house of my crew is typical – downstairs kitchen and a living room, both with tiled floors. The kitchen contains one of those weird stoves so popular here, and two water pumps. Upstairs there are, I think, three bedrooms, one very small.

We arranged to sleep in one small bedroom – the five of us – two on a double bed, and three on the floor. This was satisfactory from our point of view – palatial by comparison with the bivvy, and much better than barns and cow-sheds. But when we went to bed, we had no option but to sleep in beds – all of us. Four of us in one bedroom on two double beds, and the fifth in the small room with one of the sons on a double bed. Two other sons slept on a mattress on the floor! They had given up their beds for us! Argument is useless. It is time we had beds, they say, after sleeping so long in the open and on the floor. Very nice of them. We appreciate it. Pedder, Pestell, Slade and Ward spent the evening with a neighbour – having a 'date' as usual.

This house seems spotlessly clean, but life here is pretty crude. Food is very plain – perhaps due to war – sanitation is bad: no WC, no bath. At tea time Slade and I were chatting. He said 'there's a bloody awful stink wafting around here: can you smell it? Just like cow-shit!' I could smell it alright – but said it was from the farm about 50 yards away. I was wrong! One of the fellows asked for the lavatory and was shown a door leading from the kitchen. He opened it – and had the fright of his life: he had stepped from the kitchen into a cow-shed, and was face to face with a hulking fat cow! It lived in the next room to the kitchen! No wonder we could smell cow-shit! And, in a pen built in this cow-shed are two enormous pigs! The lavatory is next to their pen.

Some people say farmyard smells are healthy. They want to try living with them! These conditions *can't* be healthy. In this kitchen we can hear old Clara evacuating herself frequently – she is so close. And the house is full of flies. I must admit that the animals are very clean and well looked after – but pigs and cows are inherently smelly. They just can't help it. Naturally, we were horrified to find these animals in the house, but our hosts have no idea of what we think and feel. To them, it is perfectly normal and natural to live with the animals. Everyone seems to do it here.

I think our host has a fairly large family – at least four sons and a daughter, but it is difficult to sort them all out – there are so many people in the house, just coming and going as they please. What a life! The wife must work very hard – making butter, cheese, baking bread, milking the cow – and cooking all meals, etc.

Saw some local smallholders threshing their corn today – four of them beat it continually with 'flails' – poles, to the end of which are attached wooden 'clubs' by a leather thong. A very primitive business, but it seems to work. The corn is afterwards swept up from the floor. Oxen too are used here for ploughing. But there is electric light – a great blessing. The main road through the village appears to be a communal urinal – at night, anyhow!

D +134 Wednesday 18.10.44

Fairly good sleep last night – up at 7.30 a.m. Work on the vehicle until 2 p.m. Much rain today and fairly cold. Spent the afternoon by the kitchen fire. We are moving tomorrow – about 16 miles to St Leonards – and then action the following day. Depart 7.30 a.m. . . .

Spent the evening writing – Jess and Marjorie. Very difficult trying to converse with these people. Fortunately, the old lady who speaks French appeared, and that helped a bit. Awful smell in this kitchen each time anyone opens the door of Clara's room. Lads out as usual . . .

Heard 9 o'clock news. Nazis have announced formation of a 'Home Guard' today – everyone from 16 to 60 to be included!* Our magnificent failure at Arnhem is certainly giving Jerry time to postpone the coup-de-grace . . . If only . . . if—!

D +135 Thursday 19.10.44

Terrible morning: heavy rain and cold. Vehicle flooded – inside and out. Left Turnhout about 9 a.m. Route: Vosselaar, Oostmalle, then over Turnhout Canal to St Leonards for harbour. Nothing spectacular about the journey: we got very wet.

Bailey Bridge at St Leonards. Village much damaged:

* The Volkssturm was set up by the Nazi Party on the direct orders of Hitler and conscripted all able-bodied men who were not already in a military unit. Many of its older members had fought in the Great War, and some, far from the home defence for which they had been intended, found themselves in the front line.

must have been heavy fighting by Canadians: we now appear to be in their area of operations. Reached harbour by the canal about 2 p.m. Still raining very heavily: impossible to do much preparation on vehicle: sheeted up and went to billets. Mr Francis had already broken into a recently vacated private house – and we took possession, with 11 Troop. Usual signs of hurried departure by tenant: personal belongings still in cupboards, wardrobes, etc. All furniture and bedding intact: also some food – cheese, potatoes etc. We settled in and made a fire and generally tried to dry out.

Churchill crossing a Bailey bridge over the Antwerp-Turnhout canal during the attack north of Antwerp on 22 October. Note the cans carried on the front of the tank: doubtless some of the tank crews' chickens travelled like this in their compo boxes when the tanks were not in action.

Photograph © IWM B11112.

Into battle tomorrow: received orders and maps from Mr Francis. We are practically in the front line here: tomorrow, we push north, making a 3000-yd 'dent' in Jerry's line. Fairly big action is planned, of which we are only a part.*

Reveille 5 a.m. tomorrow. Cross start line 7.30 a.m. Leave harbour 6.45 a.m.

D +136 Friday 20.10.44

Managed to stow vehicle and get away on time: something of a job in the dark! Approaching start line, Mr F's vehicle was ditched: he took mine and left me with his crew. So I missed the first phase of the battle. Eventually un-ditched 10 a.m. – using two ARVs. Meanwhile, the battle had commenced: heavy artillery barrage to begin with.

Very soon, numerous farmhouses and cottages were ablaze – visible from my ditched vehicle. And then prisoners started to come in – in groups of 6 to 8, etc. Saw about 100 during couple of hours. Noticed Churchill flame-throwers (Crocodiles) also being used around farm buildings near start line.

Had difficulty in finding my way to rejoin squadron, due to mist and smoke and confusing track marks over country-side, but eventually found them as they reached final objective – 3000 yds from start. No casualties or damaged vehicles in squadron, but plenty of Jerries shot-up and captured. Changed back to my own vehicle and then commenced long wait on final objective while infantry dug

---

* Operation Rebound, spearheading 49 Division in pushing the Germans north. This was followed by Operation Thruster (26–30 October), the capture of Roosendaal.

in and AT guns arrived, etc. Amazed to see civilians coming towards us from enemy territory immediately ahead: we may easily have shot them accidentally. They were terrified – and not surprising. Their homes had probably been shelled by us: neighbouring buildings were blazing fiercely: dead cattle lay about everywhere: our artillery was still firing spasmodically: our Besas and 75s were also active: Jerry was mortaring us – and they came through the lot – about ten people, including 3 or 4 old folk, one man with a wooden leg, a couple of children – a wheelbarrow, bicycle – bundles of rags and blankets. It was a pitiful sight: they were trying to run across the rough ground – badly pitted with angry looking shell and mortar scars and deeply rutted with tank tracks. One old lady was crying: all looked terrified – but one young woman returned my hand wave with a cheery 'OK, Tommy.'

We managed to brew up – keeping one eye open for Jerry immediately ahead, but he let us have our tea in peace. Eventually, about 3 p.m., we retired about 1000 yds and took up defensive position on right flank of our salient and remained there until dark. Laagered about 7 p.m. close to Het [Het Kloester] – a Jerry strong point last night! The weather had mercifully been fine all day, but it started to rain at dusk – and didn't stop! Our move to laager done as quietly as poss, in the dark: we preserved silence throughout the night as Jerry was quite close to the east. A few odd shells and mortars fell quite close during the night, but no casualties. Too wet to sleep – and too cold, but had an hour or two in the turret. Otherwise spent the night observing and looking for Jerry patrols. A horrible night.

Learned that the day's action had all been highly

successful, and both brigs pleased with our efforts. They sent congratulations via the colonel! Felt the strain rather: first time I had been into action for many weeks.

The day's battlefield reminded me of Normandy. So many dead cattle: broken fences, shell holes – dead bodies, mostly Jerries – noise of artillery, of aircraft – burning buildings. A beastly business. At night, we counted 16 fires on the immediate horizon – 16 farms and homes ruined in a few hours ...

D +137 Saturday 21.10.44

Wretched night: practically no sleep. Stand to 6.00–6.30 a.m. – and then back again to same defence position on right flank of salient. Fortunately, the morning was fine.

Daylight and then breakfast. Spent most of morning peering through binoculars looking for Jerry. A counter attack is quite possible on this front. Many more civilians passed by during the day: some wheeling barrows and cycles piled high with bedding and blankets. All other belongings left behind. Heaven knows where they are going: into one of our refugee camps, maybe. It is awful to see so many old people trudging painfully along these devastated tracks with so much death and destruction all too apparent.

About 11 a.m., we moved forward into the flank of the salient with the major and 14 Troop. Advanced about 1500 yds – and found three well camouflaged 88s! Two in perfect order, with sighting gear, etc. These must have been the guns which fired spasmodically during last night. They won't fire any more: we smashed them up with HE and AP. A Jerry was found by one of them, crouching in his fox-hole. He looked rather scared. We took him prisoner. He must have been left as a guard or something, but it seems strange to leave one man in this manner. Presumably, the rest of the gun crews would steal back during the night and open fire.

This is the first time we have found 88s really complete: sights are usually removed. But no doubt it was thought quite safe to leave the guns, as they were very well camouflaged. Very heartening to know that three of these guns are now out of action. Quite a worthwhile morning's work.

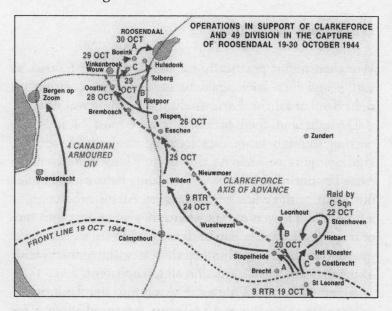

D +138 Sunday 22.10.44

No rain last night, and less enemy gunfire. Had a few hours' sleep. Usual stand to from 6.00–6.30 a.m. Very misty this morning: took extra precautions against surprise. Stray cows much more docile this morning. Several were milked by the boys. 'Simply pissed out,' according to Slade!

Had porridge (looted!) for breakfast, with plenty of sugar (looted), and fresh milk: very good. More refugees ... coming from enemy lines: the same procession of old and young – carrying barest necessities on barrows, prams and bikes: pitiful sight. A pity these youngsters have to see so many dead bodies lying around. They are all German. No time to dispose of them yet.

Eleven a.m.: major called for troop leaders: Something in the wind? Yes: Mr Francis soon returned with orders to stow everything: be ready to move into attack at twelve o'clock. This time, the plan was to make a quick raid into enemy territory, going further in than yesterday, and make a circling move north and then back west: two troops to remain behind on the defensive role ... the rest to carry out the raid, i.e. 13, 14, 15, and HQ.

It is difficult to give a description of an operation of this kind – everything happens so quickly and the enormous concentration upon one's own particular problems leaves little opportunity for observing the whole picture.

However, we crossed the start line at 12 noon, and tore past the three 88s immobilised yesterday in a few minutes. And then our firing commenced. It was like hell let loose. There were twelve vehicles, all going flat out, and firing their guns in all directions except to the rear. Hedgerows, ditches, trees, houses – any mortal thing that could provide cover for Jerries was saturated with MG fire and HE. Terrified horses were running wildly around the fields; cows scampering about, careering through ditches and barbed wire fences: our own vehicles lumbered over ditches, through hedges, across ploughed fields, turnip fields, crashed through plantations, uprooted trees: it was sheer destruction, but rather thrilling – and how terrifying for the enemy!

At one point, my troop leader's vehicle became ditched: it looked rather bad – but somehow the vehicle extricated itself, whilst Dicky and I provided some protection with our guns. This was quite open country, with houses and farm buildings lying fairly well scattered. The nearest were almost 2000 yds: we plastered them pretty well. My gunners put two belts of Besa into one house at 3000 yds, and set it on fire – adding one more blazing pile to the wreckage we were creating.

After half an hour or so, the major admitted over the air that he had lost his bearings – and wasn't sure of his position. This was not surprising. The speed of our advance, plus the type of country made map-reading practically impossible. However, we carried on and now bore to the north, thus approaching some of the area we had been shooting up.

As we neared some of the farms and houses, I was amazed to see civilians standing outside frantically waving white 'flags'. They must have been crazy to have remained in the area, knowing that it was now a battle field. Possibly we killed some of them: we certainly destroyed much of their property. Somehow, I couldn't feel sorry for them. We were fighting for our lives, and we knew that the enemy often concealed his troops and anti-tank guns in houses and farm buildings: the civilians must have known it too. We simply had to be destructive: we couldn't afford to allow sentiment to prevail when dealing with the Hun.

At one point of our journey, the major had a narrow escape. A carefully concealed 75 AT gun opened up at 50 yds – and hit the rim of his 95 gun muzzle. Luckily, the major saw the gun, and his own gun was suitably traversed. Before the enemy could fire a second shot, the major had fired a 95 HE – a direct hit ... And the Jerry gun went up in bits: two more 95s were pumped in – just to make sure! By this time, we seemed to be in an area of scattered houses – and they all had their groups of people, including children, waving white clothes. They seemed to regard these as ample protection! Dicky discovered another gun – this time a 50mm, and shot it up, using HE also on the fleeing crew! No prisoners!!

Eventually, the major gave the order to return to harbour – and so we reached the end of the most hectic two hours I have known for some time. Our 'terror raid' had involved a run of over 7 miles, instead of the four miles previously planned. No wonder the colonel seemed anxious about our whereabouts, over the air. But he congratulated all of us later, and took all details of gun positions, enemy troop locations, etc. I think we did a useful job of reconnaissance, and no doubt killed many Jerries. And we must have terrified many more. Two of them were so anxious to surrender that [*Editor's note: the third diary notebook ends at this point*] they ran after one of our tanks and more or less compelled the commander to have them! This was Frank Hodson: he was certainly amused by the incident.

Later. Today's two prisoners seemed very happy to be with us: they said that most of their comrades were anxious to surrender, but were unable to do so because of their officers' threats to shoot all intending deserters and defeatists. They were waiting for our tanks to advance, they said, to provide an excuse for surrendering. These prisoners disclosed too that there is much friction between the

Wehrmacht and the SS and that they are expected to be in open conflict before long.*

This evening, the horizon to the east is aglow with fires from our day's activities – just a few more homes destroyed: a few more refugees to join the unhappy throng.

D +139 Monday 23.10.44

A quiet night: usual stand to 6.00–6.30 a.m. A US army is taking over today on this sector – relieving 49 Div. We are moving forward – further up the salient, near to Essen on the Dutch border.

Later. Large contingent of US infantry came trudging along the lanes soon after lunch – many hundreds of them. They halted close by for a rest, and we were able to chat with them. Arrived a month ago – Cherbourg. Did not see England. Have not seen action. They seemed a breezy crowd and quite cheerful. We welcome their presence, naturally. Cannot explain their presence here: this was formally Canadian and British sector. I chatted with a few of these Americans: some of them were obviously well educated and intelligent. They were anxious to know everything about the enemy. And how easy it was for me to understand their feelings. Their eager questioning: their thirst for even the minutest detail about the enemy. Their drawn and serious faces – revealing that dreadful anxiety about the future.

---

* There were ideological tensions between the Wehrmacht – the German Army – and the SS, the military wing of the Nazi Party. Many senior Wehrmacht officers believed that Hitler was leading them to disaster, and the German military were deeply involved in the several plots to remove him.

They were now in the front line for the first time: there were many grim reminders of war's predominant feature – death and destruction. The neighbouring farms and cottages were all in ruins: dead cattle lay scattered about the fields: dead bodies too, were not hard to find. The fields were torn and scarred by shells from our barrage of a few days before. No wonder these young fellows were bewildered – and perhaps frightened.

Fortunately, they had arrived on a front where the enemy had been badly shaken and was not showing much anxiety for battle. We had learned during the day that our raid of yesterday had so scared him that he had evacuated a nearby town, and withdrawn further north. I hoped this information was correct – if only for the sake of the American patrols who had already been detailed for an operation this evening.

We departed at 4 p.m., leaving the Americans busily digging in for the night. We harboured near to Wuustwezel, in a field, and bivvied for the night. Tomorrow, we move further north to the tip of the salient – near Essen. A and B are going to stand by against counter attack – C in reserve, for a change!

Today's journey revealed much evidence of the recent battles – dead cattle and horses being very much in evidence. Most of the farmhouses and cottages are in ruins: before several of them the former inhabitants were standing, and some waved as we passed: one or two even smiled! Today, I noticed several dead cows and horses from which the hides had been stripped. It occurred to me that 'blast' was the cause, altho I had seen nothing like it before. Cattle are usually torn to fleshy fragments, or just killed, with little evidence of physical damage.

I learned later that these gruesome carcasses had been stripped by the local civilians and were being cut up for food – both cows and horses – the latter apparently being quite a common food in Belgium.

D +140 Tuesday 24.10.44

Late reveille for once . . . 7.30 a.m. On the move by 9.45 a.m. – via Wuustwezel and so up the salient to Wildert: enemy territory yesterday. A and B are standing by near Essen; we are in reserve. A battle-scarred route today: many civilians groping among the wreckage of their ruined homes. We are once again just forward of our artillery. Already, we have been treated to one or two barrages. Appalling noise – just like being in Normandy.

To bed in bivvies – accompanied by the incessant roar of our artillery.

D +141 Wednesday 25.10.44

Reveille 7 a.m.: a bad night. The enemy first shelled us about 11 p.m., necessitating a hasty retreat from the bivvy to beneath tank: horrible oily mess beneath tank, owing to oil cooler being replaced. After first shelling, three of crew transferred beds to front end of tank on the ground – another went inside: driving seat. Had to remain in bivvy myself – no room elsewhere.

We were shelled and mortared on four occasions throughout the night – and each time I dashed for rear end of tank, sprawling in the oil. Our artillery too were busy practically all night. Practically no sleep: was glad when daylight came, altho it was very cold and misty. Squadron moving to a point one and a half miles north at noon: my vehicle in fitter's hands, so cannot move – but will join squadron later.

Later. A fine evening, but cold. Work nearly finished on vehicle: will be re-joining the squadron this evening (De Loucke). Much activity by our artillery all day. Action planned for tomorrow. Heavy barrage will commence midnight tonight.

D +142 Thursday 26.10.44

Rough night: little sleep owing to barrage. Rejoined sqdn 8 o'clock last evening: barrage commenced midnight: hell let loose.

This a.m., A and B went in at 7 o'clock – A east of Nispen (in Holland again), B to the north. We went in about 10.30 a.m. to take the town. B's flank attack in woods north seemed to have scared most of Jerry from town, but he was waiting for us in nearby country north and east.

Can only describe action from point of view of my troop. We had job of clearing buildings at extreme north of town – and managed this fairly easily. Within an hour, we were among many blazing buildings, and infantry were digging in. But Jerry soon got busy: HE and mortar literally poured down around us: rather frightening, but felt fairly safe in closed turret. Meanwhile, we blazed away at nearby woods and hedges, buildings, farmhouses, etc. Usual trail of destruction and fires. Heard a few APs whizzing danger-ously close: evidently some AT guns about, but we couldn't see them. Heard various reports over the air from other troops: an 88 was reported in one area, SPs in another etc. It was evident that we were not going to be allowed to take Nispen without a fight.

For about a couple of hours, we were heavily shelled and mortared. The enemy were, as usual, completely invisible, but we kept up our fire. Much hard work in the tanks: continuous firing caused heavy fumes – sickness, headaches, etc. Kept moving about, but many of the enemy shots were dangerously close.

Late in the afternoon, 13 reported two enemy tanks firing at close range east of town. Two 13 tanks were disabled: crews baled out. Major ordered 15 to proceed to the area and give assistance. Felt horribly uncomfortable sitting out there in the open, near disabled tanks, waiting for Jerry to open up on us. But he only sent two or three loads of HE – no AP. We were lucky. Later on, a large explosion revealed that the enemy had blown bridge across river east of town: he was evidently 'pulling out'...

Towards evening was very thankful to hear major order the troop to retire to fwd. rally – other tanks of the sqdn having meanwhile been brought forward to relieve us. Don't think we could have endured much longer. Crew had worked very hard and had had no food since hurried breakfast: fumes too made matters much worse. And the strain of waiting to be 'shot up' – it is indescribable.

Cannot assess damage, but we must have punished Jerry: some prisoners taken and a few guns disabled – to say nothing of damage done by supporting artillery.

Finally withdrew about 5.30 p.m. to a point about 400 yds west of town – still very close! Days casualties might have been much worse had enemy fire been more accurate.

Sgt Tomney seriously wounded.* Also Capt Kidd (A) wounded, Sgt Virgo (B) seriously wounded.

C had two vehicles disabled, one brought in this evening, the other still to be recovered. A bad day for all of us on the whole: one of the worst we have had. Much fine work by the major, as usual.

D +143 Friday 27.10.44

Miserable night: too close to enemy to bother with bedding. Had hurried meal, and then dug holes in anticipation of mortaring during night. On guard until 1 a.m., and then tried to sleep beneath vehicle tarpaulin – with little success. Damnably cold for one thing ... and the enemy caused usual disturbance with mortar.

Stand to 6.00–6.30 a.m. Breakfast about 7.30. Troop 11 and 12 are out in fwd. position this morning. Expect we will relieve them soon. Spasmodic mortaring on Nispen this morning, but the infantry are now well consolidated, and Jerry will never shift us.

Horribly cold this morning: damp and misty. Managed to wash and shave in hot water ... but am longing for a decent hot bath, and some real warmth ...

Later: 14 and 15 moved forward to relieve 11 and 12 about 2 o'clock, but recalled an hour later to stand by for possible trouble on Essen sector.

Fair amount of mortar coming over, but mostly on village: we seem fairly safe here, 300 yds to west. Raining this

* Sergeant Tomney was later awarded the Military Medal for his part in this action.

evening: should hate to be conscious under more depressing conditions ... Have dug hole beneath vehicle – for safety against mortars.

D +144 Saturday 28.10.44

Miserable night: cold, wet and cheerless. Tried to read in turret, but too many leaks. To bed at 9.30 p.m. Called at midnight for guard: blankets saturated – oil and water running through inspection plates. Reorganised bedding after guard, but little comfort. Stand to 6.30–7.00 this morning. Weather cold and misty, but not raining. Sun came out about eight – a chance to dry bedding, if we don't move.

Fair amount of mortaring last night – our artillery very active. Something happened north ... maybe around Roosendaal. Believe we will be heading in that direction soon. 107* are reported to have met SPs!

Wish the mail would arrive: haven't heard from Jess for about five days.

D +145 Sunday 29.10.44

Two days have elapsed since I wrote the foregoing – rather bad days – and my mind is a bit confused, but I want to try and record events in sequence. We moved out last evening from Nispen at about 5 p.m., and headed westwards: we had no orders, but were aware of several rumours concerning

---

* 107 RAC (Royal Armoured Corps).

107, who were reported to have had a hammering during the day: it seemed fairly obvious that we were taking over from them on the left flank of the salient.

We eventually harboured close to the village of Wouwsche Hil – a three-mile journey through the usual scenes of destruction and death. Dead cows littered the fields: dead Germans lay by the roadsides: derelict houses and farms: smashed up telegraph poles: scarred and torn trees ... Our harbour was an open field: to our front (N) about a mile away, several buildings were blazing, the whole forward horizon was, in fact, a mass of blazing buildings. And that was where the enemy were ...

The major was obviously uneasy about the situation. We harboured in the darkness, and the absence of orders or 'information' left him in an unenviable position. The enemy may have been nearer than presumed – and it was doubtful whether there was a screen of our infantry ahead of us. And so, we had to be on the alert all night – one man in each vehicle acting as observer throughout the night.

107 had been taken by surprise the morning before, some SPs having drawn up close during the night, and they were shot up in harbour the following morning. We had to avoid a repetition of that.

We went to bed, beneath the vehicle, not knowing what the morrow held in store, but expecting the worst. There were too many signs of heavy fighting for our presence there to be merely defensive. Until late in the evening, we had witnessed signs of a battle about a mile to the west – a bitter battle, it sounded.

Reveille this morning was 5.30 a.m., with all kit stowed and vehicle ready for action by 6 a.m. – just in case some SPs tried to catch us as they had caught 107. But nothing

happened, and we were able to stand down and have breakfast at 7.30. Meanwhile, we learned of the orders which had
been issued during the night. We were going into battle that
morning – the whole battalion, each squadron having an
individual role to play. C's objective the village of
Vinkenbroek about 2000 yds due north, and 400 yds beyond
the railway running across our front. A's objective the village
of Boeiink – about 600 yds further north. B were going in to
our right – one of the suburbs of Roosendaal.

The surrounding country was very flat, and quite open,
but fairly well infested with ditches and drainage channels,
as is most of the country in this area. We know little about
the enemy, other than that he had some SPs in the area.
Our infantry were the H—shires (Crevecoeur!).* At about
12 noon, C went in. 11 and 12 took up hull down positions
behind the railway embankment to protect the right flank.
13, 14, 15 and HQ then crossed the railway and turned left
– running across the southern front of the village. This
move was made at speed, with all guns trained on the
village 400 yds away. We poured shot and shell into every
building, shed, bush and ditch which could possibly
harbour the enemy.

We ran diagonally towards the western edge of the village
– about 1000 yds run, and reached this point without trouble, altho two or three vehicles had difficulty in the heavy
ground and were ditched for a time. 15 Troop were on the
extreme left of our advance; we took up positions behind
some burning buildings on the main road through the
village. And at about this time, our infantry approached
from the railway embankment . . . I was glad to see them.

* The Hallams again.

We received orders to move a little further forward – to protect the infantry from possible enemy fire from Boeiink – and then the fun started.

My troop leader, Mr Francis, moved out to cross the road, and I followed. Through my periscope I saw Mr Francis's vehicle make a quick dash back to the protection of the house. Had he been fired at? I wasn't left long in doubt. There came a heavy bang, and bits of debris fell into the turret. My vehicle shook a bit, and the crew swore we had been hit. I ordered the driver to reverse, and the vehicle responded immediately – the hit had apparently left us undamaged. We went back painfully slowly, our right and rear being meanwhile completely exposed to the north and north east, from where the shots appeared to come.

Each second of that journey back seemed an age. Each moment I expected to be hit again: and how damnably provoking that we couldn't fire back. I had no idea of the precise location of whatever was firing – either an AT gun or an SP. The enemy were, as usual, using flashless ammo, and were exceedingly well camouflaged. I scanned the presumed location of the gun, using binoculars, but could see nothing – only houses and haystacks and innocent look-ing bushes.

Our journey in reverse was only about 40 yards, but it was one of the longest runs I have ever known. I cannot describe my relief when eventually we got round to the rear side of that house – snuggling as near to it as possible, even though it was blazing. My troop officer was already there, appar-ently unharmed.

Soon he moved forward a little and ordered me further back, to observe around the western side of the house . . . And then I noticed the major clambering from his vehicle about 30 yds ahead. He had been hit – presumably by the same gun. His crew seemed to bale out alright, altho the major had to assist one man from the track cover. Three of his crew lay down in a nearby ditch, and the major chased off to the rear – and I soon had his voice on the air again requesting medical help for his wounded crew. He had boarded another vehicle, and taken command again almost immediately. It was good to hear him over the air assuring the colonel that he was absolutely alright and unharmed.

A little later, only a minute or two, I heard the characteristic swish of an AP, followed by a terrible bang, immediately to my right . . . I looked and saw Mr Francis and some of his crew clambering from their vehicle: he had been hit and was wisely baling out instantly. Mr Francis didn't look so good. Meanwhile, Dicky Hall's vehicle, further to the right, had become ditched, and his crew had baled out and were sheltering behind their vehicle: I believe Mr Francis joined them. The next few moments were sickening. The enemy must have known my vehicle was hiding, but apparently he couldn't see me. Nevertheless, he kept firing, and hit Mr F's vehicle a second time, and followed this by a few random shots in my direction. I cannot imagine a more terrifying sound than the vicious hiss of those rounds as they whizzed by, so close to my vehicle. We seemed to have been literally condemned to death – with no chance of retaliating. Thinking became difficult: every single fibre and nerve being too occupied in trying to see from where the shots were fired. There were anxious mutterings from my crew over the IC – I could do nothing but try to reassure them: we *couldn't* bale out from an apparently undamaged vehicle. But the temptation can perhaps be imagined. During my terror-stricken searching for the enemy, I looked to the rear – back to the railway line – and my heart gave a leap as I beheld a number of tanks, followed by infantry, approaching rapidly. It was A Squadron. They had commenced their attack, and were going to pass beyond us, and so on to Boeiink beyond. How grateful I was to see those tanks, and how my heart warmed towards A . . . I didn't then know what lay in store for them . . .

About this time, Mr Francis signalled for me to lay a smoke screen to enable him to rescue the wounded from his vehicle: this was soon done. A little later, Mr Francis himself appeared on top of my vehicle – I knew instinctively that he was taking my place, and I baled out at once . . . sorry to be leaving my crew. In a few seconds I had crawled to comparative safety behind Dicky Hall's tank, stopping en route by the side door of Mr Francis's vehicle to try and drag out his co-driver, Jimmy Smith. Mr F had asked me to do this as I left him: I doubt whether I would have thought of it, even had I known Smith was still in the vehicle. But one glance convinced me that Smith was beyond earthly aid. Already his eyes were glazing and staring horribly: his mouth was open, and skin already turning that ghastly grey-yellow of death. He was on the exposed side of the vehicle, and so I wasted no time seeking cover.

Dicky's crew were all quite OK, but Mr Francis's driver, Titch Mead, was lying on the ground in a pool of blood. His left leg had been almost amputated: and his left hand badly injured – but he was conscious, and making no complaint. Dicky was fixing a tourniquet to his leg and others were improvising a rough stretcher from two gun-cleaning poles and an overcoat.

How on earth Mead was removed from his vehicle I don't know, but Dicky told me later that they had to give him two ampules of chloroform before he 'went out'. And a little later, Dicky injected a dose of morphia. How grand to have a chap like Dicky around in such an emergency. How I admired him: and what gallantry on the part of all of them in dragging Mead from that vehicle under heavy fire. It was a bit of a job to place Mead on that crude stretcher, but we managed it – and the rough splint on his leg remained in position. And now Wilde and Thomas crawled away in search of an ambulance or stretcher-bearers. Mead accepted a cigarette—!

Meanwhile, Mr Francis had drawn away in my vehicle – leaving the shelter of the house in the protection of a smoke screen. I heard nothing more of him until much later. Dicky and I crawled back to have a final glimpse of Smith, but he was now dead: we left him and crawled back to our refuge beside Dicky's tank.

Wilde and Thomas soon returned with the information that there was a first aid post in the brickworks about half a mile to our rear. It seemed a hopeless business trying to carry Mead so far on the crazy stretcher – but something had to be done, and Dicky said, 'let's go'. And that was the beginning of a horrible journey. There were six of us, besides Mead, and we learned that a human body is a heavy load, especially when the route includes ditches and ploughed fields torn by tank tracks. It must have taken us almost an hour to reach that brickworks: an hour of very unpleasant recollections, including enemy fire and fatigue. Dicky worked like a horse – and Mead made little complaint, even when we stumbled and heaved him across the ditches.

At the brickworks, the ambulance was waiting, and we parted with our colleague, thankful to have got him away from that hell on earth ... And now we returned to the tanks – the battle having moved a little further north. On this return journey, I saw a little of the price paid by A in making their advance beyond our original objective. There were at least half a dozen disabled tanks lying out in the open, and at least one blazing furiously. The crews who had baled out were returning southwards, some of them supporting wounded colleagues. God knows what had happened, but it seemed obvious that the enemy had been well prepared to deal with a tank attack.

It was some consolation to see batches of prisoners being marched back by our infantry – the latter grinning cheerfully, the former dirty and dishevelled, but seemingly quite happy.

We reached Dicky's vehicle without mishap and the crew started unloading their personal kit. Eddie Wilde, stout fella!, started to make a brew. Dicky and I and one or two others returned to Mr Francis's vehicle – and dragged out Smith. He was by now a ghastly sight. It was difficult to drag his body from the vehicle and eventually Dicky had to lever his limbs whilst two of us dragged from the outside. His body then came out – leaving most of his legs in the vehicle: he had been cut in two by an AP, and must have died from loss of blood very quickly.

We lay the body on the ground and covered it with a tarpaulin. I felt rather sick ... Back again to Dicky's tank – and a cup of tea. What a grand drink that was! By now, the battle had passed its peak, and the entire neighbourhood was a mass of blazing buildings, and damaged tanks. Major Mockford (A) appeared from somewhere on foot. He looked pretty bad and told us that he only had three tanks left! He passed on, looking for HQ. I couldn't help wondering what had happened to the rest of C – and those lads in my vehicle ...

After our cup of tea, during which several AP shots whistled overhead uncomfortably low, all personal kit was collected and the two tanks closed up. We then returned to the brickworks. Someone there had very kindly made tea, and we had another drink. It was here that I overheard the colonel of the infantry inform our 2nd in command that he had only had four casualties all day, all wounded, 'thanks to the assistance of the tanks'. He added, 'I hope you haven't many casualties'—! I was glad to hear that tribute: it is something to know that our efforts are of some use to those grand infantry lads. But I knew that our casualties would far exceed those for the infantry.

Our HQ Squadron tanks had by now taken up a position behind the railway, about half a mile from the brickworks ... and they were our next objective. Once again we had tea, provided by HQ crews from their own rations – and we answered a few questions from the colonel. And then C Squadron tanks appeared – and I was darned thankful to see almost a full squadron of tanks, including my own. The major too was with them.

I joined my crew, and a hot dinner was soon being prepared ... and yarns swapped. But everyone looked pretty ghastly. The day had left its mark, alright. The major had been hit in the head with shrapnel from an HE, but he seemed cheerful enough, and dismissed the wound very lightly. A very brave man, and a great leader. Our meal in this location was interrupted by a few rounds of HE and one or two air bursts. It was not a healthy spot, so we had to move to a harbour near our original start point. And there we eventually dug in and slept ...

Unfortunately, before bedding down, it became known that another infantry colonel (the Koyli's) had been requesting our assistance for an assault the following day on Roosendaal. This was dreadful news. We were all exhausted, and had had enough to last us for a long time. And an attack on a large town like Roosendaal—! Well, no wonder we were worried: personally, I felt terrified of going in again so soon – especially with so many SPs in the neighbourhood.

But we slept, and did our guard during the night. B's action had proceeded very well. They met little opposition, and suffered no casualties.

D +146 Monday 30.10.44

This morning, I learned a few results of yesterday's action.

C had one killed and four wounded – three of the latter in the major's tank, and one in Mr Francis's. A had eight killed and six wounded. Vehicles I am not sure of – C had the major's and Mr Francis's disabled by AP . . . both recoverable. Dicky Hall's vehicle was OK, but still badly ditched. At least one of A's burned out – a write-off. Five or six others were hit by AP, and two or three badly ditched . . .

The infantry took 80 prisoners – probably most of the enemy infantry in the villages. I don't think any of the SP crews were captured, but believe a couple of 75 ATs were knocked out.

Saw Noel Wright this morning. He has been back with tanks since Auffay. He survived yesterday's ordeal, but looked ill and much older . . .

In yesterday's action, the 'hit' on my vehicle caused a bit of amusement later. The shot had dislodged a tin box from the rear, and gone clean through the enormous bedding roll strapped to the rear of the tank: no other damage. There were four sleeping kits in that roll of bedding – and we debated upon whose blankets had been ruined. When we opened the bundle, it was found that my bedding had been hit – and what a mess it was! The blankets were a mass of large holes: my denims in shreds, and gas-cape torn to pieces. Pedder remarked philosophically that I ought to be thankful not to have been sleeping in them at the time - so 'stop ticking'. I slept in the torn blankets last night, but have had them replaced today.

We learned this morning that Roosendaal was definitely being attacked today, and that some of our vehicles were going in with the infantry, the Koylis. In view of our battered state, the tanks were pooled and about nine of them detailed for the job. The reactions of the crews can be imagined. It looked like being a hell of a battle.

I was thankful to have my vehicle left out of the first phase of the attack, but I had to stand by to go in as reserve, if necessary. The next four hours were a nightmare. We seemed to get little news over the air from the attacking force, and their fate was a mystery. Meanwhile I waited for the worst – hoping and hoping . . .

After lunch, rumours started spreading that our tanks had entered the town without opposition – a state of affairs which seemed too good to be true. But it *was* true, thank heaven. Jerry had apparently had enough and had withdrawn early that morning, demolishing a few bridges, etc. as he left. I don't know precisely what happened as our tanks entered the town, but our lads appear to have received a tremendous welcome from the inhabitants. There was not a great deal of damage, and most of the civilians were still in the place.

The easy capture of Roosendaal was a piece of great

good fortune for our lads. They were hardly in a condition to endure a further battle, and the obvious delight
and happiness of the civilians was some compensation
for their ordeal.

Mr Francis with the remainder of his crew has taken over
my vehicle – thus leaving self and Pedder and Pestell
dismounted. But later, we were put in charge of the major's
damaged vehicle, with orders to drive it back to LAD at
Essen the following day. We thus spent the night at
Wouwsche Hil alone – the unit having moved on to
Roosendaal to harbour for the night.

Dutch civilians celebrate the arrival of the first British tank to enter
Roosendaal on 30 October.

Photograph © IWM B11482.

The three of us slept in a partly derelict tavern. There was plenty of straw on the floor – and a large fire burning in the Dutch oven. The latter was a grand sight. We experienced real warmth for the first time for days. It was certainly a snug little billet. Slept without trousers for first time in about ten days. There has been much sorting out of crews etc. today in the squadron, but it will take some time for us to get reorganised. Nine dead bodies taken to Roosendaal for burying.

D +147 Tuesday 31.10.44

Slept rather too well last night. Instead of being ready to move to Essen at 8 a.m. with the major's disabled tank, we were still in bed. Had leisurely breakfast and good wash and shave, and departed about 10.30 a.m. Our five- or six-mile run to Essen seemed strangely peaceful in view of the awful battles in the vicinity but a few days before.

Nispen looked pretty battered, but many houses were still standing and the inhabitants were already clearing up the streets and repairing damaged homes. There was much traffic on the roads, too ... the same roads had been absolutely deserted last Thursday when we fought for the place. I saw no civilians either, then – but now there are plenty of them.

Reached Essen lunch time. This place too showed many scars from recent fighting, but houses were being patched up here and there. Harboured the vehicle and patched it up a bit, fitting 2 new track plates. EME has decided to tackle repairs without troubling Brig: so we are moving with his staff tomorrow to Roosendaal. Think the tank will make the journey. Am acting as driver.

Pedder and Pestell have recced civvy billets for our sleep tonight. They have found a deserted house fully furnished and am sleeping on a real mattress for a change.

Later. As usual, no lav or bathroom in the house: water by hand pump in tiny kitchen. Have discovered convenient gutter beneath bedroom window. This, plus a bucket, will obviate a cold journey out to the back during the night! Pedder and Pestell out all evening – as usual. Chatting and drinking with Belgian family. Heaven knows how they converse. The language here is Flemish.

D +148 Wednesday 1.11.44

Reveille 6 a.m., but that mattress was so comfortable: we got up at 7.25 a.m. – and our orders were to be ready to move by 8 a.m.! Bit of a flap, but we made it – and thanks to a late start, we also had breakfast. Drove vehicle to Roosendaal – no trouble, apart from losing a bogey.

Found unit billeted in schools etc. Besieged by civvies when we arrived with our little column of eight battered tanks. Much excitement caused by two gaping holes in side of my vehicle. Signed several autographs for benefit of youngsters.

Did a little work on vehicle in preparation for welding and patching. Am rejoining troop tomorrow. Mr Francis now has another vehicle, Dicky Hall's has been un-ditched, so am taking back my Ironside.* Pedder being relieved by Hopkins – don't know why. Sleeping tonight with troop in school.

---

* All the tanks in 9 RTR had names beginning with 'I'. The CO's tank was Iron Duke. Others included Iceni, Inferno and Indomitable.

D +149 Thursday 2.11.44

Slept in 'sergeants' room' last night, on wooden floor. Not bad billets, but no water or lavatories: Troops sleeping on second floor in enormous loft.

Reveille 7 a.m. – but in bed until nearly eight. Good breakfast ... and then a spot of work on the vehicle. It has been cleaned up very nicely in my absence. 13 Troop temporarily disbanded owing to shortage of vehicles, etc. Hopkins now my operator. Pedder back with 'B' Echelon. Ceased work mid-morning, and sorted kit, etc. Am hoping for a chance to do some clothes washing now that we appear to be settled down for a bit. Longing for a bath: must be three weeks since I had one – or changed my clothes.

Later. Had a shower this afternoon: rather draughty 'bathroom' in a marquee, but a godsend under the circumstances. Ensa concert this evening: quite a good show.

D +150 Friday 3.11.44

Same routine as yesterday. About an hour's work on vehicle this morning. Lecture by major on demob scheme at 11 a.m. Football match this afternoon. Wrote to Jess ... and a little reading.

Weather fairly cold – very draughty in this windowless school, but palatial by comparison with bivvies. There was a little commotion in the town last evening, and evening before. Civvies and Maquis rounding up more 'collaborators' – especially women. Saw a batch of about 50 male collaborators carrying spades and being marched under armed escort this morning. Presume they were members of the local Nazi party. Probably being forced to do excavating and repair work.

This town is still fairly lifeless. There is very little food, no gas or electricity or water supply, and all cafés and bars are closed. But believe there are one or two shops open. Some of the lads have managed to buy a few cosmetics.

My crew prepared our tea meal in the main street by the vehicle on Wednesday evening. A large crowd of civilians gathered round and the whole business became very embarrassing. Our white bread caused much comment, and one lady with two little boys asked me to let them each have half a slice of bread and butter. And then she wanted to buy some butter from us! Another lady howled with amazement when she saw Pestell using butter to fry sausages. I didn't enjoy that meal: there were too many hungry eyes upon us. Believe there will be a limited electricity supply by this evening . . .

Later. Went to an army cinema show – saw *Melody Inn*. Electricity supply is on this evening, but not in our room, altho the ground floor is lit up.

Very heavy artillery barrage all last night. Our guns are only a few miles north and their noise literally shakes this high building. Also much AA to the east last evening. It seemed a long way off, and may have been our heavy raid on Duisburg.* It was a beautiful moonlit night: cold and clear. Enjoyed gazing at the moon through binocs.

A dull day today: some rain, and fairly cold.

* Duisburg was heavily bombed on 14 and 15 October. The raid on 2 and 3 November was on Düsseldorf. Seven industrial sites were destroyed, and eighteen badly damaged, along with 5,000 houses.

D +151 Saturday 4.11.44

A fine morning: usual routine. Two of my crew going to
Brussels tomorrow morning for 48 hours leave. We are
having this leave on a rota basis: believe it is Gen
Montgomery's idea – for all troops to have 48 hours leave
after 6 months' active service.

Still no word of any further action for us. But there are
still many Germans this side of the river. Believe the country immediately north is unsuitable for us: too many canals
and ditches for heavy tanks. There must be some big move
pending. Maybe the 2nd Army and the Americans will
commence major offensive as soon as Antwerp is entirely
freed – this should be within the next day or two.

Later. Arrangements were made this morning for C to
change places with HQ at 2 p.m., i.e. C to transfer to nearby
school to allow all HQ to be housed in our school, and
under one roof. Consequently, we were all packed up ready
for the transfer at 2 p.m. . . . and then the fire started—!!! I
was in the sgts' room on the first floor and noticed a smell of
burning: about the same time somebody said, 'is the bloody
place on fire?' It certainly smelled like it. I rushed out and
down the main stairway – and there, in the large hall to the
right, on the ground floor, I noticed great tongues of flame
leaping to the ceiling, and a tremendous amount of black
heavy smoke. Breathing was difficult, and I used a hanky to
gag myself.

This was a real fire and no mistake, but why on earth
hadn't someone warned us? I was able to rush back up the
stairs and up to the second floor where most of the tank
crews were preparing their kits for the removal. By now,

some smoke had reached this upper floor, and so my fire warning was believed immediately, and most of the fellows chased down the stairs. I went back to the lower floor and found the fire now partly engulfing the main stairway – but most of our lads seemed to have got out.

The sergeants' room was by now a dense mass of smoke, but there was fresh air by the windows. I hung out my head for air, and there down below were several of my colleagues asking for their kit which had been left in the sgts' room. I started to chuck it out – valises, bedding, overcoats, haversacks – piles of the stuff went out of those windows. I was now joined by an HQ sgt and a trooper. The latter had lost himself somehow and was looking for a way down.

We quickly joined some blankets, and he slid down safely to earth. And now the sgts' room was clear of kit. I went upstairs again – groping my way through the now dense black smoke, and found that Mr Lilly was up there with one or two helpers – pouring stuff down to the lower floor, from where it was pitched through the windows. There was a great mass of stuff – including men's kit, bedding, food boxes, cookers, etc. – all the paraphernalia of the fighting members of the squadron, in fact.

We got rid of practically all of it, the smoke meanwhile becoming less dense. The wind had shifted, and was now blowing the fire away from our wing of the school. I went to the main stairway, but it was impassable. A few more fellows escaped via blanket ladders, and then someone appeared with a long ladder. This helped us to get out more kit.

The civvy fire engine arrived – and water was soon being poured into the building. I was surprised to see the fire hoses working because I understood there was no water supply in the town. Well, after about an hour, during which the entire battn staff had appeared outside, we had cleared most of the kit – and the fire seemed to be under control: I went to the main stairway and managed to get past the flames: they were now in check, thanks to the hoses. Outside, I was amazed to learn that there had been some casualties.

Apparently, some of the crews had remained on the second floor after my hurried warning. A few moments later, the terrific cloud of smoke must have scared them. They did not know that the stairway was clear to the floor below, where I was pitching out the sgts' kit. So they went to the windows – second storey windows in a high building – and jumped into blankets held by colleagues down below! A crazy business really – but fire seems to cause panic more rapidly than anything else. Anyhow, a few fellows were hurt – particularly my own troop, *viz.* Cpl Davis, broken leg, L/c Oakley fractured rib, Tpr Ward injured back (may be really serious). Also Ridgers and Gardner (14 Troop) injuries and shock.

One or two other fellows were hurt due to falling off ladders, etc., but nothing serious. The fire was ultimately put out – but there was a glorious mess of kit lying around in the mud. And what a job sorting it all out! We found most of our stuff, and transferred ourselves to the new school – and HQ had to be content with occupying the undamaged portion of our late billet. Fortunately, the fire was kept mainly on the ground floor, and only about a quarter of the building was destroyed. So HQ have the remaining three-quarters all to themselves. But it is a very smelly three-quarters now.

The fire and subsequent excitement occupied the entire afternoon. We just had time to find our new sleeping quarters before dark. C have certainly gained by the change.

Here there is electric light, water in the taps, and genuine WCs – the first I have seen since leaving England – complete with chain, etc.—! Presumably the fire will necessitate a 'court of enquiry' and the issue of much new kit. The casualties too will involve more troop changes. Ward, my driver, was due to go to Brussels for 48 hrs in the morning. Slade is now going instead. He has earned a rest anyway . . .

D +152 Sunday 5.11.44

A quiet day today. Attended a lecture this morning on the demob scheme – this time by a major who is specialising on the job. The War Office seem anxious for us to be thoroughly conversant with this business.

Tpr Ward turned up this morning – much to our amazement. We had thought of him as having an injured spine or something, but he was only shaken up, and was discharged from hospital this morning. Spent the afternoon reading newspapers . . . and a letter from Jess. Did some writing. Raining very hard. Heavy artillery barrage north – in spite of the rain.

D +153 Monday 6.11.44

Breakfast provided by cooks this a.m. First cook's meal for many weeks. C have always opposed communal cooking when in static positions because the men prefer compo packs. But Saturday's fire has forced the colonel to prohibit petrol cookers in the billets. Started the day with a parade at 8.30 a.m., and then a spot of work on the vehicle, followed by a kit check at 11 a.m. – to enable the men to indent for kit to replace that lost in the fire. Football match this afternoon . . . and a passion truck to Antwerp.

Mr Francis still absent from the troop. He sprained his leg (cartilage or something) when he baled out last week. Heard today that Ken Virgo has died from his wounds – on the 31st, I believe. It is a miracle that he has survived so long. A good bloke gone – and the only MM in the unit.

Fairly fine all day, but rather breezy and cold. It would be much warmer in this school if we had a few windows. But I s'pose we are lucky to have a roof over our heads. Electric light too is a godsend. We hang blankets across the gaping windows to serve as blackouts.

D +154 Tuesday 7.11.44

Usual morning routine. Went to Antwerp after lunch with Dicky Hall, Bob Andman, Ernie Bottoms, Reg Mead. About 28-mile run – arrived soon after 2 p.m. Practically no damage in the city, but a few houses destroyed in suburbs. Antwerp is very similar to any English city: the architecture is the same, and the shops little different – multiple stores, etc. Also trams. There appears to be no shortage of luxury goods – fountain pens, photo supplies, cosmetics, etc. Children's toys too seem plentiful, but prices are pretty high. Most of the restaurants seem to be open, but cannot say whether food is plentiful – probably not, apart from fruit and fancy cakes. The latter do seem plentiful: had several at a multiple store – we ate them like schoolboys standing at the counter. Also ice cream.

Bought first present for Barry – a rabbit. Also some scent

for Jess. Had tea in canteen for WOs and sgts – Hotel Metropole, I think. Separate Naafi for lower ranks, complete with band, etc.

Saw part of the dock area: it seemed very tidy and completely free from damage, altho I am told that Jerry is now sending rocket bombs into the town. The port should soon be in full use now that Jerry has been pushed to the north. We never realised the importance of the recent offensive when we started from St Leonard – but it has certainly been of major importance.*

D +155 Wednesday 8.11.44

Usual morning routine. We seem to be having an incredibly easy time lately: about 2 hours work on the vehicle each morning, and then we are free. Passion trucks for Antwerp each day at 1 p.m. – cinema shows, Ensa, etc. Many of the lads are (unofficially) in civvy billets and seem to be enjoying their comparative comfort. Horrible weather: wet, cold and windy. Did some shopping in Roosendaal – powder, etc. for Jess. Spent rest of day trying to keep warm – and reading.

* The capture of Antwerp and the opening up of the Scheldt Estuary provided a much-needed supply line for the Allies. It also took some of the pressure off the US VIII Corps further south along the Channel coast, where the German defence of the Brittany ports had been proving hard to crack.

D +156 Thursday 9.11.44

Usual routine. Did some writing this afternoon, but too cold to sit down for long. Received 200 ciggies from Plowman. Went to Ensa show this morning. I knew it was a classical concert – having been informed by Les Challinor who went in the afternoon. Unfortunately, the rest of the audience – some hundreds from other units – expected the usual Ensa variety show – and they did not try to conceal their disappointment. Dicky Hall and I were together, and both experienced the same feeling of shame and embarassment as the artists were 'barracked'. It was an excellent concert, but far too good for the troops. There were 6 girls and one male – *viz.* violin, cello, piano, classical dancer, soprano, contralto – and tenor. They arrived from England a week ago – all volunteers. The intention is to provide decent music for the forces. I hope their future concerts are properly advertised as classical. It is a damned shame for such fine artists to be treated almost with derision by gangs of jazz-crazy nitwits ...

D +157 Friday 10.11.44

Usual morning routine. Beastly weather – cold and windy and raining very hard. Received issue of short woollen underpants and gloves. This afternoon, went to Fort de Breendonck – an erstwhile Gestapo headquarters and torture chamber about 6 miles south of Antwerp. The party consisted of five members from each squadron: Dicky Hall, Bob Anderson, Ernie Cooper and Reg Mead were with me. The object of the trip was to allow us to see something of the methods of the Gestapo. The fort is one of a number surrounding Antwerp, built by the Belgians – presumably some time about the last war. The plaque on the entrance bears the dates 1914–1918.

The fort itself was a concrete structure, roughly about 150 yds square, and surrounded by a moat about 40 ft wide and 10 ft deep. The entrance was approached via a short roadway lined with concrete posts – all heavily draped with steel spikes and barbed wire: this barbed wire fencing encircled the entire area of the fort and moat. We crossed the moat via a drawbridge, and were immediately inside a long tunnel-like archway stretching about 70 yds ahead of us. There were various passages running off this central aisle: all concrete, cold and depressing: light was provided by electricity – no windows.

We were put in charge of a Belgian youth who spoke fairly good English: his first remarks were disappointing – he had no key to the torture chamber itself, nor was there one available just then – but he would show us around the rest of the place. First we saw some cells measuring about 6 ft x 8 ft in which five or six prisoners had to sleep: there were no windows to the cells, and the inmates had to live in complete darkness: there was no doubt about the intensity of the darkness, the walls being of reinforced concrete about 10 ft thick. We were told that prisoners usually spent four days in these cells.

We saw other cells, much smaller, each made to hold one man. And we saw the dirty and insanitary sleeping quarters of the Jews. Incidentally, the 'prison' was used for Belgian political prisoners, and anyone suspected of underground activity. The staff consisted of negroes (Belgian Congo?) supervised by Gestapo men.

From the top of the fort, we were able to see the former gun emplacements, now stripped, and the enormous amount of work put in under Gestapo supervision to unearth the main body of the fort buildings. When originally built, only the upper part of the gun emplacements, with a few air towers, were above ground – but now the entire fort is visible. It seems obvious that the moat too is German built: it cannot have been part of the original design. At the rear, we saw ten wooden pillars erected vertically in the ground – about 30 feet from the wall of the fort and 6 feet apart. To these pillars used to be strapped the bodies of men who had been condemned to be shot: a few bullet marks were quite visible in the wall behind. We were told that 400 Belgians were shot in this manner at this particular prison. Close to this shooting 'gallery', there was a crude gallows – consisting of a low stage with a trap door, and a beam overhead to carry the rope. We were told that three Belgians had been hanged on this contraption. Not having seen the underground torture chamber, I cannot describe it. But I believe the Germans destroyed most of their implements before departing. We were told that everything has been thoroughly photographed and filmed, so no doubt the world will be made aware of this frightful place.

Our troops occupied the area very quickly, and the negro staff were captured – and subsequently imprisoned with other collaborators. But the building is now being used to house some of our own troops. I don't envy them. It is a detestable place – dark and cold and evil looking.

Spent a couple of hours in Antwerp on return journey. Had tea at the sergeants' canteen – and then nearly made ourselves sick with fancy cakes and ice cream dishes at a nearby shop. Two flying bombs landed in the city as we departed.

D +158 Saturday 11.11.44

Usual morning routine – with a lecture on VD by the MO at 11 a.m. Spent afternoon reading and writing. Issued with new overall suits. Very cold: very wet: very miserable. Found bed the warmest place, especially for my feet. Squadron dance this evening. A huge success, and very large attendance – especially civvies. Perhaps the 'loudspeakers' mobile equipment which toured the town this morning brought the crowds. We were advertised as the first tanks to enter Roosendaal! Rather a blow to A and B, but quite truthful.

Male civvies had to leave at 9 p.m. owing to the curfew – and the Maquis saw that they departed! But females were allowed to stay: they were assured of a 'military escort' home later. Believe the dance finished about 12.30 a.m. Only stayed an hour myself. Sent parcel to Jess. Learned that Gardner, Ridgers and Davis are all in England now – after injuries received through baling out from blazing building last week. Gardner has sprained back or spine, Ridgers broken heel, Davis broken leg. Saw Mr Francis for first time in a week.

D +159 Sunday 12.11.44

Sunday routine: returned to bed after breakfast for warmth. Some of the fellows on church parade, others playing off rounds of the inter-troop football. A wet day – cold and windy as usual. Did more writing and reading.

D +160 Monday 13.11.44

Took vehicle for test run this morning – via Boeiink, Wouw. Was able to see our last battle ground from opposite side, Vinkenbroek, etc. Another dance organised for tomorrow evening. Spent the afternoon with a few 'pupils' who have to undergo a brigade test tomorrow:* A complete farce. They are already being paid as tradesmen – mustered on account of casualties – but they have to have this test to satisfy red-tape officialdom. Johnny 'Tiger' Boland returned to sqdn today from TDU. Had a few words with him. Doubt whether he will ever rejoin tank crews. His son now reported missing, presumed killed.

D +161 Tuesday 14.11.44

Up early this morning to take driver mechs to 147† at Sprundel for brigade test. Left them and returned to Roosendaal, and went with Boland into town – looking for 'hot sweet'! Had a queer blend of 'Koffie'. Collected 'pupils' again at 1 p.m. Pay parade this afternoon. More rounds of inter-troop football today. Dance this evening. Spent the morning in bed – writing and reading. Hot soup when the dancers returned about midnight.

D +162 Wednesday 15.11.44

Usual morning routine. Inter-troop football at 11 a.m.: 15

* Trevor was operating as an instructor to the 'driver mechs' – driver/mechanics.
† 147 Regiment, RAC (Royal Armoured Corps).

Troop beaten by HQ Troop in semi final. Last night's dance very successful – judging by all reports. We are changing into new billets after lunch. Our present school is very cold, due to broken windows: no heating system, either.

Later. It seems too good to be true. We are now in fresh billets – in centre of town. An uninhabited café cum bar cum billiard saloon with a small 'theatre' at the rear. Men are sleeping in the theatre and gallery: sgts sleeping in bedrooms. Harry Brooks and I together in tiny bedroom.

Sgts' room downstairs – where I am writing – is 'living room' of family – easy chairs, carpets, electric light, fire, etc. Very comfortable. Bar is open too, with large fire, and beer on sale to both troops and civvies. We also have a wireless set. It all seems too good to be true.

Received orders this evening regarding new courses starting tomorrow morning. I will have class of potential driver mechs. Final exam November 28th. It seems that I will have much less free time for next week or two!

Two letters from Jess today – thank goodness. Re-harboured tanks this evening, nearer to present billets.

D +163 Thursday 16.11.44

Courses commenced 8.30 this morning. Will now be working until 4.30 p.m. each day. Nothing to report.

D +164 Friday 17.11.44

Heavy frost last night. Heavy rain later – all afternoon and evening. Courses all day: beastly conditions: windowless schoolroom, very cold and wet. Several heavy explosions during today – mostly in distance. One flying bomb reported at Nispen. Radio news reports offensive by six Allied armies on Western Germany: progress satisfactory.*

Troop sergeant Reg Mead (right) of 11 Troop, C Squadron commands his tank Intensive across the Roosendaal creek. The townspeople christened this temporary bridge 'London Bridge'.

Photograph © IWM B11490.

* The Allied armies were in action along a 400-mile front from Arnhem in Holland to the borders of Switzerland in the south.

D +165 Saturday 18.11.44

Fine morning, but cold and windy. Courses until 12 noon. Indoors all afternoon – too comfortable in these billets to bother about going out. We are being well looked after – waited on hand and foot. Fires, tidying up, etc. all done by civvies. Unfortunately, none of the people in the house speak English, but we manage to converse somehow. It is really amazing how much 'conversation' is carried on by means of a few words, signs and pantomime.

Attended 15 Troop's party this evening. The troop is billeted in a separate café with quite a good dance floor. Each member of the troop invited a lady friend, making about thirty of us in all. The major and SSM were also invited. Unfortunately, we only had a portable gramophone for a 'dance band' – it was more or less useless, but the dancers managed somehow. Refreshments were surprisingly good – the lads having been scrounging and buying for a couple of days beforehand.

There was plenty of beer – from stocks in the café. We also had whisky and gin and cordial from the sergeants' mess ration. Also bully beef sandwiches – and several dozen fancy cakes bought in Antwerp yesterday. Chocolate too was fairly plentiful, thanks to the issue of 3.5 bars per man during the day. There was some dancing, and a few games, in which kissing seemed to be the principal feature. These Dutch lassies certainly enjoy kissing! The party finished about midnight, I believe.

Saw signs of a huge heavy bomber raid on Germany today. There were hundreds of bombers overhead during the afternoon: objective Munster.* We are now completely out

* Munster was the headquarters of the 6th Military District of the Wehrmacht. Much of the city was destroyed by Allied bombs.

of touch with the war here. Our first few days in Roosendaal were disturbed by heavy gunfire, but there is now complete silence – apart from the occasional roar of a bursting flying bomb in the distance.

Judging by news reports, the Belgian government [*Editor's note: the fourth diary notebook ends at this point*] is having trouble with the 'patriot army' – the latter refusing to hand in their arms, maintaining that there is still work for them to do.

From my observations of the men who constitute these Maquis forces in Belgium and France – also Holland – I am not surprised at this development. What is the nature of the work still ahead of them? To fight the enemy within? They certainly form a potential threat to any form of reactionary government – or a return to the old order of dominance by the wealthy. The Belgian govt. have offered to incorporate the 'patriots' in the regular army. This seems very much like an attempt to hoodwink them. Once in the army, they would cease to be free men able to assert themselves. The ultimatum to hand over all arms expires at midnight tonight. Meanwhile mass meetings seem to be the order of the day in Belgium.

I am living in an aroma of cheap scent at the moment. This morning, our host here – a very obliging Dutchman of 37 years – showed me a small bottle of scent – 'tis goot' he added. And then he poured some of the stuff on my hair and clothes – thinking no doubt he was doing me a favour. I had the smell with me all the evening at the party – a sickly, heavy smell: faded violets, or something.

There was some excitement in this town this afternoon ... It was caused by the arrival of the first train from Antwerp since the place was liberated. Dozens of men – civvy and army – have been working on the line during the last fortnight, clearing debris and replacing damaged permanent way. I don't know whether the damage was caused by our guns and planes – or the enemy, but the line was certainly a mess. It is now clear, and will doubtless become an important link in our supply route to Germany.

D +166 Sunday 19.11.44

Sunday routine – no parade, and late breakfast. Spent the morning listening to radio – some decent music, and the news bulletins. The general advance on the Western front appears to be going well. British troops reported fighting 3 miles inside German borders – NE of Aachen. This is a surprise, as the Second Army are already busy further north.

Attended a concert this afternoon: a piano and violin recital at a 'monastery' (St Louis Instituut) at Oudenbosch – about 7 miles east. The pianist was a monk – late organist at Amsterdam cathedral. He played several solos – Chopin, Beethoven, etc. The violinist was a young civvy: quite good artist. I believe these recitals are given each Sunday, for members of the brigade. 107 are billeted in the monastery.

Three letters from Jess this afternoon: a lucky day! There has been a fire at home, and Jess has had the job of clearing up the wreckage – and gasping for breath in the smoke laden atmosphere ...

We do seem to have parallel experiences – it was on Saturday, 4.11.44, that I was mixed up with a fire in Roosendaal – and rushing to the windows for air whilst trying to salvage kit. The post has brought me a few wisps of

Barry's hair. Jess says it is 'mousy brown and straight': he must take after me . . .

D +167 Monday 20.11.44

Cambrai Day.* A general holiday in the unit. Forty-a-side football match in the morning. Spent some time helping to arrange dining hall for the 'feast'. An excellent dinner, with officers and sergeants waiting on – as per custom. Four pigs were killed last night for the dinner. Heaven knows where they were discovered: they are worth a fortune in Holland just now. Sergeants dined in 'mess' – with hostess and son and daughter as guests: Strange to see so many luscious grapes.

Ensa cinema shows in the afternoon. Dance in men's billet after tea – music via radio-gram. Letter from Jess, and Jess A.†

D +168 Tuesday 21.11.44

Driver Mech. course again today: Cold and damp but not raining. Letter from Jess. Nothing special to report.

---

* For their part in the Battle of Cambrai in 1916 – one of the first successful uses of tanks in combat – 9 RTR was awarded the Croix de Guerre avec Palme as a regimental decoration. They were one of only four units in the British Army to have received this honour. The battalion celebrated the anniversary of Cambrai every year.

† Jess Aldcroft, wife of Jimmy.

D +169 Wednesday 22.11.44

Cold, wet and raining: miserable day. Spent couple of hours with driver mechanic class – and then left the class with Jim Bevan. Glad to get away and warm myself by fire in our café.

Pay parade at noon. C Sqdn dance this evening. Did an hour's duty on the door: a necessary precaution nowadays, otherwise the dance hall would become literally packed.

Our practice of refusing admission to civilian males is causing much bitterness, I believe. But I fail to see how it can be avoided. Even with members of the squadron and their lady friends, the place is unbearably crowded, making dancing very difficult. The bar too is a solid mass of humanity all evening.

D +170 Thursday 23.11.44

Wet day, as usual. Will it ever be fine again? D&M this morning.* Dressed myself to go to the firing range at Willemstad, but just before 2 o'clock received word that our trip was off. The morning 'shoots' had been delayed thru the weather, and our turn had been postponed until tomorrow. Pleasant news this: not much pleasure in visiting a devastated and flooded area in the pouring rain, in spite of our new rain-proof suits.

Spent the afternoon and evening reading and writing – apart from brief interlude at HQ to say *au revoir* to 'Pedlar' Palmer – the RSM. He has now left the unit and will be drafted home. He is getting on – about 46 – and has been

* Driving and maintenance.

little use since losing his two brothers during the summer. One of them was killed with the 9th, at Maltot.

D +171 Friday 24.11.44

Raining again – and misty. On parade at 8.15 with 15 Troop, HQ gunners, commanders, loaders – ready for journey to Willemstad.

Left the course in Jim Bevan's hands. About 15 miles to Willemstad. We had hardly left Roosendaal when the appalling amount of water in this area became apparent. Every field is surrounded with ditches: every road has ditches on each side – the whole damn landscape is a maze of ditches: a most depressing place. As we got nearer W, the fields gradually became more water logged – until finally they disappeared, and we found ourselves riding along elevated roadways with water all around. This was the result of the bursting of the dykes by the enemy. The countryside had become a shallow inland sea, with waves lapping against the road banking, leaving a tide mark of foam – presumably salt water.

Houses stood gaunt and desolate in this mass of water – literally a waste land. Occasionally, we passed through inhabited villages, most of them badly damaged. They appear to have been built alongside the elevated roadway purposely to avoid flooding. There were several civilians about – mostly sorting out wreckage from ruined homes. There must have been fairly heavy fighting in this almost treeless and dead flat country ... The high roads must have been blown, too, judging by the number of Bailey bridges we passed over.

Eventually reached the range – to the left of Willemstad. Did our 'shoot' in the rain, and departed for Roosendaal at noon – arriving in time for lunch. Quiet afternoon and evening – had a bath and read, and wrote ...

D +172 Saturday 25.11.44

Spent an hour with D&M pupils – and then finished, end of course presumably. Dull morning – raining and cold. Remained indoors most of day ... altho we did see some blue sky after lunch: it seems months since I saw blue in the heavens. How they must be longing for fine weather on the western front: severe battles reported, but I believe the *big push* is yet to come.

Rumoured today that we are moving Tuesday or Wednesday next. Depressing rumour. Read most of afternoon: attended 15 Troop 'party' in the evening. Quite a success: excellent refreshments under the circs.

D +173 Sunday 26.11.44

Jess's birthday: how I wish ... Surely I will be with her next year. How we will celebrate ... ! An easy day: weather dull and cold. Pete Martin departing for England this a.m. at 9 o'clock, for wireless course: Have given him my earlier notes to post to Jess. Don't think he will fail me: I so want her to have them.

Lazy afternoon – reading and writing. Ernie Cooper took photo of a group of us sgts. Sun was shining at the time!!! Sgts' mess 'party' this evening – about 30 of us in a normal living room. Much drink, also sandwiches and cakes. Tom Hamnett did some card tricks. Usual party games with much kissing. Went to bed 11 p.m., leaving several of them still drinking, etc. Certain I have a cold on the way... Confirmed this afternoon that we are departing Wednesday or Tuesday – where to ...?

D +174 Monday 27.11.44

The day after Jess's birthday – but what a hateful anniversary!* On the vehicle this morning – test run in readiness for departure. Damned things are flooded with water inside. Vehicle OK. Informed that we are departing Wednesday – a long journey: three days in Belgium en route... where to—? A round-the-world trip, judging by rumour.

Much rain this morning: cold and miserable. Before lunch, Mr Francis appeared suddenly and announced that he was leaving for England – immediately. The lucky devil: going to Lulworth on four-day gunnery course...

Sad news this afternoon – Sgt Ernie Bottoms killed in Antwerp by flying bomb. He had gone shopping with Mr Boden to buy cakes, etc. for troop party this evening. A grand fellow: a great loss to the sqdn.

Letters from Jess and Haydn – also 500 ciggies from Kath. Damned decent of K. I need ciggies at the moment, too... Dinner at 6.30 this evening provided by hostess and family. Son, Gerritt, acted as waiter. Very decent of these people. We had rabbit and potatoes and apple sauce, and custard/jam arrangement for sweet... also coffee.

---

* 27 November 1940 was the date on which Trevor was called up.

Quite a pleasant meal – ten of us present. My cold has really arrived today. Thick head this evening – but managed a few pages to Jess.

D +175 Tuesday 28.11.44

Work on vehicle this morning. Also pay parade – much speculation as to our destination. Several maps issued, including sheets for Essen and Cologne: seems ominous. Weather very bad: cold, with high wind and rain. Spent most of the day indoors – nursing my cold. Johnny Boland on medical board today: he has been recommended for CI category: hope he gets it – with a transfer to 'home service'.*

Quite a solemn air in the mess today: we all feel very depressed about leaving: the uncertainty of the future makes matters much worse. Sat up late with Gerritt, Louise, and Mrs van Aalst. I believe they are sorry we are going. Was glad to be able to give G 100 ciggies, thanks to K's parcel – also 1 pair of gloves?! He insisted on my having his lighter – and picture postcards, etc. Reveille 6 a.m. tomorrow – moving at 8.15 a.m. Letter from Jess.

D +176 Wednesday 29.11.44

Usual rush this morning – packing kit, stowing vehicles, etc. Said good-bye to the v. Aalsts. Many people to see us off – both at the harbour, and along the route. Am told there

---

* Johnny 'Tiger' Boland, who had been Trevor's driver at one point, had been injured several times and had lost his only son, who was killed at Maltot. Trevor wrote that 'his heart was no longer in it'.

were dozens of heartbreaking farewells last night – can quite believe it!

A miracle must have occurred during the night: the morning was really fine – cold, but bright and crisp – and a cloudless sky. My crew: Pedder, Slade, Ward and Crick – the latter a newcomer in Pestell's place, he having gone to Mr Francis' vehicle in place of Johnny Davies. Route: Nispen – still a shambles from our battle of some weeks ago – Essen, Wildert. Loaded on transporters about 12 miles before Antwerp. We are destined for the front – somewhere around Roermond or Geilenkirchen. Travelling round-about route to avoid heavy traffic and unsafe loads.

Passed through Antwerp, and saw damage from recent flying bombs. They are becoming much more frequent now – no doubt due to our using the docks. Am told that 400 people were killed and 2000 wounded the other day: four flying bombs hit the railway station, a cinema and other parts of the town centre. From Antwerp, passed Fort de Breendonck and then through Brussels. Saw no evidence of recent political trouble . . .

Harboured at Nossegem, on by-roads, and immediately found civvy digs – a young couple with 3 ½ month-old baby. They only have a two-roomed flat, but have gladly put their living room at the disposal of my crew – five of us will thus be sleeping on the floor. Palatial quarters by comparison with bivvies.

After dinner (5.30 p.m.) the lads adjourned to the local café . . . I chose to remain indoors with our host and hostess. They are Dutch, but managed to persuade the Gestapo to grant passage to Belgium. As a university student, (Utrecht), he was liable to be sent to 'forced labour' in Germany – in common with most Dutch students – but avoided this by transferring to Belgium to work for a relative. There must be thousands of similar cases ...

Since our occupation of Belgium, he has spent 6 weeks in prison – as a political suspect owing to his nationality. Was first arrested (by Belgian civil authority) and then released a few days later. A little later, was re-arrested, and spent 6 weeks awaiting 'trial'. Eventually he was examined and discharged immediately – there being no case against him. He informs me there are thousands of similar political suspects still awaiting trial ... and their retention without trial is partly responsible for recent disturbances. Many of them are communists – arrested for no other reason. Is history repeating itself?

Prison conditions appallingly bad – but it is the responsibility of the Belgian civil authority. I watched this fellow eat four plates full of potatoes, with a spot of dripping added – his evening meal. His wife informed me that he couldn't eat sufficient food since his release 6 days ago: he was then too weak to walk, after 6 weeks' semi-starvation. Can't imagine anyone benefitting much by potatoes and bread – seemingly their staple food. From this house, flying bombs are visible en route for Antwerp and Brussels ...

Passing thru Brussels today there was a tiny incident which illustrates the 'souvenirs' craze in this country. Our transporters were passing thru the city in column – with the tank crews sitting on top of their tanks – quite an elevated position.

Suddenly I noticed a black beret sailing to earth from one of the vehicles ahead: obviously the wind had dislodged it from the head of one of my colleagues. Almost immediately a well-dressed woman dashed into the roadway to retrieve the hat. Thinking it was her intention to hand it back to one of the following vehicles, I ordered my driver to slow down and halt by the woman. She came forward, clutching the hat to her breast and in reasonable English said, 'Let me keep it for souvenir – please, Tommy, let me keep it.'

There was something akin to frantic appeal in her voice and appearance: I was astounded. Naturally, we let her keep it ... And when later Eddie Wilde came dashing back to us at a 'halt', I had to make a diplomatic explanation as to where his hat had gone!

D +177 Thursday 30.11.44

We eventually got to bed about midnight last night – after clearing the kitchen floor, stacking chairs, etc. Our host lent us two alarm clocks to make sure we were awakened at 5.30 a.m. Breakfast 6 a.m. – then collected our kit and stowed it away. About this time, a flying bomb passed close by, its fiery tail easily visible in the darkness. It was greeted by heavy AA fire and exploded in the air.

Moved off soon after 7 a.m.: a fine morning – with a full moon still shedding plenty of light ... Between Nossegem and Louvain, saw three more flying bombs, all heading north west: plenty of AA fire, but did not see any more destroyed. Passed through outskirts of Louvain, and saw some evidence of bomb damage, but am told the centre of the city has been partly obliterated by the RAF. It was just beyond Louvain that I became aware of a pleasant change in the landscape. Instead of interminable bogs and dreary flat wastes of Holland, and part of Belgium, it was a treat to behold a few gentle undulations, with small pine forests in the vicinity.

This change continued until we reached today's harbour – Asch. We must be on much higher ground here: there is some fairly hilly moorland country just outside the town. Principal towns in today's route after Louvain: Diest, Hasselt, Zonhoven, Waterscheide (where we unloaded from transporters), and so into Asch* on tracks – arriving about 1.30 p.m.

Billets had been arranged in advance – in empty houses: neither heat, light, nor water were laid on, and all floors of a form of concrete – even the bedrooms. My crew decided to try elsewhere – and we are now in an inhabited house adjoining the tank harbour. We have the requisite comforts – light, heat and water, but unfortunately, the floors are still concrete. They seem to be fashionable here: we appear to be living on a housing estate occupied by miners. The entire town appears to be dependent upon a very large coal mine which is working undamaged. The railway too appears to be in good order: Several U-wagons† and engines in the shunting yard.

Our host family comprises wife and son, about 6 years. *They* sleep in the cellar – for safety from flying bombs which pass overhead very frequently. They are terrified of them. In view of the surplus floor space in the house, Sgt Hall and crew have joined us, so now there are eight soldiers in the house. And I am the only one with a bed – a real bed! Pedder and Crick are next door – they too have a bed. The rest are sleeping on the floors.

There has been little evidence of battle on today's route. I noticed a number of burned out vehicles lying in the

* A village on the Bosbeek river. The modern spelling is As.
† Low-loader goods wagon for the transport of exceptionally large or heavy freight items.

roadside ditches, but no more than about three dozen in as many miles. Louvain has certainly been battered, but most of that probably occurred long before the German withdrawal – and the RAF were responsible . . .

As is usual on these long road marches, our mail becomes disorganised. Have not heard from Jess since Tuesday – but am hoping for something tomorrow, Friday. This will be our only night here. Believe we cross the Maas some time tomorrow night. Once again we are among the Flemish people – and there is a babel of this language – 'Flams' – as I write. It seems to me that 90% of their vowel sounds are 'a' or 'aa': their conversation sounds like a succession of '*slaaps slaapen, taapen draagen*', etc., etc. It is not Dutch – nor is it French.

Our 'home' for tonight is a spotlessly clean place altho very badly furnished. The kitchen includes the inevitable '*kachel*' stove (by 'Smid').*

There is also a spinning wheel in the kitchen – and the 'wife' has spent much time this afternoon and evening spinning woollen thread from a bundle of sheep's wool. This seems to be part of her normal household duty, and not a war-time necessity. She makes socks, scarves, gloves, pullovers etc. from the spun wool.

D +178 Friday 1.12.44

Had a good sleep last night: my cold doesn't seem to be improving though. Another rainless morning, but dull and cloudy. I suppose we must be grateful for having had two fine days for our journey here. Believe we are moving out some

---

* The Dutch company of Harense Smid (est. 1827) still produces consumer goods today.

time this afternoon – crossing the Maas bridge at Maastricht about midnight. Some work on the vehicle this morning.

Later. Moving 10.15 p.m. – bridge 3 a.m. Fortunately it is fine ... with bright moon, but rather cold. Ensa concert this evening: umpteen tins of M&V and concentrated soup for supper. Family joined in: they seemed to enjoy it ...

D +179 Saturday 2.12.44

Moved out 10.30 last night. My cold not so good, so travelled as passenger – John Oakley commanding. Beautifully fine night: bright moonlight, rather cold, but little wind. Nothing spectacular en route: saw several flying bombs – fiery tails easily visible in darkness. Their launching sites cannot be far away.

Maas river wider than expected – it seemed almost as wide as Thames in London. Road bridge a mass of tangled wreckage, but engineers have built a fine pontoon bridge – we crossed just about 3 a.m. Fair amount of wreckage and bomb damage by bridge, but saw little other damage in outskirts of Maastricht. Eventually harboured 6.30 a.m. – on highway amidst civvy houses. Surprising number of people seemed already out of bed, and we soon had civvy billets – thanks to Slade, just beside tank.

No official breakfast laid on, but had snack at billets – and then bed. Five of us in front bedroom: two large beds, self and Pedder in one – Slade, Ward and Crick in the other. Slept until 12 noon – and then a meal. Saw MO after lunch: have to remain in bed. Wet afternoon – very miserable. We are being treated here as members of the family and with much kindness. Spent this evening in the sitting room with the family – warm and cosy. Slade out at dance with daughter.

This house is on high ground – perhaps two or three hundred feet above surrounding country. It is the first high ground I have seen in Holland. From the rear windows, looking across the town (Brunssum) with its coal mines, etc., the German frontier is clearly visible 2 or 3 kilometres away.

Am not certain of location of actual front line, but have heard distant gunfire during the day. To bed fairly early – don't feel so good.

The Bailey bridge over the River Maas at Maeseyk, built by 224 Field Company Royal Engineers. Note the twisted wreckage of the road bridge to the left. The winter of 1944–5 was a severe one, and freezing conditions made travel especially difficult for tanks.

Photograph: © IWM B14208.

D +180 Sunday 3.12.44

Am having my meals in the house – Slade is acting as my waiter. Bed collapsed this a.m. just after we were called – hell of a din – must have been Pedder's weight. Another wet day. Parade 8.30 for whole squadron – except sick–! To MO's again 10 a.m. Ordered back to bed. Eric Ward heard of father's sudden death: hope he gets leave.

D +181 Monday 4.12.44

Breakfast in bed: feel a bit screwy. MO called about noon: ordered to remain in bed tomorrow. Beastly day: raining, windy and cold. Am thankful to be indoors. Rest of squadron working on vehicles – for about an hour each morning! Spent most of day in bed.

Up at tea time – much to the disgust of our hostess. Her attentions are really embarrassing: tea or coffee every hour: two bowls of soup, etc.: whisky last evening: 'you sick', she keeps reminding me. Three former lodgers arrived this evening – 4/7, a Sherman outfit:* hell of a crowd in the house. They departed 10 o'clock. Not much peace for writing, but wrote short note to Jess. Received two letters from J.

---

* The 4th/7th Dragoon Guards, equipped with American Sherman tanks.

D +182 Tuesday 5.12.44

Another visit from MO. Have to remain in bed again tomorrow. Another beastly day: much rain and wind. Usual meals and teas and coffees in bed – also a bowl of stewed pears. Feel very guilty eating these people's meagre food reserves, but have no choice in the matter. Usual visitors – Dicky Hall, and Mr Board. SS* also came to see me yesterday, much to my surprise.

Heard some prolonged gunfire last night. A bit hazy about our precise location: have not seen detailed map since arrival. Presume we are north of Aachen, on right flank of 2nd Army. Enemy certainly cannot be very far away. Cannot get a clear impression of present battlefront. Too many rivers and canals about – *viz.* R. Maas, R. Lek, R. Meuse, R. Rhine, R. Roer, R. Saar and God knows how many canals and waterways.

Letter from Ted Hinson today, none from home. Believe there is to be some sort of celebration here this evening. Tomorrow is St Nicholas's day, a general feast day in Holland, something like our Xmas, apparently. St Nicholas Eve appears to be a time for joy and giving of presents. Will see what happens later – meanwhile our hostess is busy making cakes and waffles: she seems to have acquired the ingredients, including jam from our reserve stocks–! She has done all our washing today – a hell of a job, but she begged to be allowed to do it: we found the soap. It will be the first time my clothes have been properly washed for months. Out of bed at tea time . . .

* Probably refers here to Squadron Sergeant Major Edwards.

D +183 Wednesday 6.12.44

Mainly a present-giving ceremony among the family last evening. Followed by supper and usual party games and nonsense. The presents struck me as being rather useless knick-knacks – as so often happens with us on similar occasions. We soldier guests – five of my crew, and three former lodgers from 4/7 DG* were each given a souvenir – a small wall plaque labelled 'Brunssum'.

A fairly fine day today. MO called again: temperature still above normal: have to remain in bed (officially!). No mail from home. Wrote to Jess. Hostess again giving me too much attention – coffees and teas and soup and fruit. Don't know how on earth to repay her for her great kindness.

This seems to be a general holiday in Holland – St Nicholas Day. None of family at work today. Mr S† has two nights off duty from the mine.

D +184 Thursday 7.12.44

MO's visit this morning. Temperature now normal but have to remain in bed today and tomorrow. Announced today that unit moving tomorrow into Germany: defensive role for a start, with C in reserve – location immediately north of Geilenkirchen, only about 10 miles from here. Hope the echelon aren't moving – otherwise will have to find new billets, or go into hospital.

Xmas cards issued today: am sending ten . . . First number

---

* 4th/7th Royal Dragoon Guards, as above.
† Mr Stikkelbroek, the father of the family with whom Trevor was billeted. Mr S was a coalminer.

of 9th News Letter also issued today. Don't think much of
it. It sounds more like an officers' Rag manual to me. Feel
almost ashamed to send it home.

Bad day again – very rainy and misty . . . Two letters from
Jess, thank goodness. My tank today crewed by Cpl Pete
Davies, Raeburn, Poulter, Egan, and Slade. Poor Dave is the
only member of the regular crew on board – Pedder and I
'sick', Crick on troop leader's tank in place of Pestell (sick)
– Eric Ward departed for England today on compassionate
leave. Am very glad this leave has been granted.

Possibility of 7 days' leave early in new year: yesterday's
rumour of leave scheme now confirmed on radio.

D +185 Friday 8.12.44

Tanks departed about nine this morning – for Germany. All
local families out to see them off. Am now attached to echelon: we have moved about a mile from former area to make
room for 147 returning from front. Said good-bye to
Stikkelbroek family about 2 o'clock.

Am now billeted with Mr and Mrs Boh – a very decent
middle aged couple: he is a miner, in common with most of
men in this town. They hail from Yugoslavia, but have lived
in Holland many years. Neither of them speaks English.

Was introduced to them as a 'sick man' and have since
been almost killed by kindness. Was made to occupy only
easy chair in living room: blanket over my legs: warmed
slippers: warmed cushion: footstool: fire lit specially: dirty
boots cleaned for me: hot water bottle in bed: dose of whisky
at bedtime . . .

Can hardly lift my finger without being fussed around by

my hostess. She is a female counterpart of Falstaff.* A buxom, smiling and happy Dutch housewife. The first 'typical' house-*vrouw*† I have seen, and she is not really Dutch–!

Surprised to see a £5 banknote: Mr Boh produced 19 of them from his wife's handbag when I commented upon their value. Wondered whether I was dreaming: thought the darned things were extinct. Mrs B. shrieked with laughter when explaining how she had outwitted the Bosch by burying the money in the cellar.

Cold wet day – but damnably warm in these Dutch homes. They use inclosed slow combustion stoves in their rooms. These produce an almost overpowering closeness in the atmosphere. The open fireplace around which our home lives are spent are unknown here. To us, the open hearth and cheerful flame are an essential part of comfort: a part of our happy homes. But in Holland, the stove is simply a means of producing heat, and is usually relegated to an obscure corner of the room.

The Hollanders' evenings seem to be spent around a table in the centre of the room: and inevitably, there is a yellow or orange-coloured silk or parchment shaded lamp immediately above the table. Believe my host is a good accordionist: he has an instrument here, but seems loath to play it during the war, 'whilst so many soldiers are being killed'.

Dickens of a strain trying to converse this evening: almost regretted being alone here – they are two to one against me. We have made use of five languages this evening – Dutch, French, German, Yugoslav, and English! A sort of international conference.

---

* Sir John Falstaff, a Shakespearean character notable for his jollity, rotundity and fondness for good food and drink.
† Housewife.

D +186 Saturday 9.12.44

Little to report. Cold wet day: only ventured out for meals. C tank crews are living in cellars of ruined houses in front line: believe the entire front area is a sea of mud. A and B further forward than C . . . some of them sleeping beneath tanks!

MO is forward with HQ – don't know when I will see him again. Feel better, but still have cough and headaches. Perhaps the latter are caused by my efforts to understand Mr and Mrs Boh! It certainly is a hell of an ordeal trying to speak with them.

D +187 Sunday 10.12.44

Still living life of idleness – spend my time indoors, apart from trip to cookhouse for meals. This echelon life is vastly different from that of tank crews: quite safe – little work – plenty of spare time, etc. . . . Mr and Mrs B. still trying to drive me crazy, but am just about holding my own. Have borrowed an English–Dutch dictionary from Tom Hamnett: this helps a lot with the language problem. Mr B. has spent most of today copying words – seems to be compiling a miniature dictionary for his own use.

Mrs B. proudly demonstrated her cellar today. Usual rows of shelves filled with potted and preserved foods – *viz.* cherries, gooseberries, plums, tomatoes, mushrooms, sprouts, cabbage, rabbit, chicken, beans, peas, onions, beetroot, apples, pears and heaven knows what else. She has 200 large bottles of these preserves. Seems to be a major occupation of Dutch housewives: practically every derelict Dutch home

I have entered has had its stock, usually intact, of these bottles of preserves. They certainly do the job in a big way over here. Have managed to scrounge a little food for them – including butter, white bread, and tinned milk. It is three or four years since they saw any butter. Haven't seen any fresh milk at all in this town. They drink their coffee without milk. Mrs B. makes her own coffee – with acorns! She has a sack of the latter hanging over the kitchen stove. Periodically, she slices a batch of acorns and toasts them over a hot plate, and then grinds them up in the typical coffee grinder found on the wall of all Dutch kitchens. This 'coffee' has a bitter flavour of its own, but has a slight resemblance to coffee.

Mr B. has been preparing his own (ersatz) tobacco today – large green leaves, something like docks. He rolls them up and cuts off slices and then dries them in the oven. The result is a slightly 'snuffy' smelling weed, which may have a faint tobacco flavour. Being a miner, he takes it with him down the pit for chewing.

Scrounged some genuine tea today for Mrs B. from Tony. Must have been about a pound. Her eyes boggled at the sight of it. I think there was about a five years' supply on the basis of their present ration! They are fond of tea, in common with all Dutch people. It seems to be equally as popular here as coffee. Wrote to Aunt G., Ted Hinson, Kath, and Jess.

D +188 Monday 11.12.44

Dull day, but a little warmer than of late. Fixed a couple of lights in cookhouse and Jock Wilson's room. Jock still on the echelon – must have been here about two weeks now.

Seems to be having very easy time. Tanks still static at the front – defensive position: very close to enemy ... Spent the day reading and writing. Letter from Jess, and postcard from Les Stanley.

D +189 Tuesday 12.12.44

Nothing to report. Still at Brunssum – on sick list – living with Bohs. Dull day, wet, but not cold. No activity at the front. Tank crews having leisurely time, but strict guards.

D +190 Wednesday 13.12.44

Nothing to report. Living very lazy life here in Brunssum: Have wired one or two more lights today for office and SSM.

Went to see Mr and Mrs Stikkelbroek this afternoon. Promised to go again tomorrow. Assisted Mr and Mrs Boh to write Xmas card to Jess: at least an hour's job! Weather mild, but damp. Much mud at the front.

D +191 Thursday 14.12.44

Usual routine. Breakfast about 8 a.m. Went to Stikkelbroeks for lunch: back here for tea. Had a chat with Mrs S. about problems in Brunssum since arrival of Allied troops. Most of young girls appear to have become infatuated with soldiers. Dutch youths naturally resentful. Her own daughter, Christine, has broken off courtship with Dutch youth because of his 'jealousy' of English soldiers! Only one of the minor problems of this war.

Some heavy gunfire close by today: houses vibrated alarmingly. Must be some large guns about, as the front line is some miles away. Believe our lads are being shelled occasionally, but nothing heavy – no casualties. Something big brewing up out there! Leave 'draw' took place today. My number is 35, and that means I may get away a month after scheme commences – unless rumoured leave rate is increased. At the moment, rumour has it that one man per squadron per day will be the rate. Of total sqdn strength of 160, 104 qualify for leave scheme, so am comparatively lucky with my number.

Political news appears bad. Trouble in Greece shows no improvement. Must be heavy fighting to justify reported British reinforcements from Italy. What are we doing to Greece? Reports from America very unfavourable. Mr Stettinius, Hull's successor, pretty outspoken in his condemnation of our Greek policy – and our mysterious attitude towards Italian Count Sforza. Are we trying to 'impose' suitable governments upon liberated territories? It seems like it. Churchill has not brought much glory upon himself in recent days. His defence of our Greek policy very weak. 'Poor old England'—! What a phrase! And what a weak attempt to 'explain' his former sympathetic comments about Franco. What has happened to the latter? Press reports say he has resigned.*

---

* Edward R. Stettinius, Jr. was US Secretary of State 1944–5. Count Carlo Sforza was a prominent Italian anti-fascist who had returned to Italy after it had surrendered in 1943, and subsequently joined the provisional anti-fascist government. Trevor's remarks are clarified in a letter to Jess in which he asks, 'was Churchill misinformed when he spoke in the Commons about ELAS [the Greek Resistance] being bandits? I cannot believe that he still holds this view.'

Still struggling along with this darned Dutch language. Have been trying to understand their time. What a job! For instance, 6.20 becomes in Dutch 'tien for half zeven'. Literally: 'ten (minutes) before half an hour to seven'.

Played Ludo with Mr and Mrs B until late this evening. They seem to regard it as a grand game!

D +192 Friday 15.12.44

Usual routine. Went for bath this morning to Hendrik coal mine. Allied soldiers have been allowed use of miners' shower baths. Excellent showers ... in warm building. Interesting system of clothes racks – literally hoisted to ceiling during shower.

Bitter weather today ... clear and frosty. Sammy Stubbs back from tanks today – with rheumatism. Sleeping here tonight in separate bedroom.

Still no letters. Learn today that there has officially been a hold up in letter mails ... due to weather?

More heavy gunfire today from local guns. Enemy plane over last night – heard local sirens! Played Ludo until late – four of us this time, including Sammy Stubbs.

D +193 Saturday 16.12.44

Usual routine. More heavy frost last night – but much warmer during day, with some rain, so now we are back again with the wind. Pending events at front cancelled today. Weather?

Received one letter from Jess today – must be several en

route somewhere. Also received Xmas present from Marjorie and Fred – 100 Players [cigarettes] and pair of gloves. Wedding anniversary tomorrow . . .

More Ludo – until midnight! Am sick of the game, but the Bohs seem to revel in it: can't very well refuse to play. Barry's first tooth arrived December 10th!

D +194 Sunday 17.12.44

December 17th! Dear Jess . . .*

Usual routine: am spending most of my time now away from this house – away from Mrs B. She is pestering me to death: can't stand it much longer. Jock Wilson and the SSM have fixed up a sergeants' mess in an empty house, furnished with loot from Germany. There is less comfort there – but no Dutch people and no interruptions. Can at least read in comfort. For heat, we have a Valor oil stove – and electric light.

Several enemy air raids last night. Also similar activity this evening: have heard the sirens four times already. The Bosch seems to have found a few planes, altho they only come over in ones and twos – but bombs are being dropped fairly close. Letter from Jess today . . .

D +195 Monday 18.12.44

Much enemy air activity last night. Presume this has some connection with the large German counter offensive

* Their wedding anniversary.

launched on the American sector, a few miles south of this place. Received word today of impending move – believe we are going on Wednesday.

More air raids this evening. Heard a German jet-propelled plane.* The powerful 'whine' sounded like a falling bomb, and gave me a hell of a fright until I realised what it was. The enemy have certainly found many planes for their recent raids.

Spent the day in the sergeants' mess, returning to my billet at 9 p.m. NO Ludo this evening: read a book instead, in spite of Mrs B's efforts to monopolise my attention. Sammy did most of the talking, and I was thankful for his presence. Usual tea and tart for supper – and then bed about midnight. Wrote to Ediswans,† Marjorie – and Jess.

D +196 Tuesday 19.12.44

Usual routine. Had an undisturbed sleep last night in spite of enemy bombers, but most units here seem to have had a stand-to during the early hours – including the tank crews at the front. This was due to a report that 70 enemy gliders had passed overhead – but nothing further appears to have been heard of them. Presume the authorities are now 'glider conscious' after the recent paratroop landings behind the American lines.‡

* In 1944 Germany had produced both the first fully operational jet fighter, the Messerschmidt Me 262, and the first jet bomber, the Arado Ar 234.

† The Ediswan Electric Company Ltd., where Trevor worked in his civilian life.

‡ The Battle of the Bulge, also known as the Ardennes Offensive, which lasted from 16 December 1944–25 January 1945. The initial German action took the Allies by surprise, and the Germans caused confusion by landing paratroopers disguised in US uniforms.

Tomorrow's move officially confirmed today. I shall be with the echelon, departing at 5.30 a.m. Believe the tanks have moved out today. This will be my first journey with the echelon since coming from England. Have already packed most of my kit. The Bohs seem genuinely sorry to be losing us. Personally, have mixed feelings about leaving this house. Mrs B. is certainly too much for any man ... but the place is spotlessly clean, and we have been well looked after – perhaps too well 'mothered' to be pleasant. I shall never be able to dissociate these Dutch homes from the sickly-rancid smell of apples. They all have the same smell due to the large stocks of apples kept in the cellars or bedrooms. The people seem to eat large quantities of apples – but whether this is merely a wartime avenue of cheap food I cannot say.

Letter from Jess today. Visited Stikkelbroeks this evening, to say good-bye, and leave some food in payment for coat alterations by Chris. Left them all busily chewing apples!

News this evening reveals that counter measures against German attack are showing signs of being successful!! But it seems certain that Jerry has now advanced about 20 miles on a 60-mile front. May be a good thing in the long run. Weather very mild today – but very muddy under foot.

D +197 Wednesday 20.12.44

Rather a glum atmosphere in the house last evening: our impending departure seemed to have upset Mr and Mrs B. Had our usual supper of tea and apple tart – with a bully-beef sandwich. Called this morning at 4.15 a.m. Breakfast 4.45. A damp, misty morning, but not cold. A hurried breakfast, and then back 'home' to say good-bye – a painful business. As I shook hands with Mr B he turned away and was too upset to look at me: he spoke quietly, in an unsteady voice. His wife was in tears, which she made no attempt to hide. We finally got away, after shaking hands three times!

On the vehicles at 5.30 a.m. – myself in the cab of a three tonner with Sharman [?] driving. Route cards were issued, and I found the DP to be Leopoldsburg, Belgium! Finally got away about 5.45 a.m. We were part of a very large convoy, and progress was slow – advisedly so, on account of the mist (visibility about 40 yds) and the damp greasy condition of the roads: the earlier passage of the tanks had left much mud on the roads, making them more dangerous.

We had hardly travelled a mile before we started passing casualties – vehicles lying partly on their sides in the ditches. And before daylight, we passed dozens of them. A good demonstration of the treacherous nature of many of these Dutch and Belgian roads – if a vehicle happened to leave the road 'metalling', perhaps to allow another vehicle to pass, it almost certainly became ditched ... hopelessly so.

The first two hours of the journey were decidedly unpleasant, due to the weather and the roads, but matters became easier around 8 a.m. Progress was spasmodic, with several long halts, but we eventually reached Asch [As] in Belgium and found ourselves in the midst of an enormous concentration of vehicles. Something was definitely 'up'. We parked by the roadside and awaited orders. Rumours came thick and fast – but after being stationary for an hour or so, it seemed that our march programme had been abandoned – and this turned out to be the case.

The tanks were still in Asch from the night before – having abandoned *their* day's programme before starting it! Yes, something was in the wind – and there were very few who weren't convinced that the German offensive on the American sector was the cause. Had they at last asked for British assistance? The answer seemed obvious. The cooks managed to prepare a dinner on the roadside, and this was very welcome.

During the afternoon, it was confirmed that we would remain in Asch for the night, and so we parked the vehicles as far as possible off the main highway. The lads drifted into neighbouring cafés, etc., and as usual, made friends with householders in the locality. Unfortunately, they were not allowed to find their own billets: these were found under squadron arrangements, so as to have the men as far as possible under one roof, in the event of a sudden order to move.

By nightfall, everyone had a bed-space and everything seemed to be well organised. And then damned rumour started again – we were moving at 8.30 p.m. Could it be true? Where were we going? To Ch. [*indecipherable*] But it was only a half truth. Orders had come through for the *tanks* to move at 8.30 p.m., not the 'soft' vehicles of the echelons. We echelon fellows breathed a sigh of relief – and I felt a wave of sincere sympathy for the tank crews. They would have to do one of those appalling night marches to God knows where, whilst others were allowed to remain comfortably ensconced in billets before warm fires, etc. The tank crews always seem to get the raw end of the deal. I suppose it is inevitable. But at 8 o'clock my sympathy had turned to damned annoyance. I had just negotiated a comfortable private billet, contrary to orders, when the SSM 'asked' me to take charge of two petrol lorries which had to accompany the tanks. Just my blasted luck! What a business! The lorries had been parked in daylight off the road – between trees and ditches and houses, etc. – and they were scattered over a quarter of a mile of roadway – a roadway which had become literally seething with traffic since dark. Lorries by the hundred were rolling and roaring past, all heading in one direction – infantry lorries full of singing troops, artillery lorries trailing their guns, ammunition, petrol, water – all and every conceivable type of vehicle. It had been a remarkably consistent flow of men and weapons, and it merely confirmed our earlier conviction that British troops were going to assist the Yanks.

Presumably, this ceaseless flow of vehicles would be interrupted to allow our convoy of tanks and lorries to gain the highway. In the near distance, above the noise of traffic, I could hear Churchill engines roaring as they were being warmed up for the journey. [*Editor's note: the fifth diary notebook ends at this point.*] This sound is not unpleasant in itself, but it is never welcome to me, so often has it been the prelude to a dawn attack – memories, unpleasant . . . dreadful . . .

At 8.30, the tanks commenced to move out – slowly nosing their way from the harbours on the roadside, and moving along past the lines of parked lorries. It was pitch dark – horrible conditions for the tank drivers on those narrow congested roads, but somehow there were no accidents. By now, I had located our two petrol lorries, plus the water cart, and had their drivers standing by ready to join on to the end of the tank column. We had a long wait. It is no mean job to organise a night march for a battalion of tanks, and progress was inevitably slow. But after about an hour, the tail end of the tank column rumbled past, and we quickly tacked on to the last vehicle – before any other vehicle had time to squeeze us out of our column.

Fortunately, side and tail lights were being used, so it was reasonably easy to keep in touch with the vehicle ahead.

And so we moved off into the night, not knowing definitely where we were bound – but grimly conscious that the enemy lay somewhere ahead, and that a minor crisis in the war had arisen. After some hours of slow progress, we finally halted by a railway yard in what appeared to be a small town – Bilzen. It was about 2 a.m. I had to enquire about accommodation for the drivers and co-drivers of my three vehicles: six of us, all told. Nothing had been organised, but I ultimately found room in a small factory for four men. Bill Awcock and I slept in the driving cabs of two lorries.

Ultimately got to sleep about 4 a.m., after listening to a few flying bombs overhead, and three heavily laden goods trains puffing their way to Maastricht . . .

D +198 Thursday 21.12.44

Not much sleep last night – too cramped and cold. Had breakfast 8 a.m., and then delivered petrol to the tanks – renewing acquaintance with the tank crews after about a fortnight's absence . . .

Finished my job after a couple of hours, and then returned with the lorries to Asch. Found the echelon being reorganised – all C personnel (echelon) being transferred to a nearby school, and thus billeted literally under one roof. We sergeants have a small room at the rear of the school and are quite comfortable – altho sleeping on a wooden floor again is a bit hard after the luxury of soft beds. But we are under cover, we have a fire and electric light – and must be grateful for this luxury. I only wish the tank crews had similar accommodation.

Spent the afternoon attending to the lighting, and eventually had all lights working OK. Had to purchase our own bulbs – luckily, there is an electrical shop close by, and I was able to barter 150 Players for five 100W lamps. (We only have Dutch money, not accepted in Belgium.) Was served by a pretty girl – fair hair and blue eyes! – the most English-looking girl I have seen since coming over here. Jock Wilson much amused by my description of this girl. Perhaps he thinks I have fallen for her!

Had to make another lorry journey to the tanks after tea, to deliver a cooker for the officers' mess. A twelve-mile run, but managed to avoid getting lost. Returned about 8 p.m. Made a 'brew' – wrote to Jess – and bed. Weather quite mild, but a little rain and mist.

News of the German offensive still very scarce, but they appear to have advanced about 20 miles into Belgium. Judging by traffic in this area alone, something very hard is going to hit the Jerries before long – but it is bound to take a few days to muster all our weapons and supplies.

Rumour today that Gen Montgomery has superseded Gen Bradley.*

Looking back upon yesterday, am forced to admire the manner in which our column was halted – and then redirected. There seemed to be complete confusion at the time, but it must have been an enormous job to reorganise the entire movement, bearing in mind the colossal amount of stuff using the roads. Our convoy, a *very* small part of the forces involved, covered a distance of 35 miles! Received 200 Players from Phyl.

---

* General Omar Bradley was in Luxembourg when Germany launched the Ardennes Offensive, and hence was cut off from a key part of his forces. Eisenhower transferred temporary command of the US First and Ninth Armies to Montgomery for operational reasons, in spite of Bradley's strenuous objections.

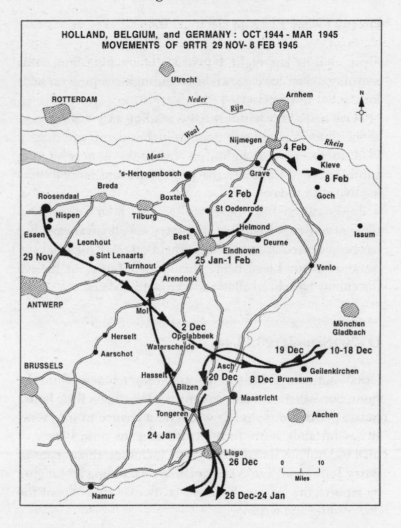

HOLLAND, BELGIUM, and GERMANY : OCT 1944 - MAR 1945
MOVEMENTS OF 9RTR 29 NOV- 8 FEB 1945

D +199 Friday 22.12.44

Slept soundly last night, but had a few aching bones this morning. Must have grown 'soft' through sleeping on beds for the last few weeks . . . !

Have had a very leisurely day – reading and writing most of the time. Weather still quite mild, but damp and drizzly. Had to fix another light for the cooks – necessitating another visit to the charming young lady, and more bartering. No mail today.

Tanks still at Bilzen and still on one hour's notice. No signs of any flap. Reported that Jerry is still advancing, but has been slowed up, and is being held on the flanks. Several rumours about Liège being surrounded, but don't believe the enemy have been allowed to cross the Maas.

D +200 Saturday 23.12.44

Usual routine, and little to report. Not much news from the front, but everyone seems optimistic. Weather a little better today: perhaps our aircraft will have a chance to intervene. It has certainly been 'Jerry' weather up to now. Plenty of mail today. Four letters from Jess – including three snaps of Barry. Jolly good! Tanks still at Bilzen – standing by. Judging by reports, the lads are having a fairly easy time. Spent the day reading and writing.

D +201 Sunday 24.12.44

Xmas Eve! A grand morning: cloudless sky, no wind, and heavy frost – very cold. At last our aircraft will have a chance to assist in the battle. Jerry reported to have advanced 40 miles into Belgium, but Liège has not fallen. More mail today: letter from Jess (and Mr Morgan), Mr Cornelese (with photo) – card from Wilf. Wrote to Jess, Cornelese, and Dorothy . . . Report that squadron is moving back, but nothing definite – usual rumours.

Later. Our aircraft have been busy all day – particularly fighters, Typhoons, etc.: not so good for Jerry. Weather excellent: cloudless sky all day, and good visibility. Yesterday's newspapers report another call-up in England: 250,000 men will be affected: this is good news to us. Bit of a shock for those who thought the war was as good as over!

Now reported that tanks are not moving, but the echelon joining them tomorrow. We have orders to be ready to move at 10 a.m. Bit of a nuisance having to move on Xmas Day!

A little excitement this evening. A young lady burst into the men's billet in a semi-exhausted state. She gasped 'Germans', and waved her arms wildly. She only spoke 'Flams', but we learned that three Jerries had broken into her next-door neighbour's house and demanded food. The neighbour had somehow signalled to her through the wall – and she immediately mounted her bike and rode the half mile to our billet. There were only about half a dozen of us in the place, the rest of the lads being out celebrating Xmas eve. We grabbed our arms and followed the girl. The night was bitterly cold, with bright moonlight, and already the ground was white with frost. After quarter of an hour's walking, we found ourselves in a lonely country area, with a few scattered cottages straggling along the narrow country lane. One of them, 150 yards ahead, had lighted windows, and this was pointed out as our objective.

We went forward quietly, with weapons cocked, not knowing what was in store for us – whether fanatical Nazis dropped by parachute in the present offensive, or the more docile Jerry, willing to surrender on sight. When quite close to the house, I noticed a dark object moving in the shadow of a barn adjoining the house. I decided to investigate, fearing an ambush. But the 'object' soon moved forward into the moonlight, and I beheld a woman. I had withheld my fire, fortunately . . . Almost simultaneously, I heard a thump and the house door flew open, revealing Ginger Young and two others standing in the beam of light from the house. They started a hell of a hullabaloo, inviting the 'bastards' to give themselves up. There was a rush inside by four of us, and I noticed three terrified-looking Jerries raising their hands as they rose from the table at which they were having supper! No doubt we looked pretty desperate, and all had arms. We quickly searched the prisoners, removing all papers, etc. They had no arms. They were unshaven and looked very dirty. Their clothing too was in rags and totally inadequate for the cold weather. None of them wore an overcoat.

I have dim recollection of two other people in the room – probably the husband and wife – but was too busy searching the prisoners, and on the *qui-vive*** for treachery, to pay any attention to them. We soon had the prisoners outside, and marched them back to our billet. We detained them whilst transport and an escort was organised, and then

---

* On the alert, on the lookout. The phrase has its origins in a traditional French sentries' challenge, meaning 'long live who?'

dispatched them to the POW camp at Hasselt. I was glad to see them go. Had they been in the billet when any of our semi-drunk lads returned, there may have been trouble.

After this incident, I returned to my writing. But not for long. The SSM turned up at midnight half drunk – and required some attention. And then Jock Wilson appeared, really drunk: finally got him to bed at 1 a.m. – and followed suit. Jock seems to have been celebrating his impending departure to Bovington* as a gunnery instructor. It is now about three months since the major dispensed with him, and he has been on the echelon ever since, doing very little. His transfer to England makes one feel very envious. I will be the last of the 'old 'uns' as a sergeant on the tanks. Les Challinor and Tom Hamnett are still with me in the mess, but they are not in the tank crews.

D +202 Monday 25.12.44

Xmas day. Damnably cold last night, but another beautiful morning: cloudless sky, no wind, and everywhere frozen. Should be another good day for our aircraft. I believe there were 7,000 of them over the enemy yesterday.

Echelon moved to join up with tank crews for Xmas dinner: new location small village near Bilzen. Billeted with typical Flemish peasant family: pigs, manure heap, clogs and tiles. Dinner 7 p.m. – very good. Bed 10.30. No time for writing.

---

* Bovington Camp in Dorset was the home of the Royal Armoured Corps, of which RTR was a part. Today, Bovington also houses the Tank Museum.

D +203 Tuesday 26.12.44

Awakened 6.30 a.m. – squadron departing 7.15 a.m.! Hell
of a flap. Said good-bye to Jock Wilson about 7 a.m.: he
departs for England today. Delivered Brussels leave party to
Waterschei – then back to Bilzen. Scrounged breakfast from
Cornwall [?]* unit.

On to Liège via Tongres.† (billets Ougrée). Saw a flying
bomb drop en route. Liège civvies seem pleased to see us –
much hand-waving, etc. They must have had an anxious
time lately, and our presence is no doubt very reassuring.
Much damage in Liège from flying bombs – also from allied
bombers. Most of inhabitants seem to be living in cellars.
Rather queer to see rows of small metal chimneys protruding from cellar windows and air vents just above level of
pavement. In civvy billet with SSM, Sgts Challinor and
Hamnett. Rest of echelon sleeping in damaged school: very
bad accommodation.

Weather bitterly cold with heavy frost all day, but good
visibility and dry. Plenty of our aircraft overhead. Flying
bombs too frequent for my liking – they seem to arrive every
half hour. Usually preceded by 'siren' giving a few seconds
warning. As soon as bomb motor becomes audible, the
family in this house stand by the cellar door ready to dive
down below, in case the thing heads for this locality. A
beastly business, terrifying for everyone.

Slept up in bedroom, but spent a few uneasy hours listening for the ominous roar, and then waiting the crash as the

---

* Trevor's compact handwriting, never easy to read, is especially difficult to deci-
pher here.
† Also known as Tongeren. In common with many Belgian towns, Tongres had
both a French and a Flemish name.

engine cuts out . . . Managed to get a few hours' sleep. Have to re-learn French again now. We are out of Flanders.

D +204 Wednesday 27.12.44

Bitterly cold again: more heavy frost last night. Tanks still standing by, about five miles from echelon. Saw MO today: to see him again in 4 days. Had a trip to tank harbour to collect another leave party, including Dicky Hall. Saw Dave Lubick. Believe we will be moving again tomorrow. Spent the evening again with a house full of people here: impossible to write. Still confused with the change in language, but am improving.

Sleeping in kitchen tonight: safer and warmer – a bit of a squeeze for four of us, but we managed it.

D +205 Thursday 28.12.44

Still very cold: freezing again this morning in spite of light snowfall during the night: very misty down here in the valley of the Meuse. It must be clear on the high ground above as our aircraft seem to be passing overhead in large formations.

We are leaving this place (Ougrée, suburb of Liège) at 1.30 p.m. today. The tanks are moving nearer to the enemy – and the echelon will follow. Our hostess, Mrs Maertens, seems genuinely sorry to be losing us. She has this morning been recounting the details of her cheerless existence. The usual story of a selfish and uninteresting husband who regards his wife as his servant and plaything. Have heard the same thing so often over here . . . Perhaps it is no wonder that so many wives have allowed American – and British – soldiers to become intimate. It is at least a change for these women!

Later. Mrs M. very upset when we parted – a depressing business. Departed 1.30: unpleasant journey in lorries owing to frozen snow on roads, heavy mist, and dangerous roads – very hilly locality. Echelon remained in rear of tanks, and so the journey was very slow. Fortunately, we only moved about 10 miles to Limont: even so, it was after 7 p.m. when we arrived.

Soon found civvy billets for everyone. Even out here in the country, the people are sleeping in their cellars on account of the flying bombs, so there are unoccupied beds in practically every house. Am billeted with Les Challinor and Tom Hamnett. We each have a separate bed!!

Typical Belgian country people: the old 'mama' has been busy spinning wool all evening, using the primitive hand spinning wheel. The lives of these people must be very drab – completely devoid of any cultural pursuits whatever. Books seem to be unheard of – apart from the bible.

D +206 Friday 29.12.44

Still very cold – in spite of light snowfall during the night. Very little to report today. Tank crews in civvy billets: seem to be quite comfortable. No incoming mail. Wrote to Jess. Flying bombs still dropping in this area, but mostly towards Liège. No electric light this evening.

D +207 Saturday 30.12.44

Usual routine: we have today installed the sgts' mess radio in this house: it works quite well – too well for my liking: the incessant jazz is a bit nerve racking. George Rathke today took over from SQMS Dobinson.

Still very cold: fairly heavy snowfall this afternoon. German assault now appears to have been halted – according to today's news, their spearhead has been pushed back 9 miles to Rochfort. Churchill and Eden appear to have returned from Greece – and have advised the Greek king to appoint a regent, the Archbishop ... Have rejoined the troop today, but am remaining in same billet, and dining with the echelon. No incoming mail again today.

D +208 Sunday 31.12.44

New Year's Eve. Usual routine. Very cold. Roads now very dangerous owing to frozen snow. No sign of any further movement: doubt whether the vehicles could move on these roads.

The family here invited us to dine with them this evening – we had waffles and coffee!! Hard luck on Tom Hamnett who expected a real feed, and so omitted to have his army tea at 4.30.

Expecting a bit of a binge here this evening. SSM has got some drink still on hand!!

316 D-Day to Victory

D +209 Monday 1.1.45

Usual routine. Visited MO this evening. Still freezing: roads
very bad ... Some heavy drinking here last evening. Several
family relations turned up, and they joined in with the
SSM's whisky and beer. By midnight, several were drunk –
viz. SSM, SQMS, and at least two of the relations, including
the 'Gremlin'.*

Heard the radio at midnight – including a few phrases of
Hitler's broadcast – and the Solemn Melody: lovely to hear
such music after the row of the evening.†

Low flying enemy plane over the tanks this morning –
Fw 190. Usual flying bombs about every half hour. Several
of the darned things passed by last evening and exploded in
the Liège area. We may move tomorrow – but imagine this
will depend upon the roads. No mail again today – last letter
from Jess Xmas Eve ... According to the Q, we are no
longer with 34 Tank Brigade but attached to 51 HD.‡
Presume we are now on our own as a battalion. Another
invitation for this evening – this time to the house of the
cousin – the Gremlin.

D +210 Tuesday 2.1.45

* In a letter, Trevor describes the Gremlin as a cousin of the family. He does not
explain how he came by the nickname.
† It was Hitler's custom to broadcast an address to the German nation on New
Year's Day. The *Solemn Melody* was a popular classical piece by Sir Henry Walford
Davies, who died in 1941. Appointed musical director to the newly created Royal
Air Force in 1918, his other compositions include the *RAF March Past*.
‡ According to the 9 RTR War Diary, on Boxing Day the battalion detached
from 34 Tank Brigade and came under command of 51 (Highland) Division.
Subsequently, on 7 January 51 HD began to move and 9 RTR came under
command of 53 (Welsh) Division. On 29 January, they also moved and 9 RTR
reverted to the control of 34 Armoured Brigade, which had by then changed its
designation. Such complicated changes of higher formation were not unusual.

Very cold again this morning – roads impassable for tanks: definite that we cannot move under these conditions. Plenty of our aircraft during the morning, but NO flying bombs!! Commenced to snow lunch time, quite heavily. Tank crews working on the roads this afternoon, sprinkling dirt to make them safer for pedestrians.

Fairly quiet 'party' last evening, altho there was some drinking. Gremlin rather subdued: his orgy of the previous night responsible. Our meal consisted of huge chunks of apple tart and coffee. Bit of a problem handling the tart as no plates were provided. Tom Hamnett entertained as usual with card tricks.

Later. Had a visit this afternoon from a batch of Scotties (51 Hd Infantry) to inspect the tanks. Quite a cheerful and enthusiastic lot of lads. Received some free home comforts, *viz.* a pair of gloves, scarf, woollen stockings (for gumboots). Very useful, especially the latter. Also received some ciggies from 'British Commonwealth Society of Peru', Patriotic Fund Lima, Peru!

Still no mail – no mail!

D +211 Wednesday 3.1.45

Usual routine. Nothing to report. Much snow today: must have been a heavy fall during the night. Still no mail.

D +212 Thursday 4.1.45

Usual routine – first parade 9 a.m., work on vehicles for about an hour. Received pair of gumboots today – very useful, especially in this deep snow. Spending most of my time reading.

D +213 Friday 5.1.45

Usual routine. Visit to MO's 2.30 for inoculation. Mail arrived today – eight letters from Jess!!

D +214 Saturday 6.1.45

Am too sore and stiff for work. Remained indoors all day. Major departed on leave this a.m. Another letter from Jess. Still very cold – the countryside is white, with a 3-inch carpet of snow. Flying bombs still very frequent – some landing uncomfortably close.

D +215 Sunday 7.1.45

Little to report. Still cold and icy. Dance this evening.

D +216 Monday 8.1.45

Little to report. Still on usual routine – first tank parade, and then occasional jobs during the day. Division concert party.

D +217 Tuesday 9.1.45

Usual routine. Brains trust* this evening: Capt Link, Mr Wood, Mr Young, Tpr Low, Cpl Adams, Sammy Stubbs and self. Not a bad effort – plenty of fun. Believe we are now with 53 Div!†

D +218 Wednesday 10.1.45

Usual routine. Not many flying bombs for last few days. Weather, maybe? Still very cold.

D +219 Thursday 11.1.45

Heavy snowfall last night – average of 8 inches, but drifts 2 or 3 feet deep at all street corners. Presume mail will again be held up due to this . . . Squadron concert this evening.

D +220 Friday 12.1.45

More snow last night – about 2 inches. And the previous heavy fall hasn't even commenced to thaw yet! Floods seem to be indicated if there is a quick thaw. More flying bombs last night and today: damn them!

* *The Brains Trust* was a popular radio programme in the 1940s, in which listeners would send in questions on an eclectic range of topics for the panel to answer. Later transferred to television, it was the forerunner of many subsequent panel discussion formats.

† The 53rd Welsh Infantry Division.

Successful concert last evening. Hall packed as usual. Most of villagers seemed to be there. Took up small part in sergeants' sketch. Another brains trust this evening – with Capt Link, Mr Young, Mr Lilly, Sgt Brooks, Tprs Etheridge, Fitzpatrick, and Mr LeBrun.

D +221 Saturday 13.1.45

Usual routine: still very cold. Short test run with tank this a.m. – progress difficult: brakes useless due to icy conditions. Les Challinor departed for England today . . . Had a bath in tin tub.

D +222 Sunday 14.1.45

Usual routine: beautiful day - cold but sunny. Hundreds of US bombers heading east* – sky a mass of vapour trails after they had departed. Good news from Russia: after two days, their offensive has breached the enemy defences between Warsaw and Cracow, and advanced 25 miles on 40-mile front. Is this Stalin's battle for Berlin?

D +223 Monday 15.1.45

Much colder today: one report – via the Q – says the thermometer was reading 3 deg F at lunch time (about minus

---

* The strategic bombing raid on oil installations at Derben, near Berlin. The USAF fighters protecting the B-17 bombers engaged more than 200 German fighter planes in a major aerial battle, shooting down 56 of them, the highest single day's tally of the war by the US Eighth Air Force.

16 deg Celsius). 29 deg of frost? Seems unlikely to me, but it has been well below freezing all day. Cinema show this afternoon – could only stick it for an hour – usual tripe ... Eddie Wilde back from leave.

D +224 Tuesday 16.1.45

Usual routine: still very cold: still snowed up: still at Limont – struggling to understand Francois and the family.* Pantomime today somewhere in this area. Quite good, according to reports. Very good news from Moscow.† Red Army appears to have overwhelmed entire German front south of Warsaw. Is this the beginning of the drive for Berlin? One Moscow commentator stated 'we alone will judge our torturers'?!!

D +225 Wednesday 17.1.45

A little warmer today: thawing slightly, but there is a cold wind. Usual routine on vehicles this morning.

---

* Trevor was billeted with this family in Limont from 28 December until 24 January. In a letter home dated 18 January he writes: 'with this letter I will enclose ... two snaps which the family here insist upon my having as souvenirs. They show the old lady, 'mama', her daughters Irma and Maria, and Francois, Maria's husband. I like Francois best of all. He is so genuine and kind ...'

† The commencement of the Soviet advance across Eastern Europe, which began with the Vistula–Oder Offensive on 12 January 1945.

D +226 Thursday 18.1.45

Tremendous news last evening. Warsaw captured by Red Army: also terrific advances all along the front from East Prussia to Carpathians. BBC celebrated news by playing Polish and Russian national anthems.

Still thawing slightly. Roads very treacherous due to snow, etc. Very cold on guard last evening. Announced suddenly today that we are moving tomorrow. No details yet. Local roads being sprinkled with granite this afternoon, especially on fairly steep decline to main road.

D +227 Friday 19.1.45

Echelon moved out at 12 noon today, but tanks following later – don't yet know when, but rumour says a few days time. Echelon to Mol.* Meanwhile,

Editor's note: the entry ends here, unfinished.

D +228 Saturday 20.1.45

Usual routine. Nothing to report, apart from more snow.

D +229 Sunday 21.1.45

Usual routine. Nothing to report.

---

* A town in Belgium, about 35 miles east of Antwerp.

D +230 Monday 22.1.45

Usual routine. Received four letters from Jess – including snaps of Barry. A grand surprise. More snow. Very cold.

D +231 Tuesday 23.1.45

We are moving tomorrow. Spent couple of hours this a.m. removing centre section of track covers to prevent snow piling beneath turret ring. The people of Limont seem very sad today. We have been almost four weeks in the village, and the civilians have got used to us. Weather and road conditions seem very bad for tanks – but we are moving. Apparently there is now no need for us in the Ardennes. Dicky and I had a farewell drink of cognac with Francois this evening. Reveille tomorrow 6 a.m. Breakfast 6.30. Ready to move 7.30 a.m. A cold business in this arctic climate.

D +232 Wednesday 24.1.45

Had breakfast with the family this a.m. – two eggs! Francois very kindly helped carry my kit, etc. More snow during the night.

Departed about 8 a.m. . . . all Limont out to see us off. Many tears, etc. Today's destination western outskirts of Liège. Ten or twelve-mile journey. Seemed doubtful whether we would make it at the start. Tanks behaved very erratically on hills, etc. Out of control several times – especially on steep descent. Had to resort to logs and shrubs on the roads:

they were solid ice beneath the snow of last night. No accident, much to my amazement.

Difficulties too on long decline into Liège: Spare track plate came in handy for preventing skid on corners. Bitterly cold journey – well below freezing all day. More difficulties on steep and long incline out of Liège, but eventually made harbour about 4 p.m., damned cold and hungry, and fed up with the journey. Usual working class area for billets, but have found a remarkable billet for myself and Ward and Edmunds. The house resembles all others here from the exterior, but the interior is a remarkable contrast, and the host obviously has means. Also here, for the first time on this continent, I have found a decent bathroom, including bath, washbowl, lav., etc., and hot and cold water! The house is centrally heated and very warm, in spite of coal shortage.

Very fine radio-gram – and plenty of jazz records. Ward and Edmunds have been playing the latter all evening, with port wine, coffee and biscuits also laid on. Family sleeping in the cellar, due to 'robots',* so we have bedrooms and beds. We are practically in Liège here, so robot menace is more acute. Some structural damage to this house, but it is still quite habitable. Couple of robots over this evening, but the things have been far less frequent for the last week or so.

Hope to have a bath this evening – a genuine bath for the first time in about ten months. Reveille tomorrow 7.30 a.m.: breakfast 8 a.m. Tanks 8.45, ready to move 9.30 a.m. Boarding transporters somewhere in the locality. Remainder of my crew, Pedder and Slade, have found their own billet – they would!!

* The local name for flying bombs.

D +233 Thursday 25.1.45

Had a bath last night – marvellous! Boarded transporters this a.m. close to Liège, and eventually moved off somewhere around noon. Bitterly cold: we all had to ride outside, either on tanks, rear of transporter cab, or anywhere else we fancied.

What a journey! Snow everywhere: roads icy: freezing all day. Heaven knows how we survived. I found it bitter travelling on the front wing of the vehicle, ahead of the driver, with my back to the wind. And I remained there all the way to Eindhoven – where we landed around 11.30 p.m. But by the time we had found billets it was after midnight. Accommodation had been reserved in advance, but many of the civvies had gone to bed – no doubt tired of waiting for us.

Found myself billeted with Eddie Wilde: the daughter was waiting up for us, and 'ma' came down soon after our arrival – 'pa' stayed in bed! Had a cup of coffee, and then bed – to try and get warm. Vehicles parked outside the front doors of our billets! Today's journey via Hasselt.

D +234 Friday 26.1.45

A little work on the vehicle this morning, but spent most of day indoors trying to keep warm. Children seem to be enjoying much skating on a nearby pond. Usual difficulties with the Dutch language. None of the civvies in my billet speak a word of English – and I have forgotten what little Dutch I ever knew. Unfortunately, they will persist in talking to me, and I can only 'reply' by looking gormless: I have to do this in self defence.

Saw Mr Cornelese this evening. Unfortunately I cannot stay with him as HQ are billeted in his area – but am staying quite close. Was made very welcome. Also met a Dutchman who spoke perfect English. Had an interesting conversation with him.

D +235 Saturday 27.1.45

Usual hour or two on the vehicles in the morning and then 'rest'. The SSM has organised a sergeants' mess, and we have today dined in civilised style with tablecloth, cutlery, cruets, etc. The mess comprises two ground floor rooms of a comfortably furnished home. The husband and wife seem to be living in the kitchen. Lynch is cooking for us in a small building at the rear.

Saw Mr C. again this evening. Had to accept a child's picture as a present for Barry. Intend to take it with me on leave, but carrying it will be a problem.

D +236 Sunday 28.1.45

Spent most of today in our comfortable mess. Nothing to report: Skating is now in full swing and many of the lads are joining in with borrowed skates.

D +237 Monday 29.1.45

Usual routine: still very cold. One or two flying bombs seem to pass this area, but they do not land here. News from

Russia still excellent. HQ and C holding combined dance tomorrow evening in the town. Am i/c bar for officers and sgts. Spent all afternoon arranging the bar, etc.

D +238 Tuesday 30.1.45

Usual routine: still very cold and roads icy and dangerous. Some vehicles being fitted with 'ice-bar' tracks. Dance this evening: seemed quite successful, but bit of a shambles in the bar, as usual. SSM in a fight!!

D +239 Wednesday 31.1.45

Warmer today and some rain. It has cleared away much of the snow and put an end to ice skating. Usual routine on vehicles, but spent most of day in mess – after clearing up in the dance hall this morning.

D +240 Thursday 1.2.45

Usual routine: still warmer – little snow left now, but much mud, etc. Rumoured that we are moving Saturday. Still having bother with the language. Am constantly being pressed to have food in my 'house' – but have to refuse, even at the risk of being rude. They will not take no for an answer! Leave drawing nearer. Scheduled to go on 13th, but may go on 11th, due to Cpl Spencer's trouble.* SSM goes tomorrow.

---

* Trevor does not elaborate as to what this 'trouble' was.

D +241 Friday 2.2.45

Much hard work today for tank crews – removing replaced tracks, etc. Am orderly sgt for the day and have been chasing fatigue men all day. Definitely moving tomorrow: much bustling about – especially among officers.

Bath parade this afternoon. SSM left for England this morning. Dicky Hall acting SSM today. Saw Mr C. this evening. Promised to call again tomorrow – for photo enlargement and Barry's present. Weather much warmer: very little snow about now.

D +242 Saturday 3.2.45

Normal routine during the day – said *au revoir* to Mr C, also Mr Slaats. Received 'souvenir' from the Garenfeld family. Tanks ready to move 5.30 p.m. – an all night journey to Nijmegen. Route via Best, 'S Hertogenbosch, Grave, Nijmegen, Malden. Bit of a nightmare journey owing to speed. No lights allowed: much secrecy concerning this move. My driver succeeded in destroying two wooden cable pylons!

Grave Bridge – intact: a marvellous job; can't understand why its capture wasn't given more publicity* – likewise dual rail and road bridge just south of Nijmegen. From N, proceeded about 3 miles south-east to Malden for harbour. Arrived about 4 a.m. Spent remainder of night sitting in cookhouse – drinking tea!

---

* The 600-metre bridge over the Maas at Grave was taken by E Company of the 2nd Battalion, 504th Parachute Infantry Regiment, 82nd US Airborne Division in a dramatic assault led by Colonel Reuben H. Tucker on 17 September 1944.

D +243 Sunday 4.2.45

Civvy billets – but I think we have rather commandeered the accommodation than asked permission. Little work today: we have to remain out of sight as much as possible for secrecy. All unit signs, clothing signs, cap badges etc. removed. Something very big is brewing – very big.*

---

* This was the push through the Reichswald Forest into Germany, the last major action that Trevor was involved in, and one which left a profound impression on him.

Part Three

Into Germany

situation acute. Slept in tanks all night
cold & wet — little sleep
Sat. 10.2.45

Much stuff passed thru us during day — heading E.
Recce corps, 43 div etc
Some sniping, mines etc.
Many mines' wait for ... — pretty foul. Last
water contains damages by Jerry Pt. ...
Briefed in the evening for further advance tomorrow.
S. this time — about 3 miles — of same ...
(53 H. Div)

Sun 11
Mon. 12.2.45

Advance in daylight this time; terrible ... thru
extremely dense forest. Tanks performed ...
A. knocked out a Jagd Panther — but in ...
the second, no trace.
Finally harbour about 7.0 pm in dark — cold &
wet. Infantry dug in by tanks. Pretty forlorn
position here.
About 10.0 then saw flash ... by roar of bazooka
Learned later that Sgt Mead killed by Jerry patrol

The entries for 8.2.45 to 12.2.45 indicate the extreme pressure
Trevor was under during the Reichswald action.

D +244 Monday 5.2.45

Usual routine: no definite news yet – but it can't be long now – too many conferences, maps, etc.

D +245 Tuesday 6.2.45

Departed for Helmond, beyond Eindhoven, 2.30 p.m. Arrived 6.30. About 50 miles: hell of a journey owing to road traffic: indescribable amount of stuff pouring towards Nijmegen.

Did our night training in the forest: a horrible business. Departed for Malden 10.30 p.m. – arrived 8.30 a.m. Terrible journey owing to priority traffic: one hold up lasted 5 hours!

D +246 Wednesday 7.2.45

Some information today: not long now for the 'big thing'. My leave! Am due to go in three or four days – but have to go through with the attack. Feel wretched about it.

I do so want to see Jess and Barry ...

Editor's note: The diary entries become scrappy, staccato, less legible, and even a little confused, at this point, with corrections to dates and times. It has the appearance of having been written in great haste or under pressure. This is almost certainly the reason, as will be clear from reading the next few days' entries. Such was the haste, that Trevor abandoned the D-Day count that has preceded every date entry so far. The changed appearance of the diary – impossible to capture in this transcription – speaks more eloquently than the actual text about what the next few days were like.

Thursday 8.2.45

Barrage 5 a.m. We moved off 8.30 a.m. – Destination W edge of Reichswald Forest – to break thru along N edge and emerge E side by dawn. Start delayed – eventually 11 p.m. Remained at first halt awaiting A. They appeared at dawn and went thru us with more infantry.

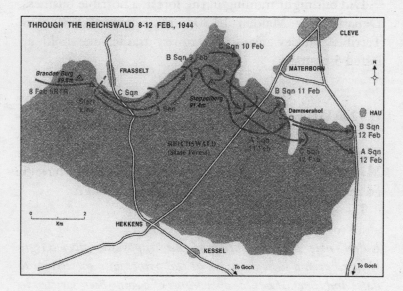

Friday 9.2.45

About half doz prisoners last night. We moved off mid-morning to pass thru A to final objective at far edge of wood. Hundreds of prisoners started rolling in soon after A left us for their advance.

Ultimately reached final obj during afternoon – and found a few dozen more prisoners. Very gratifying to see so much stuff passing thru us early in the morning with A – good night's work. Remained on final objective with infantry. Stonked two or three times by Jerry. Our water situation acute. 'Slept' in tanks all night, cold and wet – little sleep.

Saturday 10.2.45

Much stuff passed thru us during day – heading east. Recce corps, 43 Div*, etc. Some sniping, etc. Using 'rusty' water for drinks – pretty foul. Last water container damaged by Jerry HE. Briefed in the evening for further advance tomorrow. South this time – about 3 miles – with same infantry (53 Welsh Div).

* The 43rd (Wessex) Infantry Division.

Churchills at the start of the Reichswald battle, 9 February 1945.
It was stands of trees such as these that the tanks were used
to plough straight through.

Photograph © IWM B14422.

Sunday 11.2.45

Advance in daylight this time: terrible journey thru
extremely dense forest. Tanks performed miracles.* A
knocked out a Jack Panther – but we missed the second: no
trace. Finally harboured about 7 p.m. in dark. Cold and wet.
Infantry dug in by tanks. Pretty perilous position here.

About ten or eleven saw flash accompanied by roar of

---

* Lt Col Berry Veale, CO of 9 RTR, wrote in his report: 'The ability of the
Churchill tank to give close support to infantry through forests of the Reichswald
type, both day and night, was proven. It is believed that no other Allied tank now
in service could have done as well, or even have reached the forest over the same
country.'

bazooka. Learned later that Sgt Mead* killed by Jerry patrol. Entire crews on guard all night afterwards. Wretched conditions – cold and wet, no water for tea. Heard Jerry tank during night.

Monday 12.2.45

Pete Davies appeared at dawn to inform me he had been sent to relieve me. Leave at last! Departed almost immediately for echelon. Arr. echelon about 7 p.m. (Malden). Terrible journey thru flooded road – with SSM Tomlinson and Johnny. Welcomed by Les and Tom, and slept in old billet. Everyone very kind. Damned glad to get back.

Tuesday 13.2.45

Departed 1 p.m. for echelon at Eindhoven with Q Rathke. Arrived about 3.30 – and started sorting kit, etc. Collected new coat, beret, boots, etc. from RK [*unidentified*].

Now have Leave pass, cash, etc. Sleeping in civvy billets tonight – Burg Leopold tomorrow.

Wednesday 14.2.45

By road to Burg Leopold: arr. 10.30 a.m. Bath, haircut, etc. Entrained 5 p.m. – departed 6 p.m. Arr. Calais 5.15 a.m. – detrained 6 a.m.

* Sergeant Michael 'Reg' Mead: not the same person as Alfred 'Titch' Mead who was badly injured at Vinkenbroek (D +145 29.10.44).

Miserable journey – very uncomfortable carriages. Exchanged cash, etc. at Calais Transit Camp – breakfast, meal ticket, etc. – and then waited for sailing orders ... Waited until 3 p.m. and then loudspeakers announced cancellation of day's sailings. We remain here for the night. Drew extra blankets, etc.

Editor's note: The sixth diary notebook ends at this point, with many unused notebook pages left. There are no diary entries for the duration of Trevor's leave – understandably. The diary resumes again in the seventh and last notebook, after an interval of nine days.

Saturday 24.2.45

Last day of leave: said good-bye to Jess and Barry about 1.30 p.m. To London via 2.25 Edgeley – arr. Euston 7 p.m. Marjorie and Fred awaiting. Dined with them at Coventry Street Corner House.

Reported Victoria 10.30 p.m. – thousands of troops waiting – depressing sight. Ultimately reached Folkestone about 1 a.m. – then herded to Transit camp (Hotel). To bed about 2 a.m.

Sunday 25.2.45

Reveille about 5.30 a.m. Good breakfast – then to landing stage: changed cash – proceeded on board. Lunch and tea at Calais. Entrained for Burg Leopold about 8.30 p.m. All-night journey in wooden carriages: little room or comfort.

Monday 26.2.45

Arr. BL about 6 a.m. Had breakfast and lunch at transit camp. Unit lorry departed 1 p.m. Called at Mr C's house in Eindhoven [Mr Cornelese] – left presents. Joined up with rear echelons at Malden, Nr. Nijmegen. Arr. about 6 p.m. Slept in same billet with Les Challinor.

Tuesday 27.2.45

Remained at Malden: probably rejoining tanks tomorrow. Saw *Song of Russia* film this evening.

Wednesday 28.2.45

Travelled with echelon to small village a mile west of Goch – and rejoined tanks. Temporarily attached 13 Troop. Some German civvies still living in cellars in this area. Houses terribly battered. Usual scenes of destruction – furniture, etc. in gardens and roadways. Reminds me of Normandy.

Plenty of our artillery close by. Also a German 'fort' and blockhouse. Former apparently designed for the MGs only. Enormous concrete structure. Blockhouse very strongly built: walls about 10ft thick with sloping sides. Triple steel doors: air conditioning plant: hand pump for water: bunks, etc.: gas stop in fire chimney. Slept in partly wrecked bedroom of cottage. Little sleep owing to artillery barrage during night.

Thursday 1.3.45

Moved forward this morning to village of Hulm, about 2 miles south of Goch. Goch itself a terrible shambles: practically every building and house damaged: Centre of town almost wiped out. Our bombers raided this town (and Kleve) the night before present offensive started.

Precise location of enemy not certain, but we are under fire here. Only a few cottages in Hulm – and remains of the village church. My troop harboured in church: several gaping holes in roof and walls, but we have found one or two sheltered corners in the place.

Friday 2.3.45

Remained at Hulm all day. Crews very busy hunting chickens, ducks, eggs, etc. Some civvies in the area. They seem quite docile.

Slept on floor between 2 rows of pews last night. We have a huge brazier made from dustbin for warmth – located in centre of main aisle: plenty of timber for fuel. Chickens and ducks for lunch – roasted in ammo tin over brazier: graveyard surrounding church now resembles a poultry farm. Several crews are keeping live hens for eggs – wire netting enclosures around gravestones.

In between graves – many hit by HE – infantry have dug slit trenches. Whole scene is rather fantastic and unreal. Dead horse among graves: wooden cross now serving as hen-perch: steel helmet in slit trench containing portion of man's head: church tapestries, carpets, etc. being used for bedding: steel safe in vestry still locked in spite of infantry's efforts to burst it open with AP rounds.*

Front has moved forward today, so we may have quieter night tonight – and easier guard! Jerry 88 close by – now wrecked – also 75 mortar. Dicky and I 'spiked' the latter.

The German town of Kleve, photographed from a low-flying Auster aircraft, a few days after the major Bomber Command raid on 7–8 February 1945.

Photograph © IWM C4964.

---

* In a letter Trevor adds: 'the churchyard is littered with ... shell holes ... The numerous graves have been somewhat disturbed. To quote one of our wits, it looks as though there has been a "bloody resurrection"!'

Saturday 3.3.45

Still at Hulm. May move forward today but not certain: too much stuff on main roads. Recce officer's Honey went up on a mine this a.m., seeking a route to the front.

Later. No move today: perhaps tomorrow. Believe the tanks are temporarily 'frozen' owing to enormous demand on the roads. And moving across country is impossible in this land of ditches, bogs, floods, rivers, mines and tank ditches: also, practically all bridges are blown.

Tank crews having a good time looting in this locality. There are many empty houses – mostly well battered – and much stuff is being unearthed, particularly clothing, sheets, towels, pillow cases, etc. – mostly new – and, significantly, bearing Dutch labels. It would appear that the looters are now being looted!! Some of the houses are still occupied, but the civvies seem quite docile. In this connection, I have seen a few German males of about 30 years, and apparently quite healthy, calmly idling about the farms and cottages. Cannot help wondering whether they are deserters from their army. Food seems quite plentiful with these Germans. Several of our lads have asked for, and received, home-cured bacon and ham. And in the empty houses, large quantities of lard and bottled foods have been found – and used!

Several dead cattle in this locality – also a few bodies. One of the latter – a mutilated German – was being eaten by a hen and a cat simultaneously today.

Sunday 4.3.45

We left Hulm at 11.30 today en route for Walbeck, about 20 miles south, but we only travelled about 7 miles and were then stopped on the main Venlo–Nijmegen road and 'frozen' again. So we are now harboured in various cottages just off the main road. A wretched day – heavy rain and cold. We all got soaked on the journey. Depressing countryside too, terribly flat, badly waterlogged, ditches by the mile: all road bridges blown, but now 'Bailey bridged'. Much damage to property: roads also very badly cut up: mines are plentiful too, and many of the roads bear the horrible sign 'verge not checked'. Have today seen more of Jerry's Siegfried defences – mostly trenches – endless miles of them, also tank ditches, mostly flooded.

The cottages we are now occupying – in Holland – are badly damaged, but we have made them habitable after clearing tons of debris. Had a job finding a stove, but eventually rigged up a crude stove from bits of scrap iron found in neighbouring barns, etc. Today's departure caused a complication with the live hens, but the lads never seem to be daunted. My crew packed their two hens in a compo box, and J— [*name illegible*] packed his cock and five hens in a sack!! When 'unpacked', our two had laid one egg – broken, but J's had laid two – unbroken!!

Two letters from Jess today. Sleeping on a wooden form tonight. Too many mice in the house for my liking. Our room is leaking water – but we hope for a fine night! Still doing guards every night. Capt Link now temporary OC – whilst Major Holden is battn 2 i/c in Major Massy's absence on leave.

Monday 5.3.45

Five letters from Jess today – but four of them were written before my leave. Still 'frozen' – no move today. Weather fine, but cloudy. Rumours of Yanks having crossed Rhine, but official reports only speak of action along western bank.

Visited nearby village today: completely deserted, not even occupied by soldiers. Terribly depressing to see so many homes so deserted and wrecked. The recent floods seem to have inundated this area.

Tuesday 6.3.45

Still 'frozen' off roads: no sign of move. Spent the day reading and writing – also a little work on vehicle.

Wednesday 7.3.45

Still static: may remain here a few days. Not very comfortable in the billet, but we are at least 'indoors'. My bed consists of a long form, with four chairs laid sideways to provide extra width.

Crews doing usual scrounging and looting from derelict houses: but no food in this area (Holland). Chickens are now laying. Rumour that we may be static here for 10–14 days – but anything is possible. Wrote to Jess. Terribly cramped here – ten of us packed into a small room. Using candles looted from church in previous harbour. CO's Inspection of billets today.

Thursday 8.3.45

Usual routine on vehicles this morning. Officially informed of 'tank-head memorial service and march past Brigadier' for Sunday. Usual palaver and spit and polish. Preparatory parade tomorrow and Saturday morning. Fitted up electric light in billet from tank. News from General Patton's army – officially reported across Rhine somewhere around Bonn.* This news from Brigade – probably true.

Later. Much better light this evening. Sunday's parade now cancelled. We are moving tomorrow – probably to Wezel area where German pocket is still resisting strongly. Reveille 6.30, ready to move 9 a.m. Damnable billet this: two crews in one small room for 'recreation': very noisy.

Later. Tomorrow's move now timed for 6.15 a.m.: reveille 4 a.m.! 9 o'clock news confirmed bridgehead over Rhine. Americans crossed at 4.30 p.m. yesterday. Good news.

Friday 9.3.45

At midnight last night, we were informed that previous orders concerning anticipated move should be ignored. Reveille 7.30 a.m., etc. But we were awakened at 4 a.m. by the guard – and informed that the move was now definitely ON – depart 6.15 a.m.! Damnable.

Usual chaos and rushing about to stow our belongings on

* A colourful and frequently controversial figure, General George S. Patton was commander of the US Third Army, leading it to some spectacular successes between August 1944 and May 1945.

the vehicles – not so easy in the dark –! Morning cold, but not raining.

Moved off 6.15 a.m. and travelled towards Wezel, via Geldern and Issum. The former place is a ruin – presumably bombed out of existence. Halted about 2 miles east of Issum and not far from the front line. Much artillery and aerial activity. These Jerries in the Wezel 'pocket' are certainly proving a damned nuisance.

Saw several Jerry civvies today – mostly elderly women – but a few girls and young men. Also noticed masses of 'safe conduct' leaflets dropped by Allied planes in Geldern area.* Usual scenes of destruction, but not so bad in the country. It appears to be a rich agricultural area: thousands of hens. And we are still carrying 4 live ones on the vehicle. Pestell appears to have become attached to them, but will have to insist on disposing of them if we go into action.

Later. Moved about 2 miles nearer front at 4 p.m. Now harboured beside a large pine forest. We are relieving the 13/18 Hussars† either at midnight or dawn tomorrow. Meanwhile, this is not a very healthy spot. We are well within mortar range, and Jerry is still fighting stubbornly.

* Enormous numbers of these leaflets were dropped by the Allies from June 1944 onwards to encourage the German forces to surrender. Signed by General Eisenhower, each one began, 'Who carries this safe conduct is using it as a sign of his genuine wish to give himself up. He is to be disarmed, to be well looked after, to receive food and medical attention as required, and to be removed from the danger zone as soon as possible.' The leaflets Trevor saw were most likely the standard ZG61, of which more than 65,000,000 were dropped between September 1944 and March 1945.

† The 13/18 Hussars (Queen Mary's Own) were an RAC regiment which formed part of 8 Armoured Brigade.

Watched a heavy attack by our Thunderbolt fighter bombers this evening. They certainly played havoc with something a mile or two ahead of us. Jerry must have been in occupation here yesterday. There is a German dead body in the field close behind my vehicle. If we remain here until dawn, will probably spend the night beneath the vehicle – cold, but fairly safe.

Saturday 10.3.45

Remained static last night – in the tank. Moved out 6 a.m. with 11 Troop to take up defensive position east of Alpen. The latter supposed to have been cleared of remaining snipers yesterday. Increased signs of heavy fighting along the road as we neared Alpen – dead cattle, Jerries, etc. Many trees blasted down as road blocks: some of them still standing with undetonated charges still attached near base of trunk.

The area seems to be infested with mines: not safe to wander off the road on to verges. Some road craters, but already roughly filled in. Alpen itself still under shell and mortar fire: the place has been badly battered – with usual chaos on roads – *viz*. rubble, wreckage, furniture, sewing machines, pianos, clothing. No civvies about – perhaps we are too early for them. Barely daylight when we arrived. Proceeded through town, and took up position adjoining large house on eastern outskirts. Crews immediately dismounted and carried out recce of house: soon had breakfast on the way. Meanwhile the lads enjoy an orgy of looting – bicycles, wireless sets, clothing, linen, pots and pans, etc.

Two male civvies dead on rear cellar steps; one body

intact, the other badly mutilated. The house itself very badly damaged. Appears to have belonged to an ardent Nazi. Civvy neighbour appeared during morning – and started removing some of the household effects: we let him carry on.

Meanwhile, fair amount of HE was falling, but none nearer than about 200 yds. Saw an enormous number of civvies filing from a 'hole in the hillside' about 400 yds ahead of us during the morning. This must have been an air raid shelter. They all returned to the town – mostly carrying bundles, etc. – and mostly women and children. Saw huge batch of prisoners coming forward about lunch time.

Several rumours during afternoon: Jerry reported to have pulled out and blown remaining bridges at Wezel this morning. Things certainly became quieter towards evening. Even our artillery seemed to fade out. We remained on observation awaiting further orders. 11 Troop called in about tea time. 13 Troop withdrawn about 6 p.m. – and rejoining rest of squadron harboured along roadside in Alpen.

Everyone seems to have had a great day – so far as looting is concerned. The tanks must be bulging with the stuff. Several civvies appeared in town, particularly towards evening, mostly women and children. Some queer sights in the town: troops wearing silk hats, etc. – and generally celebrating.

Sleeping tonight in derelict house – formerly the home of a doctor. Piles of debris in the place, and remains of much good furniture. Believe we are moving out tomorrow, but no definite orders. Presume our immediate future will depend upon the enemy. If he has withdrawn, there will be nothing for us to do on this sector west of the Rhine.

Sunday 11.3.45

Early reveille, and all vehicles stowed ready for moving at 7 a.m. – but soon learned that we are remaining in Alpen a further day. It now seems definite that Jerry has withdrawn. Military government of the place has been installed today – so looting is now definitely taboo. Seem to be more civvies here now – pitiful creatures, many in tears. Presumably they have lost everything in the battle for the town. Some mail arrived today – thank goodness. Sleeping in same ruined house tonight. Everyone seems very cheerful and in high spirits. The lads have an amazing variety of preserved food from the local houses. The Germans here were evidently far from starving.

Moving tomorrow: received orders late tonight. Destination Venlo on tracks, and then to Deurne, near Helmond, by transporter. Reveille 5 a.m. Move 7 a.m.

Monday 12.3.45

Usual rush and hurry: breakfast prepared in the dark – and everything stowed on vehicles. Moved off at 7 a.m. Some confusion en route. The squadron missed the left hand turn at Issum and had to turn back at Geldern. This caused delay which must have upset movement control programme very seriously. We got mixed up with many convoys, particularly American, and caused some chaos.

Eventually reached Venlo in late afternoon and ultimately got across the Maas via the amazingly long Bailey bridge – 413 yds! Harboured west side of river – our late arrival has involved a day's delay: the rest of the unit moved off via transporters, but we cannot now move until tomorrow. Sleeping in bivvys tonight. The lads have already done much bartering with local civvies – Several wireless sets and bicycles etc. have changed hands this evening. The harbour resembled a market place!

Tuesday 13.3.45

Luckily, it was fine and not very cold last night, otherwise the bivvies would have provided little comfort. We slept in a minefield which had not been cleared – but the mines were presumably of the anti-tank variety: We had no trouble from them.

Reveille 5.30 a.m. – and moved on to transporters at 7 a.m. And that was the beginning of one of the most boring of all our rides. We actually travelled about 80 miles by road, but finished up at Deurne – not more than 25 miles as the crow flies from our start point. The long detour, via Belgium, Eindhoven and Helmond was necessitated on account of the weight of the transporters – we had to have a Class 70 route.

After the usual halts for punctures and minor repairs, we reached Deurne about 4.30 in the afternoon and ultimately harboured and found our billets. Most of us have civvy billets – a rare treat after the rough conditions of the last two weeks. During today's transport journey, I saw Monty for the first time. First a jeep came whizzing by, containing four MPs* – three of them standing up and waving to other traffic to clear the road. An electric siren and flashing light

* Military Police.

assisted them. And then came the low fast car with four brass hats, including Monty, sitting by the driver. He waved cheerily to the troops around. Late this afternoon, Gen Dempsey* visited the colonel and carried out a brief inspection.

Wednesday 14.3.45

We anticipate some hard work today, but Capt Link (acting o/c) gave us a lecture on first parade and announced a rest day to get settled in! He also passed on some complimentary criticisms of the unit by Gen Dempsey and the Brig.

Passion trucks this evening to Asten and Helmond, also cinema shows in Deurne. Saw a large force of Lancasters this afternoon and afterwards heard on radio that they dropped our new 22000 lb bombs on Germany for the first time. Some bomb!†

Thursday 15.3.45

Best BD parade this a.m. for clothing exchange – preparatory to a round of 'bullshit' parades and inspections, presumably. This parade was followed by a battalion parade for an address by the colonel.

* Lieutenant General Sir Miles Dempsey was commander of the British Second Army in the Normandy campaign. Dempsey was knighted by George VI during the King's visit to the Second Army in October 1944, and was the first British Army commander to cross the Rhine, on 23 March 1945.
† The 22,000 lb Grand Slam earthquake bomb or 'Ten Ton Tess' was designed by Barnes Wallis of Dambusters fame, and was used to great effect against bridges and viaducts in the final stages of the war.

He repeated some of the compliments mentioned by Capt Link – *viz.* 53 Div had had to be relieved before completing their offensive towards Wezel. We had been detached from them a few days previously. One of the division officers stated that they would easily have reached the Rhine in three days had the 9th Battn RTR been with them!

Other compliments about the brigade came also from Gen Dempsey and Gen Horrocks,* and the former spoke of the 9th as a fine regiment on his visit yesterday.

But the most interesting part of today's little ceremony was the colonel's announcement that the King has confirmed the award of the DSO to Major Holden. A high honour for the unit, but particularly for C Squadron. The colonel pinned the medal on Ronnie's breast alongside his earlier MC. I haven't heard a soul speak disparagingly of this award to the major. If any man has earned it, he has.

After dismissal, we carried on with work on the vehicles. Sgts' mess opened today.

Friday 16.3.45

Routine maintenance on vehicles and major overhauls where necessary.

Saturday 17.3.45

Routine maintenance, etc.

* Lieutenant General Sir Brian Horrocks earned high praise from Eisenhower, who called him 'the best of Montgomery's British generals'.

Sunday 18.3.45

Church parade and 'march past': otherwise a 'day off'.

Monday 19.3.45

Usual routine: the locality now looks like a Churchill scrap yard, so many vehicles are partly dismantled for major repairs – tracks, final drives, bogies, etc.

Tuesday 20.3.45

Usual routine. Dicky Hall, Bob Anderson, Capt Link, Lt Lilly left today for 60 hrs in Paris. Weather now very fine. Brig visited vehicle park today.

Wednesday 21.3.45

Usual routine. Have to carry out AFV inspection on three troop vehicles in Mr Lilly's absence: to be done by Saturday. Night exercise tomorrow evening.

Thursday 22.3.45

Usual routine today: beautiful weather. Exercise this evening – seems to have been evolved by Colonel: 'silent' approach on enemy strongpoint, using tank searchlight, etc. as target. It is worth trying, but may only work once.

On German soil. These are the Churchills of 9 RTR on the road towards
Goch. Note the bomb crater in the foreground, courtesy of the RAF.

Photograph © IWM B14726.

Friday 23.3.45

Usual routine today: beautiful day. Rumours of another
Rhine bridgehead, this time by American 3rd Army.
Exercise again this evening – this time we acted as infantry
for B Sqdn. A boring business: vehicles travelled far too
slowly. Audience included Brigadier.

Saturday 24.3.45

Usual routine: Further Rhine bridgehead by Americans
officially confirmed. They crossed about 10 p.m. Thursday
evening. Beautiful morning – still warm, and cloudless.

One of the historic days of this war.

About 9.30 a.m., we saw a few groups of low-flying Dakotas heading for Germany – 30 or 40 planes in each group. An unusual sight here, in spite of recent terrific aerial activity. Very soon, it became obvious that something really big was occurring. The Dakotas continued to appear in large groups – must have been hundreds of them in half an hour. What else could they be carrying but airborne paratroopers? It was an inspiring sight in the clear and vivid light of this beautiful morning. The Dakotas were followed by a more amazing sight still – hundreds of them came over, this time towing gliders! Obviously our airborne army. The gliders were of at least two types, and armour was presumably being carried.

This amazing procession of aircraft continued until about 1 p.m. – finishing up with Sterlings and Halifaxes towing gliders – and Liberators flying solo, presumably with supplies. Meanwhile, the sky above was alive with fighters protecting this modern armada.

Confirmed on 1 o'clock radio news that our land forces, assisted by RAF and Navy* had crossed the Rhine in Wezel area last night. Today's aerial pageant must have been a sort of 'second phase'!

Am glad to have seen it: to my mind, one of the really outstanding days of the war. And how exhilarating! Everyone seemed immensely cheerful this morning: the tension has certainly been relaxed now.

---

* The Navy provided landing craft, pontoon bridges and booms across the river to guard against German midget submarines, explosive boats and saboteur swimmers.

Sunday 25.3.45

Fine weather persists. Bridgehead appears to be going well: opposition less than anticipated. No signs of a move here: very little work today. Much eager enquiring after news at the front.

Monday 26.3.45

Usual routine. Bridgehead still expanding: Everything going well. This fine weather a great help – especially in the air. Lloyd George dead.*

Tuesday 27.3.45

Cold and misty this morning: but news from the front still excellent. Several bridges now – and more bridgeheads on US sector. Usual routine here.

Harry Brooks and Frank Hodson now back from UK. Presume I will rejoin 15 Troop.

Wednesday 28.3.45

Usual routine this morning: still misty and cold. Later – Conference with major at noon: all officers and sergeants present. Announced that Br. definitely frozen here for three

* Prime minister from 1916 to 1922 and instrumental in the creation of the welfare state, David Lloyd George was a towering figure in early twentieth-century politics.

weeks – but each battn providing a sqdn for special duties: 1 sqdn for L of C protection:* 1 sqdn for army HQ defence: 1 sqdn for 'riot' troops. With providing latter – C Sqdn!

Vehicles for our use – Honeys, scout cars, half-tracks – 15 cwts† – mechanised infantry!! It appears that our job will be to fight against guerillas and snipers etc. behind our lines. Not a pleasant prospect – but the major seems enthusiastic – perhaps because we will now cross the Rhine!! We are expected to move within 48 hours.

Thursday 29.3.45

Troop training today – as infantry. Did one or two attacks – with Mr Feathers.‡ Much sorting out of ammo, equipment, etc. to comply with 'light squadron' establishment.

Friday 30.3.45

More infantry training today – this time with vehicles including Honeys: far too strenuous for my liking. Spent half the day performing like a human caterpillar – crawling over ploughed fields, etc.

---

* The lines of communication between the rear supporting areas and the front line formations needed additional protection in hostile or potentially hostile country, as the transport units, radio operators and so on had little to defend themselves with.

† Hundredweight. In the British imperial system of weights and measures, there were 20 hundredweight in a ton.

‡ Lieutenant Featherstonehaugh, who was standing in as troop leader.

Saturday 31.3.45

Announced today that 'light squadron' business is off – pro
tem. We are now moving as a battn to new location. Move
tomorrow – tanks depart from Deurne about 10 a.m. –
somewhere in Venlo area.

Sunday 1.4.45

Arrived Sevenum today – about 6 miles west of Venlo.
Route via Liessel and Maasbree: evidence of much heavy
fighting in Liessel area. Billeted with elderly Dutch couple.
Dicky and I sleeping on floor. Huge petrol dump along road
east of Venlo.

Monday 2.4.45

An hour or two on vehicles this morning. Spent much time
in sgts' mess, reading and writing.

Tuesday 3.4.45

Usual routine: Liberty trucks to Eindhoven. Chief local
entertainment appears to be antics of bulls in local stud
farm!

Wednesday 4.4.45

Usual routine. Much rain: spent the day in the mess.

Thursday 5.4.45

Usual routine. Believe we are moving from here on Saturday, but no preparation as yet. Later. Informed at 10.30 p.m. that we are moving tomorrow.

Friday 6.4.45

Awakened at 1.30 a.m. and informed that we move at 9.30 a.m. today. Departed to schedule. Route via Venlo, Uedem (in ruins: absolute chaos) Hochwald Forest, and Marienbaum for night's harbour. Evidence of heavy fighting in the forest. Slept in deserted and partly ruined German house. Marienbaum badly battered and completely deserted, apart from a few troops. We cross the Rhine tomorrow at Rees.

Saturday 7.4.45

Leisurely morning: beautiful day. Ready to move at 3 p.m. Journey under strict orders of MC due to bridges. Eventually the battn got away about 4 p.m. Journey to Rhine thru perfectly flat country, with a few German farmers working in the fields. But much evidence of recent heavy fighting, including piles of unused ammo still to be collected. Also plenty of evidence of 'smoke screen' over 2nd Army during assault preparation. Hundreds of canisters, etc. littering the fields.

Crossed Rhine about 6 p.m. at Rees. River much tamer looking than expected. Perfectly flat country each side and comparatively smooth flowing water. There were three Bailey bridges in use at Rees, and much bridge building equipment on west side of river. A much larger bridge appears to be under construction. The town of Rees is completely battered – a mass of ruins: we passed through without halting.

Beyond Rees, country very flat and uninteresting with much evidence of recent fighting – ruined farm buildings, burned out vehicles etc. And so to Bocholt, a one-time fairly large town, but now a mass of ruins. The RAF must have plastered the place fairly recently.* Hardly a building left in the town – only gaunt and blackened walls and heaps of rubble.

Saw several groups of civilians searching amongst the wreckage and pushing all kinds of wheeled vehicles from prams to handcarts. Scenes very typical of France, Belgium and Holland – but now the Herrenvolk are having a taste of war with a vengeance.

From Bocholt, across Dutch frontier and so to Winterswijk – a small Dutch town where we were given a great welcome. The place was only liberated a week ago, so troops in khaki are still a novelty. The town is gaily decorated with flags, streamers, etc. Practically every house and shop has a flag flying. This place has suffered little damage from the war – the railway sidings only appear to have been bombed.

* There was an RAF raid on Bocholt on 21 March.

Civilians appear to be well dressed and well fed: they are obviously far from starving. Our harbour is in a good class residential quarter and we are billeted with local civilians. It is almost strange to see rows of well built and new houses perfectly intact – there aren't any broken windows even.

Dicky and I sleeping in same house. Good bed, with sheets! Wash-bowl in bedroom, carpets, etc. Also a decent WC, piano, etc. It is a well equipped home and very comfortable. Noticed a complete absence of religious junk, and presume we must now be in a Protestant area.

Sunday 8.4.45

Some work on the tanks this morning, but spent most of the day 'settling in'. Host and hostess (Lammers) do not speak English, but we manage to converse somehow. Believe there was a strong pro-German element in the town, and about 600 of them are now in gaol: but there are many more Dutch Nazis still at large.

SSM already has sgts' mess functioning: a fully furnished house – home of a former collaborator.

Monday 9.4.45

Went out in the tanks today (15 Troop). Just a 'patrol' in neighbouring areas: returned in time for tea.

Fine day – beautiful, spring-like weather.

Tuesday 10.4.45

Out again this morning – this time in lorries with 12 Troop – an 'infantry' patrol seeking suspected Jerries in a nearby wood. But we found nothing. Given the job of lighting up the dance hall today. Proposed using batteries, etc., but the SSM rolled up with a first-class German generating plant and this solved the problem. Excellent machine, 6 cylinder petrol engine, 8KW dynamo, 85/150 V – perfectly new and in good working order. It was 'found' in a local Nazi ordnance dump – and there are six more of them! Obviously field searchlight units. Spent afternoon and evening with the plant, wiring up dance hall, etc.

Few civvies in the mess this evening.

Wednesday 11.4.45

Spent most of today providing electric light for cookhouse, sgts' mess, etc. The latter involved overhead cable over main road. Utilised house wiring, and fitted 130V lamps. We now have an all electric home! More civvies in the mess this evening – dancing, etc! Beautiful weather – warm and sunny.

Thursday 12.4.45

Announced this morning that we are moving tomorrow. A horrible blow! Learned of death of President Roosevelt. Terrible news.*

---

* Franklin D. Roosevelt, the only US president to have served three terms in office, had been in declining health for some time, although his death was

Friday 13.4.45

Move postponed: probably depart tomorrow.

Saturday 14.4.45

Reveille 4 a.m. Depart 6 a.m. – Destination Schüttorf in Germany. Route via Enschede. Arrived Schüttorf about 10.30 a.m. Billeted in large house (15 and 12 Troops). Civvies had been given notice to quit by major on preceding day. They were still carting masses of furniture from the garden when we arrived. Sergeants' mess in fully furnished house: a large place and quite luxurious. Plenty of books – including amazing collection of works on Nazi party, etc.: officers' mess in large modern house next door. Previous tenant, obviously wealthy, kicked out by major previous day.

Very gratifying to see lorry loads of prisoners passing by. Local authority is repairing electric supply, but have wired up our own plant as reserve. Several orders issued outlining our activities here, *viz*: riot sqdn, road and curfew patrol, tank park guard, billet guard, etc. We are certainly going to have a less restful time than in Holland.

Sunday 15.4.45

Roosevelt funeral today ...
  Did little all day apart from work on the generating plant

---

unexpected. Roosevelt had described his convictions as being 'left of centre', a position which accorded with Trevor's own.

– But at 7.30 p.m., the troop had to pack up and prepare for immediate departure to Nordhorn, about 10 miles north, to act as bridge guard.

Found on arrival that the CMP had departed the previous night, leaving the town and three important Bailey bridges unguarded. There was a local scare due to sabotaging of some lorries in nearby village a day or two earlier. Also, mysterious chalked notice had appeared on a wall in Nordhorn regarding radio broadcast by 'Radio Wolf'. It may have been written by a 'Werewolf'.*

Temporary HQ with RAF security unit in main hotel of the town: mattresses provided for beds – quite comfortable. Did a turn on one of the bridges around midnight: rather uncomfortable experience. Hope we are relieved tomorrow.

Monday 16.4.45

Carried on with bridge patrol all day. Saw many more loads of prisoners – including a convoy of them during the night. Also a lorry of freed slaves – Italians and Russians. Vehicle driver seemed unable to get rid of them.

Some of the lads have spent most of the day repairing a looted car – a three-wheeler. Finally repaired it – and drove it back to Schüttorf! The patrolmen seem to have enjoyed accosting Germans – particularly prosperous looking ones – and demanding passes during the day. Weather very warm

---

* Werwolf (the German spelling) was intended to be an underground commando or guerilla force which would resist the Allied advance into Germany. In reality it was ill equipped, poorly supported and ineffective, dwindling rapidly to isolated handfuls of Nazi fanatics; but its propaganda outlet, Radio Werwolf, achieved some success in making it seem a greater threat than it was.

– like midsummer. Relieved about 8 p.m. by HQA* – glad to get back to the unit.

Tuesday 17.4.45

Learned today that Barry's operation 'quite successful'. Good news.

On 24-hour guard from 9 a.m. Announced this evening that we are soon moving again: this time to Dortmund–Ems canal – probably be under canvas.

This was the final entry in the diary. The war in Europe was over, and three weeks later on 8 May the Allies formally accepted Germany's unconditional surrender.

There was, however, a great deal of work to be done establishing the peace, and 9 RTR remained in Germany until December 1945, at which time the regiment was disbanded. Apart from several weeks in June and July, during which he was seconded to the British Army Exhibition in Paris, Trevor was kept busy with a combination of guard, patrol and administrative duties, enforcing curfews or checking the passes of German civilian workers. This was a role with which he was ill at ease, but which he accepted had to be done, as the first steps in rebuilding a shattered Europe.

He continued to write home to Jess almost every day. His letter of 13 November is marked 'D –17', the 'D' in this instance standing for his demobilisation, and the countdown continues to D minus 2 on 29 November. On 1 December 1945, his last day as a serving soldier, he was finally able to write to her: 'I am now … on my way home.'

---

* Possibly refers to the HQ Squadron 'A' tank and its crew.

Trevor, King of the Tea Brewers. Drawn by Bert Cousins, also in C Squadron, who no doubt shared many a brew of 'hot sweet' with Trevor.

Photograph © The Trevor Greenwood Archive.

9 RTR in Normandy, 1944

by John Delaney

Background

9 RTR was first formed in December 1916 as the 9th Battalion, Heavy Branch Machine Gun Corps. The battalion served at the Battle of Cambrai in November 1917 where, along with III Corps of the Third British Army, it achieved complete surprise and dealt the Germans a major defeat.

Cambrai was the first large-scale tank battle in history, and went a long way to proving the theories of the advocates of mechanised warfare, who argued that the tank would in future become an invaluable asset on the battlefield.

Throughout the remainder of the Great War, 9 RTR were used to great effect supporting large-scale infantry operations. As a result of their close and effective coopera-tion with French forces in the field they were awarded the Croix de Guerre avec Palme as a regimental decoration.

The battalion was also awarded the honour of wearing the badge of General Bourgon's 3rd Division for their support of French troops during the Battle of Moreuil in July 1918; a replica of which was worn on the sleeve of everyone serving in 9 RTR. From this the battalion took their unofficial motto: '*Qui s'y frotte, s'y brûle*', which trans-lates as '*Touch me, and you burn*'.

At the end of the war the Tank Corps was reduced to a much smaller force of only four fighting battalions, and the 9th Battalion was disbanded.

So when it was re-formed, 9 RTR was very much a 'junior' battalion in the view of the British Army establishment. The Royal Tank Regiment as a whole only dated back some twenty-three years. It was not seen as glamorous, nor did it have the backbone of tradition that informed so much of the way things were done in other regiments.

From the very start, 9 RTR attracted officers who wanted to get away from the 'bull' and the ingrained conservatism of well-established units: those who said they were interested in fighting Hitler, as opposed to those interested in a career in the military. The Royal Tank Regiment as a whole welcomed this sort of officer and even turned it to its advantage, presenting itself as an alternative home for those who were interested in 'proper soldiering' (i.e. winning the war), as well as attracting those with backgrounds in engineering or mechanics who were interested in the tanks.

These found that 9 RTR was a much more comfortable place for the citizen soldier; the battalion was much more welcoming, less stuffy, and less rigid, than many of the cavalry units that had recently been re-equipped with tanks. The disadvantage of this philosophy was that, when it finally came to facing up to the enemy, 9 RTR perhaps lacked something of the military professionalism and élan that saw other units through. However, what 9 RTR might have lacked in this regard it more than made up for in terms of its technical professionalism and its ability to make newcomers feel at home and part of a larger military family.

Training at Charing Tank Park, spring 1944. Relaxed but ready, reflecting the ethos of 9 RTR. Trevor is standing, second left.

Photograph © The Trevor Greenwood Archive.

After the disaster at Dunkirk, it was imperative that new tank units were raised to replace those lost in France. Britain was open to invasion and there were virtually no tank units left on the Home Front. As a result, 9 RTR was re-formed, at Gateshead, in November 1940.

It was not until mid-1941, however, when the regiment was based at Otley in Yorkshire, that 9 RTR received the tanks it was to use in its role as a Heavy Tank Unit. The battalion was one of the first units to be equipped with Churchill Infantry Tanks, and it stuck with them until the end of the war.

Between 1941 and 1944 the regiment moved around the country, from Otley, to Eastbourne, South Lancing, Charing, and eventually Aldershot. Along with this, tanks and tank crews often moved around the country to various gunnery ranges, such as Bovington Camp, Castlemartin in Wales and Kirkcudbright in Dumfriesshire. By mid-1944, they felt they were as well rehearsed as they could be, and were itching to get at the enemy.

9 RTR finally saw combat in Normandy shortly after D-Day. Their first action against the enemy was as part of Operation Epsom, launched to punch a hole in the German line and create the opportunity for the mass breakout from the beachhead.

The Army Tank Brigade and the Infantry Tank

In the 1930s the British Army foresaw a requirement for tanks to carry out two distinct roles on the battlefield of the future.

The first, that of reconnaissance and exploitation, was the role that had formerly been allotted to the cavalry. These tank units, in large part made up of regiments that up until recently had been horse mounted, were to be equipped with fast (and therefore lightly armoured) tanks. Their job was to seek out the enemy and report back their positions and numbers. They would then be withdrawn into reserve, ready to be unleashed when the infantry had done their job of punching a hole through the enemy defensive line. When released, they would dash through the gap created and into the rear, creating havoc within enemy supply lines and attacking headquarters and rear area units. This would precipitate a retreat and, importantly, keep any battles fluid, avoiding trench deadlock.

To enable this role to be carried out, British tank designers created a series of light, fast tanks called 'cruisers'. Typical examples of the wartime cruiser tank were the Crusader and the Covenanter. But by 1944, it was clear that these tanks were far too flimsy to be effective on the battlefield; and they had to a great extent been superseded by US-built, lend-lease medium tanks like the Sherman.

The second role, that of battlefield assault, was to overcome this presumed 'primacy of the defensive'. Heavily armoured (and thus slow-moving) tanks would assist the infantry to break into the enemy's main line of defence, to help overcome dug-in anti-tank guns, pillboxes and entrenched positions. The Royal Tank Regiment battalions were in large part allotted this distinctly less glamorous role. And it was for this task that the Churchill tank was designed.

The Churchill, or to give it its formal designation the Tank, Infantry, Mk IV (A22), was the heaviest British battle tank of the Second World War. It carried much thicker armour than the mainstay of the German Panzer divisions, the Panzer IV, but it was much slower moving (after all, it was theoretically not required to go above the walking pace of the infantry it was to accompany).

Earlier in the war the Churchill had carried a two-pounder tank gun, but this was quickly found to be inadequate, and by 1944 most were fitted with 75mm guns. In a stand-up fight a Churchill would usually beat a Panzer IV. However, by 1944 increasing numbers of German Panther and Tiger tanks were being deployed within Panzer units. Both of these were far superior to the Churchill, both in terms of armour and armament (although not in terms of mechanical reliability). They could easily stand off at a distance and destroy oncoming Churchills well before their 75mm guns became effective. The Tiger, armed with the feared 88mm gun, could pick Churchills off at ranges of over 1,000 yards. Attacking Allied tanks in effect became sitting ducks, at least until they could get really close, or around the flank of the German Panthers or Tigers.

It became a rule of thumb in the Allied armies that five British or American tanks would be needed to destroy one Panther or Tiger, as the German tank was sure to knock out several Allied vehicles before they could narrow the range down to 100 or 200 yards, when they might stand a chance of destroying the heavily armoured German vehicles.

Having been convinced of the argument for two distinct types of tank, the Army naturally began to think that two different types of tank unit would be needed, each one specialising in one of the above roles. This led to the creation of armoured brigades (to carry out fast-moving exploitation) and tank brigades (to carry out set-piece assaults in coordination with the infantry). 9 RTR was, along with 7 RTR, assigned to the newly created 31 Army Tank Brigade.

The idea behind the tank brigades was that they would be semi-independent, in that they would normally remain as a reserve unit not assigned to a particular fighting formation. When plans for a particular assault were drawn up and a requirement for extra heavy armour to help the infantry was identified, the tank brigade would be assigned for that operation, and that operation only. It would then be withdrawn back into reserve to be used again when the next assault became necessary.

Of course the reality of war showed the premise that lay behind a lot of this thinking to be false.

German forces adopted the Blitzkrieg strategy to keep the battlefront mobile and to use tanks to penetrate deep into the enemy rear. They found, however, that the answer lay not in two specialised types of tank, but in one good all-rounder; a tank that could conceivably deal with any situation it might find itself in on the battlefield.

As will be seen from the following examination of the Normandy battles, 9 RTR Churchills often became involved in long-distance gunnery exchanges with German panzers, something for which they were not designed. They were supposed to be taking on the dug-in infantry and anti-tank guns. The Second World War battlefield could not be as easily compartmentalised as the theorists wished. Tank battles were inevitably mixed up with infantry combat.

Normandy also highlighted a fundamental weakness in the tank brigade concept, in that to create the desired hole in the enemy defensive line very close coordination and cooperation was needed between infantry and tanks. Apart from the fact that the wireless technology of the day militated against this, and the fact that when closed down (i.e. with all hatches shut) it was virtually impossible for infantrymen to communicate with tank crews, it rapidly became clear that allotting heavy tanks for single operations did not really work. This was because the tank unit would be assigned to work alongside an infantry unit it didn't know, that it had probably never trained with, and with whom it had no empathy or understanding. It was this lack of familiarity that, time and again, led to battlefield setbacks and a lot of unnecessary casualties.

Organisation

A heavy tank battalion such as 9 RTR was subdivided into smaller units called squadrons, and in turn squadrons were again subdivided into sub-units called troops. Theoretically, the battalion would usually be assigned a single battlefield task but, as was discovered in Normandy, more often than not individual squadrons were assigned battlefield objectives, often several miles apart and with different geographical targets.

9 RTR was made of four squadrons; three fighting squadrons identified as A, B and C, and one Battalion Headquarters squadron, which could (and was) called upon to fight in the front line from time to time, but whose primary role was to coordinate the activities of the three fighting squadrons on the battlefield. As well as numerous non-armoured vehicles, half-tracks and scout cars assigned to other headquarters sub-units such as its ambulance unit, its signals company and its REME workshop, Battalion HQ contained five Churchill tanks; for the commanding officer, his second in command, the battalion intelligence officer, and two tanks assigned to Royal Artillery observers to assist with the accurate placement of indirect artillery fire support.

Each fighting squadron was made up of six troops, each of three Churchills. Each squadron had an HQ troop, to which an armoured recovery vehicle was attached (to pull out bogged-down tanks, or to take damaged tanks to the rear for repair). But unlike the battalion HQ, the squadron HQ was seen as a front-line fighting unit, and always accompanied the other troops into battle. The non-HQ troops in 9 RTR were numbered sequentially from 1 to 15 (1 to 5 being in A Squadron, 6 to 10 in B Squadron and 11 to 15 in C Squadron). So when a 9 RTR squadron went into action, it was usual for it to contain eighteen battle tanks.

It was usual practice for British tanks to move across the battlefield in a stop-start fashion. A tank would move forward to a designated position, then stop and scan for the enemy. A second tank would then transit to the same area, with the third tank remaining stationary at the troop's point of departure on what was called overwatch, keeping a lookout. This way only one tank was moving at any one given moment. This was important, because tanks were not fitted with gyro-stabilisers; that is, the tank's main gun bounced up and down as it crossed the uneven countryside. Because of this it was almost impossible to get off anything like an accurate shot unless the tank was stationary. If one tank from a troop was lost, the two remaining tanks could still leapfrog forward, each giving the other covering fire. Thus a troop of three vehicles was thought to be the smallest practicable unit that could operate successfully on the field of battle.

Each Churchill contained a crew of five (wireless operator, gunner, driver, commander and co-driver/machine-gunner), so in effect a team of fifteen men operated as a close-knit unit. Because of this and the fact that tank crews could be bottled up together in their vehicles for hours, sometimes even days, at a stretch, friendships were strong and the camaraderie was intense. A small number of losses, just one or two men from a troop, would be keenly felt in a unit so compact.

And as the unit's experiences in Normandy were to show, a steady rate of tank crew losses per action was the norm. A squadron in action could expect to lose ten per cent of its men per day at best. Sometimes, as during Operation Jupiter, this could rise to twenty-five per cent or more.

Operation Epsom (26–29 June 1944)

Background
Field Marshal Montgomery's strategic plan for D-Day called for the historic city of Caen, some ten miles inland from the beaches, to be captured within twenty-four hours of the initial landings. Yet by 26 June 1944, twenty days into the campaign, it was still in enemy hands.

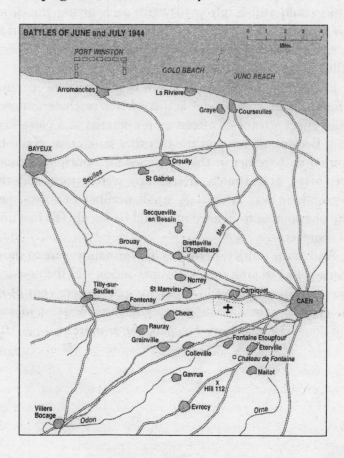

Montgomery's first attempt to break the deadlock in this sector, to encircle Caen from both east and west, finally ended in failure on 18 June. Operation Epsom, his second attempt, was less ambitious. Instead of attacking Caen from both sides, one much bigger breakthrough effort would be made to the west of the city. XXX Corps would take and hold the high ground on the right flank of the advance (Operation Martlet), while VIII Corps, just off the boat from England and completely new to combat, carried out the main thrust towards the River Odon. When the river was crossed the attackers would swing to the east and encircle Caen from the south.

The Plan

VIII Corps' plan was for 15 Scottish Division to lead the assault, supported by 31 Tank Brigade. The units in this force would break into the enemy defences from the north, creating the hole that would then be exploited by 11 Armoured Division, who would pass through and carry out the actual encirclement.

The bad weather (persistent rain and low cloud) which dogged almost the entire operation meant that no close air support was available to help the attackers smash through the defenders and in particular to stop German reinforcements reaching the main battle area. A high degree of emphasis was therefore placed on the artillery support. VIII Corps could call on a total of 272 medium and heavy artillery pieces for immediate fire-support and a further 440 guns could be made available from flanking corps to assist with the breakthrough as and when required. This tremendous weight of firepower was a major factor in enabling the operation to succeed to the extent that it did.

15 Scottish Division was designated to attack in two phases. Phase 1 was to commence with a standard textbook assault on the German line: two of its three constituent infantry brigades (44 and 46) attacking, with the third (227) held in reserve. When 44 and 46 Brigades had achieved their objectives, 227 Infantry Brigade would pass through them commencing Phase 2, during which it was hoped a crossing over the River Odon would be captured, thus releasing 11 Armoured Division in the exploitation phase.

To support 15 Scottish Division 31 Tank Brigade was split, 9 RTR (less one squadron) to support the attack of 44 Infantry Brigade on the left of the 15th Scottish line and 7 RTR to support 46 Infantry Brigade on the right.

For the operation 9 RTR was itself broken down into its three constituent squadrons. A Squadron was designated to support the attack of 8th Royal Scots to capture the area around the hamlet of La Gaule, astride one of the few north–south roads that ran across the battlefield; while B Squadron operated on their left, supporting the attack of 6th Royal Scots Fusiliers on the village of St Manvieu. C Squadron (Trevor Greenwood's squadron) stayed in reserve with 227 Infantry Brigade. They were to attack with them later on in the afternoon, passing through 44 Infantry Brigade lines and pressing on to the Phase 2 objectives of Colleville and Mondrainville, and a potential bridge over the Odon nearby.

The Opposition

Unfortunately for the inexperienced 9 RTR, their advance was against perhaps the best, certainly the most fanatical of the German forces in Normandy, the men of the 12th SS Panzer Division Hitlerjugend. Most of these men were in fact teenagers, eighteen and nineteen years old, who had volunteered to transfer to the fighting forces from the Hitler Youth. They had never known anything but life under Nazi rule; and thus they were thoroughly indoctrinated and possessed of the self-belief that they were indeed supermen, and that their cause was right and just. To cap it all, for a German field division they were very well equipped, well supplied, and could count on the battlefield support of several attached Luftwaffe flak batteries equipped with the feared '88' dual-purpose gun.

Terrain

Assisting the SS diehards considerably was the fact that the ground Epsom was fought over was perfect for defence. It consisted of a number of villages and farms, most of the buildings within them being of sturdy stone construction, many further fortified and turned into strongpoints by the defenders. They were surrounded by a network of orchards and copses, each of which was in turn surrounded by high-banked and deep-hedged fields – the infamous *bocage* hedgerow. This was particularly problematical for tanks trying to give close support to the infantry storming the villages beyond the fields, as smashing through the hedge whilst climbing up and over a very steep bank inevitably blinded the tank crew to what was immediately in front of it and at the same time exposed the very thinly armoured belly of the tank to anti-tank guns or Panzerfaust troops – the German equivalent of the bazooka – hidden behind (or sometimes inside) the hedgerow.

The country between the villages was open cornfield, with corn about four to five feet high. This provided plenty of cover for infantry and anti-tank guns but nothing for tanks, which stuck up out of the top of the corn like ships at sea.

Very few roads ran north to south (the direction of the attack) and those that did inevitably joined other roads at the villages or farms turned into strongpoints. This created massive bottlenecks for the advancing forces. Motorised transport (things like ambulances, artillery tractors and supply trucks) and armour (tanks making their way to the front line) all tried to use the very limited road network at the same time, often while villages were still partially occupied by the enemy holding on to isolated fortified buildings.

Day one: 26 June

9 RTR's three squadrons' first experiences of battle were markedly different from one another.

A Squadron's attack on the hamlet of La Gaule started at 07.30 a.m., both the tanks and infantry following closely behind the massive rolling barrage being laid down in front of them. Early morning mist was particularly problematic in this area and it was difficult for the advancing troops to see just how far in front the barrage was falling, and indeed, in which direction the advance should be made. Some units lost their way and went off course, while others advanced too quickly and caught the tail end of their own barrage.

Luckily for A Squadron, their attack hit the German defensive line at the boundary of the sections of front held by the 12th SS Pioneer Battalion and the 26th SS Panzergrenadier Regiment. Consequently resistance was less well coordinated than it might have been. By 09.30 hours the advance had reached the road 2,000 yards forward of the start line, and within the hour the hamlet had been cleared of the enemy.

A Squadron had run into no enemy anti-tank guns or tanks but had suffered its first casualties, two troopers wounded and one killed by artillery fire (quite possibly friendly).

B Squadron, to the left of A Squadron, also started the attack at 07.30 a.m. in support of the attack on the village of St Manvieu. This village was heavily fortified and contained the headquarters of the 1st Battalion 26th SS Panzergrenadier Regiment.

B Squadron's advance almost stalled at the very start when the tanks inadvertently ran into a belt of anti-tank mines laid by Canadian troops not marked on anyone's maps. Two tanks lost their tracks and were put out of action. Once through the mines, they tried to catch up with the infantry who were still advancing towards St Manvieu through the mist. As a result some tanks pressed on too quickly and ran into the rolling barrage.

The village had been turned into a series of interlocking fortified positions, each giving covering fire over its neighbour. The fields surrounding the village were heavily entrenched with several dug-in anti-tank guns. The tanks of 9 RTR enveloped the village and provided supporting fire. But they were discouraged from going too close because of the anti-tank gun threat. Even after this was neutralised, RTR tanks elected to stay back from the buildings, their reasoning being that it was easy to destroy tanks with magnetic mines and Panzerfausts if infantry could get within a few yards.

The problem for the attacking British infantry was that they didn't need long-range gunfire support against the buildings on the periphery of the village; they needed accurate close-range fire against the fortified strongpoints in the centre.

As the day wore on, the buildings slowly fell to the attackers, partly because ammunition was running out for the defenders but mostly because two Churchill Crocodile (flamethrower) tanks were brought forward to help destroy the fortifications. B Squadron 9 RTR lost a total of five tanks in the action, all of which were recovered and repaired. There were no fatalities, which is testament to the thick frontal armour of the Churchill. But the early morning mist and the difficult battle for St Manvieu had slowed down the advance.

To regain momentum, the VIII Corps commander took the decision to prematurely launch 11 Armoured Division through the 15th Division line, in the hope of turning a limited advance into a decisive breakout. Thus the advance of 227 Infantry Brigade (with C Squadron 9 RTR in support) was further delayed.

The delay caused by the earlier setbacks and the fact that 11 Armoured Division and 15 Scottish Division vehicles were now all trying to use the same few country lanes gave the overstretched Germans time to react. Twenty-five Panzer IV tanks on the far left of the line were ordered to break off their defensive action and move as fast as they could to the east, to cover the area south of Cheux/La Gaule/St Manvieu against the expected continued British offensive.

The first Panzers arrived at their new defensive positions at 14.30, just as the lead tanks of 11 Armoured Division topped the ridge just south of Cheux right in front of them.

A major tank battle ensued, with over seventy Sherman and Cromwell tanks being committed to action. 11 Armoured Division failed to break through.

Finally, at 18.00 hours the last squadron of 9 RTR to see

action (C Squadron, Greenwood's squadron) was launched forwards from a start line to the south-east of Cheux: behind the ridge line and thus not visible to the Germans. They were to support 2nd Battalion Gordon Highlanders in an attack on Colleville, a village sitting astride the east–west railway line, about two miles north of the Odon.

No air support was forthcoming for the attack. The weather had got worse as the day had gone on, and it was now raining steadily.

All went well with the advance until the Churchill tanks topped the ridge. Their bulky forms stood out on the skyline out of the top of the corn; perfect targets for the anti-tank guns and Flak 88s concealed in the woods on the outskirts of Colleville. Within minutes several were knocked out. Visibility was poor, with the rain hampering attempts to sight the camouflaged enemy gun positions. But the infantry pressed on and a decision was taken to support them with half the squadron moving forward, the other half remaining on the forward slope of the ridge, trying to silence the anti-tank fire.

Trevor Greenwood's tank was the only one of his troop (No. 15 Troop) to get safely over the ridge and down the frontal slope, keeping up with the advancing Gordon Highlanders. Several tanks, Greenwood's included, pressed on and supported the lead infantry company into Colleville. Visibility was seriously impaired by the now torrential rain. This was a bonus in that the German anti-tank guns could no longer target tanks, even those relatively close to their positions, but it also bred a mood of caution amongst the tank crews, who were even less inclined to enter any built-up area.

After losing a tank at the entrance to the village, the

remaining C Squadron tanks contented themselves with standing back, pouring fire into the buildings and surrounding woods and orchards. This undoubtedly helped the Gordons but it also meant, as it had at St Manvieu, that a foothold could not be turned into a victory, as buildings in the village interior could not be subjected to tank fire. By about 21.00, with the light beginning to fade and no sign of further reinforcements, the Gordons decided they could no longer hold on and the order was given to pull back to Cheux.

C Squadron stayed in the line covering the withdrawal until 22.30, when it was finally too dark to see. They then made their way back to Cheux, carrying as many wounded as they could on the tanks.

The assault had gained no ground. C Squadron had shown bravery by continuing to push on towards Colleville even after significant tank losses, but also naivety in electing for some vehicles to remain on the ridge in a vain attempt to search out the well-camouflaged anti-tank guns, which simply picked them off. C Squadron lost eight out of eighteen tanks committed. Fortuitously only three men were killed, with a further fifteen wounded: a casualty rate of almost twenty-five per cent.

Back at 21st Army Group HQ Montgomery reported 'weather very bad with heavy rain and low cloud but very good progress was made and leading troops now on railway line at Colleville' (which was incorrect). But he knew he could commit fresh troops to action on 27 June, whereas by and large the German forces would be those that had survived the previous day's fighting. One thing was certain from Montgomery's report; Epsom was to continue.

Day two: 27 June

A and B Squadrons were committed to action again, supporting a thrust south from Cheux towards the Odon. A Squadron pushed south towards Colleville, supporting a combined attack by both the 2nd Battalion Argyll and Sutherland Highlanders and 7th Battalion Seaforth Highlanders. B Squadron advanced on their right towards the village of Grainville sur Odon, advancing on the flank of an assault by 10th Battalion Highland Light Infantry (HLI).

All the British infantry units committed to action were fresh and at full strength but for all of them it was to be their first time in action. Even though the HLI attack was against remnant groups of SS infantry supported by the last few remaining Panzer IV tanks, all of whom were exhausted having survived the onslaught of the day before, the attack went disastrously wrong almost from the start.

Despite significantly outnumbering the dog-tired defenders the attack by the inexperienced British infantry was soon pinned down. And despite being supported by the heavy Churchills, the advance stopped and then turned into a panic-driven rout. B Squadron could not advance on Grainville without infantry support, so their attack stalled too. It was not until later on that afternoon that the HLI, now accompanied by a company of Gordon Highlanders, managed to resume the offensive.

It was only at this point that B Squadron met anything other than a modicum of resistance. The 2nd Panzer Division, like many other units, had been dashing to the front as fast as they could to relieve the hard-pressed German forces. In fact they 'rushed' so much that the seventeen Panther tanks of their lead unit inadvertently passed straight through the

German front line and blundered into the British troops west of Cheux, near the hamlet of Le Haut du Bosq. They had no infantry with them and soon found themselves surrounded by tank-hunting teams of soldiers armed with PIATs (the British equivalent to the bazooka).

While the majority of these Panthers crashed into the British line to the north of B Squadron, one or two hit the line to their front. It was this inadvertent reinforcement of the Grainville defences that led to B Squadron's losses for the day. One tank from No. 10 Troop was lost on its way to Grainville (two crew killed and the other three wounded), while another two from No. 9 Troop were destroyed by gunfire on its outskirts.

This was the first time 9 RTR tanks had seen action against heavy German tanks and they soon realised that it was almost impossible to destroy them in a stand-up gunnery battle. But as in Le Haut de Bosq further north there was simply not enough German infantry left to hold the ground, and the Panthers had to withdraw as they soon found themselves surrounded by swarms of British infantry. Grainville was eventually taken.

A Squadron further to the east supported the Argyll and Sutherland Highlander attack on Colleville, passing over the same ground, driving past the destroyed tanks of C Squadron, lost the day before. This time a determined attack by the Argylls overcame the German defences quickly. The village was clear by 15.00 hours. Seizing the initiative, the Argylls' commander sent a company to dash a mile or two further to the south, and captured a tentative bridgehead over the Odon at Tourmauville.

Not one tank was lost by A Squadron during the day's fighting. But their luck was not to hold.

Day three: 28 June

With British troops across the Odon, German commanders now reasoned the only way to halt the advance was to attack the base of the salient from both sides in an attempt to cut off the advance. Thus the main assault on 28 June fell on sections of the front well away from 9 RTR.

A Squadron did see some action, assisting with the placement of a battalion of Cameron Highlanders on a vital crossroads just to the south of Grainville. As the operation got underway two tanks were lost to fire from a Panther tank which was thought to have been knocked out the previous day. Unbeknown to the British, the crew had sneaked back inside the immobilised tank during the night and opened up on the Churchills at very short range.

A Squadron lost nine men wounded during the day. But the bridgehead was held and furthermore the German counter-attacks to the north on the base of the salient failed.

Day four: 29 June

C Squadron had been left out of the line for two days to help them recover from the mauling they had received on 26 June, but now they were back in the line. The squadron was assigned the role of helping with the defence of Valtru just south of Grainville, held by 7th Seaforth Highlanders.

Ultra decryptions of German signals had informed Montgomery that the Germans were planning yet another counterstrike, this time by the 9th Hohenstaufen and 10th Frundsberg SS Panzer Divisions, newly arrived from the Russian Front. He also knew where the attackers were to assemble. The German assault was planned to fall on the right-hand flank of the salient, and C Squadron were slap bang in the projected line of advance of the SS troops.

For the first time since the opening of Epsom, the weather was fine and air operations unhindered. Wave after wave of USAAF Thunderbolt and RAF Typhoon ground-attack aircraft strafed, bombed and rocketed the German assault formations as they formed up. As a consequence the shell-shocked German troops didn't perform anywhere near as well as expected.

Fortuitously for C Squadron, the point in the line held by them was not attacked by a Panther or Tiger formation but by the half-tracks and infantry of the 19th Panzergrenadier Regiment, supported by several Panzer III flamethrower tanks. With their thick frontal armour the RTR crews had a field day, picking off the lighter enemy armour with ease. Fortunately for them, when the Germans had converted these old tanks to take flame-throwers they had removed the main gun armament, so they could not hope to destroy the Churchills unless they got within thirty yards or so.

C Squadron survived the day without losing a single tank, and suffered only one casualty.

29 June saw the beginning of the end for Operation Epsom: over the next forty-eight hours the front stabilised and quietened down, with the British in possession of a signifi-cant salient in the German line, but without the decisive breakthrough they wanted.

Operation Jupiter (10 July 1944)

By 9 July Ultra intercepts had made it clear to Montgomery that his 'new' plan to hold the German Panzer divisions in place in front of the British was in danger of failing. The 2nd

SS Das Reich Panzer Division had already been transferred away to the American sector, and now the Panzer Lehr Division was on the move that way too.

What was needed was a holding attack to make sure that no further panzer formations moved to the US front, to enable them to undertake the major breakthrough operation. This meant hitting the German line where the Panzer divisions were strongest, and this in turn dictated another attack in the same area as Epsom had been launched just two weeks previously.

This time the assault was to be led by 43 Wessex Division, another British formation to be blooded for the first time. The attack was to be launched from the Tourmauville bridgehead seized during the previous operation. The general lie of the land and terrain encountered would be the same as that encountered during Epsom.

The objective was Hill 112 to the south-east of Colleville (fought over on the last day of Epsom) and the villages of Eterville and Maltot, which lay to the east of the hill. It was hoped that the attack would hold at least three SS Panzer divisions in position to the front of the British forces.

9 RTR was given the role of supporting 130 Infantry Brigade in its attacks on Eterville and Maltot. As was becoming the norm in Normandy operations, 9 RTR was split up, each squadron supporting a different aspect of the assault.

B Squadron was to advance in support of the 5th Dorsets and attack and take the Château de Fontaine, a country house and associated complex of buildings which lay to the north of Maltot. This initial assault was to commence at daybreak, 05.00 hours. Seventy-five minutes later C Squadron was to advance in support of 4th Dorsets in their attack on Eterville to the east of the château. And 100 minutes later A Squadron was to advance through the new front line (i.e. between the chateau and Eterville) and attack Maltot in support of 7th Hampshires.

Unfortunately the attack also drew into combat another German unit that had only arrived at the Normandy front at 02.45 that very morning. The thirty-plus Tiger tanks of the 102nd SS Heavy Tank Battalion had been eighteen days on the road from Holland and had just stopped for an overnight rest at the little village of St Martin, just south of Maltot.

As soon as the battle was joined, two out of three companies of Tigers raced to Hill 112 to assist with its defence. The remaining Tigers were held in reserve at St Martin.

The 5th Dorsets advanced on the Château de Fontaine, keeping as close to the edge of the rolling barrage that preceded their assault as they could. The château was defended by the 2nd Battalion, 21st Panzergrenadier Regiment, part of the 10th SS Frundsberg Division. They fought hard, but without any tank support the buildings around the chateau soon fell.

B Squadron lost just one tank in this attack, destroyed by a roaming Panzer IV.

The report of the 5th Dorsets' success reached their sister battalion just as they were to launch their assault on Eterville. The left flank of this advance was covered by a huge smoke-screen. Fortuitously the smoke barrage was laid along the wooded river line of the Orne and in the trees sheltered the last remaining few Panzers of the 12th SS Hitlerjugend Division. Effectively blinded, they took little part in the opening phases of the battle, and as a consequence C Squadron did not lose a single tank in the attack on Eterville, successfully dealing with the two anti-tank guns sited on the outskirts.

Maltot was separated from Eterville by a low ridge, and as the A Squadron tanks topped the rise to follow the Hampshires down into the town, they were met with a torrent of anti-tank fire from four or five Panzer IVs stationed along the Orne and several concealed anti-tank guns within Maltot itself. The smokescreen, although it had masked the advance on Eterville, had not extended far enough down the riverbank to cover the approaches to Maltot.

But now another, even bigger problem became apparent.

The attack on Hill 112 had been repulsed with heavy casualties. Tiger tanks stationed on the rear slope of the hill could now look to their right and see A Squadron advancing on Maltot in the distance. The 88mm gun of the Tiger was designed for just such long-range fire. The Churchills were also presenting their weaker side armour to the Tigers, in part due to the fact they didn't realise they were being observed, since they assumed British troops would be in control of the hill, and of course they were distracted by the much closer-range gunfire to their front.

At 11.56 hours only nine tanks of A Squadron were left. Within five minutes of the Tiger tanks turning their guns on the Churchills A Squadron was down to just four tanks. The survivors retired back over the ridgeline, leaving the Hampshires to hold Maltot without any tank support.

This was when the divisional commander of the Frundsberg released his reserve armoured battalion of Panzergrenadiers (mounted in half-tracks) from a holding position south of Maltot. They were accompanied by the remaining Tigers from St Martin: maybe a dozen tanks in all. They smashed headlong into the Hampshires now defending Maltot.

Miraculously the Hampshires held out. But knowing that they could not withstand a second assault, at about 15.00 hours permission was given for them to withdraw, the Dorsets (both 4th and 5th) pushing forward to take their place.

It was at this point the British troops made a grave error. The Hampshires, receiving permission to withdraw, moved with alacrity and abandoned Maltot. The Dorsets following up behind them for some reason did not get their orders until the Hampshires had started to fall back. The result was that when the Dorsets arrived in Maltot to take over, they found Tigers and Panzergrenadiers waiting. The battle to clear the streets had to begin all over again.

Both C Squadron and the HQ Squadron had been tasked with supporting the Dorsets into Maltot. And they ran into exactly the same problems as had A Squadron, with the added discomfort that not only did they have Tigers on Hill 112 to their flank, they now had Tigers to their front as well.

For three hours the battle raged in and around Maltot. But the Dorsets and the Churchills simply could not hold against Tigers and infantry.

Casualties had been extremely heavy on both sides. Of the 500 men of the 4th Dorsets who had gone into battle that morning, only five officers and eighty men struggled back through the lines at day's end. During the day's fighting 9 RTR took sixty-five casualties, more than a quarter of the total suffered by the battalion in the whole campaign. They lost twenty-two tanks, of which six were recovered and repaired.

At the end of the day Hill 112 was still in enemy hands, so was Maltot.

It had been conclusively proven to the battalion that their

Churchills were no match for the Tiger. But, crucially, the Germans had been forced to commit their last panzer reserves, and they knew they could not afford to weaken the front to send any tank units to the American sector: not if they wanted to hold the line in front of the British. Operation Cobra, the planned US breakout further to the west, was as assured of success as it could be.

A Tiger II tank or Königstiger as it was known, abandoned in France. With its 88mm gun and massive armour, this was the most feared of all the German tanks.

Photograph © IWM STT7029.

9 RTR in Normandy

As can be seen from the problems encountered during both Epsom and Jupiter, 9 RTR had great difficulty coordinating its activities effectively with the infantry battalions it was assigned to support.

This was due in part to inexperience. 9 RTR simply had not had the time to develop the field craft needed to cooperate effectively. Problems were exacerbated by poor wireless equipment, which limited communication between formations, even when they were only a few hundred yards away. And of course when closed down no amount of shouting and banging on the side of the tank could persuade the crew inside to open up. What if they were Germans intent on dropping a grenade through the hatch?

Some Churchills were provided with a telephone set on the rear, so that infantry could ring up the crew inside. However, these were rarely, if ever, used. Tanks had the nasty habit of suddenly moving off, reversing or turning on the spot. No infantryman wanted to be crushed to death. So although they were generally glad to have friendly tanks nearby, they did not want them too close. Friendly tanks also inevitably attracted enemy artillery fire. Just close enough to provide effective gunfire support was what was required.

This poor coordination could have been ameliorated by officers getting together and going through the battle plan in detail well in advance of the action to be fought. But operational constraints almost always meant that this planning time was never available.

Another option would have been to team up a tank battalion with an infantry unit and to try and make sure they always operated together, so mutual understanding and trust could be built up. And this is indeed what tended to happen later in the war.

But for the Normandy campaign at least, British tank units did seem to be operating with a quite different understanding of their role than that supposed by the infantry. Tanks saw it as their job to get the infantry to the objective.

Once that was done their job was over and they could stand off. The infantry wanted, and expected, the tanks to drive into the enemy line with them, providing short-range fire support against German fortified positions.

Tank crews knew just how vulnerable they were to Panzerfausts and magnetic anti-tank mines and not unnaturally wanted to stay as far as possible away from the enemy infantry who wielded them. But to the infantry they were supposed to be supporting, this hanging back seemed almost treacherous.

It took a while for the tank crews to realise that the best way of ending the battle quickly was to get in close and take that risk. Doing so ensured much more rapid success (less time in battle meant less casualties overall) and built up mutual trust with the infantry, who were then, in response, far more likely to take on and take out enemy anti-tank guns and Panzerfaust teams.

To be fair to 9 RTR, for the majority of the time they were on the offensive, against defenders who had both fortified the terrain and cleared pre-selected avenues of fire. Churchill tanks literally drove into the cross hairs of concealed and waiting anti-tank guns and tanks. When stationary and awaiting a German assault, as on the last day of Epsom when C Squadron saw off a mechanised assault by SS Panzergrenadiers with relative ease, 9 RTR crews performed much better.

So perhaps it should be concluded that the technology of the time favoured the tank in defence. The tank in attack was at a disadvantage, with its inability to fire on the move, its limited ability to communicate with others, and its very restricted ability to see what was going on around it. This was much magnified when British tanks faced a foe equipped with tanks which had a much longer-range gun, with more penetrative power, and much thicker armour. No doubt this perceived inferiority led to the almost universal assumption that any Panzer faced on the battlefield was either a Panther or Tiger, whereas in truth only a very small proportion of German tanks were of these types.

Montgomery was exasperated by this habit, and he went so far as to ban his officers talking about the supposed superiority of the Panther and Tiger, telling them it did nothing but spread fear and angst amongst the troops (which indeed it did). But banning talking about the enemy's superiority doesn't stop him having it.

It must be remembered that in Normandy the inexperienced citizen soldiers of 9 RTR faced an experienced and in some cases a fanatical enemy, led by veteran officers, in well dug-in and often fortified positions. And that they did in fact (and not just through false assumption) face up to a very large proportion of the total number of Panther and Tiger tanks present in Normandy.

Bearing all that in mind, 9 RTR did remarkably well. And the experience gained turned them into a veteran unit, ready for the next phase of the war, the push through the Low Countries and into Germany: a phase of operations in which they were to further distinguish themselves.

Index

(page numbers in italic type indicate illustrations)